Spider Woman

A LOOM STANDS

Spider Woman

A Story of Navajo Weavers and Chanters

Gladys A. Reichard

Introduction by Louise Lamphere

*"Spider Woman instructed the Navajo women how
to weave on a loom which Spider Man told them how to make.
The crosspoles were made of sky and earth cords, the warp sticks of
sun rays, the healds of rock crystal and sheet lightning. The batten was a
sun halo, white shell made the comb. There were four spindles; one a stick
of zigzag lightning with a whorl of cannel coal; one a stick of flash lightning
with a whorl of turquoise; a third had a stick of sheet lightning with
a whorl of abalone; a rain streamer formed the stick of the fourth,
and its whorl was withe shell." (Navajo Legend)*

University of New Mexico Press
Albuquerque

Reichard, Gladys Amanda 1893–1955.
Spider woman : a story of Navajo weavers and chanters /
Gladys A. Reichard.
p. cm.
Originally published: New York : Macmillan, 1934.
With new introd. Includes bibliographical references and index.
ISBN 0-8263-1793-6
1. Navajo Indians.
2. Navajo textile fabrics.
I. Title.
E99.N3R4   1997
746.1'089'972 —dc20
96-43353
CIP

INTRODUCTION

GLADYS Reichard opens *Spider Woman,* her ethnography of Navajo family life in the 1930s, with an account of her first visit to White-Sands (Séí ligai). She has come with Roman Hubbell, the trader at Hubbell's Trading Post in Ganado, Arizona, known in her book by his Navajo name, Old Mexican's Son [Naakaii sání biye'], to locate a family to help her learn to weave. The picture she paints of the extended family residence is that of an outsider, allowing the reader to view Navajo life through "white eyes." There is the cluck of a hen giving herself a "dust bath," a horde of mongrel dogs, and a description of a large dome-shaped "hut" with a closed door and a lock hanging loose in its hasp. Hubbell and Reichard find a woman sitting at her loom weaving "a dull thump thump, the sound of the comb pounding firmly, regularly, and rapidly the yarn which is becoming a Navajo rug" (p. 2).

Hubbell and Reichard know that they should "stand respectfully at the doorway for a time" while the woman continues to weave, "thumping her comb, as if we did not exist, her way of greeting us respectfully." This is the first indication of a different set of culturally prescribed behaviors that Reichard will introduce to us, Anglo-American readers of the book, who begin as unfamiliar with Navajo culture as Reichard presumably is.

As this chapter and the next continue, we are introduced to the members of the family—Red Point or Miguelito who is a Navajo chanter or singer (hataałii), and his wife, Maria Antonia, and their married daughters, Atlnaba (the weaver described earlier), Marie (who is to be Reichard's teacher), and a third daughter known as "Yikadezba's mother" (who does not live in the White Sands residence group).

The next Monday morning Reichard moves into the family storage dugout, which provides a cool room with enough light for weaving and a place for her bedroll and trunk. Soon we learn that Atlnaba is married to Curley's Son, and Marie is married to his brother Tom. Both sons-in-law avoid and never "see" their mother-in-law, a custom which some Navajo continued to practice until the 1960s, but which is beginning to change in the 1930s as Reichard describes in her book (see pp. 135–36). During the afternoon, Tom constructs a loom for Reichard, and Marie helps her to string the warp threads.

By the end of the day, Reichard sits back to enjoy her surroundings, an Easterner who never loses her enthusiasm for the beauty of the Navajo Reservation. A letter to Elsie Clews Parsons echoes her feelings for the Southwest as described on that first day at Red Point's residence group (pp. 13–14): "I want you to know that there is a kind of unexplainable balm about the Southwest—you doubtless know it already. I found it last summer and needed it even more this. There is a peace which comes to us at evening when the air is cool and the sun sets, the mountains become purple rose and blue—we are high in cedar and piñon country, a most comfortable setting—and night settles down with the sheep in the corral and the stars and the moon and the air. Most people would hate the quiet—it *is* quiet—but I love it. It is the sort of thing some writers (a few) have gotten across, but somehow needs experiencing" (ECP: GR to ECP, 7/6/30).

From her early contacts with these Navajo, we see Reichard's relation with Red Point's family change, and with it our knowledge of Navajo daily life. By the end of the book we have shared the ceremonies that Red Point has performed for family members, trips to the trading post, Navajo tribal council meetings, sheep dips, and the deaths of Red Point's wife and youngest daughter.

As an ethnography or a description of a culture, *Spider Woman* is perhaps fifty years ahead of its time. Ethnographic depictions of the daily lives of "native" peoples reached their classic form in the writings of Bronislaw Malinowski and Margaret Mead. Both pioneered this genre of "scientific writing" which attempts to record the life of a people in a systematic and distanced way. As James Clifford has described this style, observations and dialogue gathered in particular places and at particular times are assembled into a text containing a unified voice, that of the ethnographer representing beliefs, practices, and behaviors of a whole culture (Clifford 1988:38–40).

Spider Woman is much more experimental, using textual strategies that are now becoming the vogue in anthropology as ethnographers attempt to create "dialogic texts" that try to capture conversations between outsider and native consultant and that take a particular point of view. In *Spider Woman* we are always conscious that we are seeing the Navajo from Reichard's standpoint, that of an Eastern white woman who wants to understand Navajo life but clearly has her own opinions and prejudices. This is not the distanced, unified voice of an ethnographer who presents the beliefs, practices, and behaviors of a whole culture and pronounces (using the ethnographic present), "Among the Navajo, x is the case." Rather we see a wide range of people interacting with Reichard and with each other.

In the last ten years, anthropologists (see Clifford and Marcus 1986, Rosaldo 1989) have critiqued the classic ethnographic text and called for more dialogical approaches. Likewise, several contemporary feminists (e.g. Ruth Behar in her biography of a Mexican street vendor, *Translated Woman* [1993] and Lila Abu-Lughod in her ethnography of Bedouin women [1993]) have experimented with texts that incorporate their own presence, utilize dialogue, or draw on the tape-recorded narratives of their subjects. In this they are adopting textual strategies pioneered by Reichard in *Spider Woman.*

Reichard's World: Anthropology in the 1930s

By the time Reichard arrived at Red Point's residence group in the summer of 1930, she was a thirty-seven-year-old assistant professor of anthropology at Barnard College and had conducted field research on the Navajo reservation for three summers. The daughter of a respected small-town physician, she was of Pennsylvania Dutch (German) heritage, raised as a Quaker. After graduating from high school, she taught in a country school for two years and then returned to her home town of Bangor, Pennsylvania, to teach for four more years. She enrolled in Swarthmore College at the age of twenty-two and received an A.B. degree in 1919. She had intended to be come a doctor, but in her senior year, after hearing several lectures by Dr. Spencer Trotter, an anthropologist trained by Franz Boas, she enthusiastically converted to anthropology. In the fall of 1919 she received a Lucretia Mott Fellowship to enter Columbia University. Reichard received her M.A. in 1920 and her Ph.D. in 1925, both from Columbia. Her dissertation was a grammar of the Wiyot Indians of California, among whom she had done field work in 1922–23.

The Columbia Anthropology Department of the early 1920s revolved around Franz Boas, widely known as the "father" of American anthropology. Boas rejected the evolutionary frameworks of nineteenth-century anthropologists. He took a position of cultural relativism, arguing that each culture should be judged on its own terms rather than by some Western standard. Instead of building grand explanatory schemes that placed the "civilized" at the top of an evolutionary ladder and the "savages" at the bottom, Boas advocated empirical research and careful description as the basis of anthropology as a science. He urged his students to study and document the languages, material cultures, social organizations, religious practices, and mythologies of the vast array of Native American cultures which he felt were rapidly disappearing. His own monographs and articles on the Eskimo and the Kwakiutl of the Northwest Coast were examples of the kind of description Boas encouraged, down to the pages devoted to the decorative designs of Alaskan needlecases (Boas 1908) and his account of the Kwakiutl Winter Ceremonial in 1895 (Boas 1966).

Reichard was one of a number of women anthropologists who were part of Boas's circle. Others included Elsie Clews Parsons, a wealthy feminist who became Reichard's patron, Ruth Benedict, Margaret Mead, Ruth Bunzel, and Esther Goldfrank. All except Mead conducted substantial research in the Southwest.

By the early 1920s gender roles in American society were growing flexible. There was much less emphasis on female chastity and chaperonage and, of course, the "new woman" of the 1920s drove a car, smoked in public, and wore short skirts. This change of gender roles may have supported the recruitment of women to anthropology and eventually to field work in the Southwest. By 1930 when Reichard went to live with Miguelito's family, it was not unusual for a woman to drive her own car and conduct field research on her own. Though women professionals were gaining more acceptance, it was still difficult to combine work and marriage. Although Parsons and Mead were married for a good part of their professional lives, Benedict was divorced, and Reichard, like Bunzel and Underhill, remained single.

Boas was particularly protective of his women students, taking a kindly paternalist stance toward them. Reichard became an instructor at Barnard in 1923, while she was still working on her dissertation, a job Boas arranged. Thus Reichard received the first permanent job held by any of the women in the Columbia circle. Boas was especially concerned that, unlike Ruth Benedict, who was still married, Reichard had no male to support her.

Reichard was almost a member of the Boas family, living at the Boas house during the winter and engaging in field research during the summer. Remaining a daughter and continuing to live with aging parents or, in this case, a mentor, was one of the acceptable strategies young women adopted as they entered the professions. In 1931 and 1932 during the winters between the second and third summers Reichard spent with Red Point's family, Boas was both depressed and ill, "withering away and with no spirit at all." Reichard hauled Boas and his books back and forth from department to home in her car and discussed the progress of his recovery in letters to Parsons(ECP:GR/ECP 2/24/31; ECP:GR/ECP 1/25/32). As a devoted resident in the household, Reichard took the role of someone who communicated his emotional and physical situation to other close friends, a position women frequently assume in families. She often personally attended to her aging mentor's wishes, particularly those that pertained to his work.

Sometime in 1923, when she was thirty, Reichard began a close relationship with Pliny Earle Goddard, curator of ethnology at the American Museum of Natural History. She accompanied Goddard on a field trip to the Navajo reservation in 1923 and returned with him in 1924 and 1925. It is part of anthropological folklore that Reichard had an affair with Goddard, a much older married man with a family. Certainly she was close to him, enjoyed her field work with him, and continued his work after his death.

These first summers of research, as well as subsequent field trips, were funded by Parsons through her Southwest Society. Parsons's role of mentor and confidante to Reichard emerges in their correspondence and shows that Parsons took a hand in directing the research as well as financing it. She suggested, for example, that Reichard visit the Pueblos and attend a Navajo Fire Dance, and she encouraged Gladys in her interest in studying Navajo clanship and chieftaincy. Reichard's continued intellectual debt to Parsons (as well as her financial assistance) is acknowledged in the dedication of *Spider Woman* to the Southwest Society, the foundation established with Parsons's money that funded Reichard's research.

Reichard and Goddard, traveling together, used what were then traditional field techniques. They covered several communities each summer, hired an interpreter, and worked with informants, collecting genealogies, data on Navajo clans, kin terms, Navajo names, and folklore. This approach to field research was quite different from her later experience living with a Navajo family and learning to weave, which is described in *Spider Woman.* As a result of these three field trips, Reichard published *The Social Life of the Navajo Indians* (1928). But during the years following these summer trips, her research took her away from Navajo studies. She spent 1926–27 in Hamburg, Germany, on a Guggenheim Fellowship, where she studied Melanesian design. In 1928 she went to Idaho to gather data on Coeur d'Alene grammar for the *Handbook of American Indian Languages* (Reichard 1938). That year Pliny Goddard died suddenly at the Newtown, Connecticut, house that Reichard owned. As a result their relationship came to the attention of Dean Gildersleeve of Barnard College. Reichard may have been threatened with dismissal and had difficulties with promotions and benefits later because of this incident. In 1930, when she returned to the Navajo Reservation, she was at a point where she needed to break with her past, utilize her experiences on the Navajo reservation, and try something new. As she said in her unpublished manuscript *Another Look at the Navajo,* a number of factors led to her new approach to field research.

I had started the study of Navaho social structure by accident, the genealogical method being used by my sponsor [Parsons]. After working three summers at the job, it seemed that I had come to know a good deal about Navaho clans, linked clans, marriage and related abstractions, but little about the Navaho themselves. (Personality was not largely used at this time). I concluded that a study of structure is indispensable for any kind of social study, but that is by no means enough for the understanding of behavior, attitude, and motivation. . . I was interested in crafts and decided that learning to weave would be a way of developing the trust of the women, as well as of learning to weave and to speak the language. By this attempt I would put myself under the family aegis; my work would at first deal primarily with women, and I could observe the daily round as a participant, rather than a mere onlooker. (Reichard n.d.a: handwritten insert, p. 1)

Reichard may have obtained an assistant professorship and traveled to the Southwest by herself to begin her field research, but her experiences with Dean Gildersleeve and her encounters in 1930 with Father Berard Haile, a Franciscan missionary and ethnographer, indicate that even the gender changes of the 1920s had their limits. Father Berard had been very helpful to Goddard and Reichard during their trips in 1923 and 1924, probably providing them with interpreters and even informants during their stays in Lukachukai where he lived. Although Berard was critical of Reichard's *Social Life of the Navajo Indians,* he was downright condescending when she wrote to him during the winter of 1930 asking about a singer and family she could live with.

I thought he had my point of view. He answers at length & with great detail saying he doesn't think I know enough even to wash behind the ears! Holds up Mrs. Armer as a model of how to do work among the Navajo! Even mentions a nice house with curtains, easy armchair, etc. I guess except for linguistic help I can count him out. (ECP: GR/ECP 2/24/37)

INTRODUCTION

Haile seemed to think that a young Anglo-American woman was incapable of living with a family in rather "primitive conditions." She spent a week in the early summer working with Haile's interpreter, Albert "Chic" Sandoval, but given Haile's sense that she needed a place with "window curtains," Reichard went on to Ganado with Ann Morris to ask trader Roman Hubbell's assistance in finding a family to live with. This is how she was introduced to Red Point's family as described in the first few pages of *Spider Woman*.

Red Point's World

Red Point, a well-known singer and traditionalist, had had extensive contact with the white world by the time Gladys Reichard came to spend the summer months with the family. He and his wife and daughters had worked for Fred Harvey, demonstrating weaving for tourists. The family traveled to San Francisco and San Diego for exhibitions in 1915, remaining in California for the greater part of two years. After returning to the reservation, Red Point apprenticed himself to a number of singers, learning several important Navajo ceremonies over the years. In 1923 he participated in the dedication of the El Navajo Hotel in Gallup (Parezo 1983). Mary Colter, who designed the interior, used sandpainting motifs based on reproductions by Red Point and other Navajo singers.

Reichard's visits during the summers of 1930–33 came on the eve of a time of great change on the Navajo Reservation. John Collier became head of the Bureau of Indian Affairs (BIA) in 1932, and ushered in a new era of U.S. Indian policy. The Navajo Reservation had suffered several drought years, and range land seemed seriously overgrazed. Collier felt strongly that the Navajos needed to reduce the size of their herds.

In 1930, the Navajo had almost a million sheep and over 300,000 goats. Collier met with the Tribal Council in the fall of 1933 and got them to agree in principle to stock reduction, citing the damage soil erosion was doing to Boulder Dam. The first sale of sheep in early 1934 resulted in only an 8 percent reduction in total herd size. By July, the Tribal Council agreed to accept the sale of 150,000 goats and up to 50,000 sheep. The sale, in the fall of 1934, was badly mismanaged. "Agents in some areas," according to Aberle, "put heavy pressure on owners, and often on small owners, to sell. It proved impossible to deliver all the goats to the railhead. So some were slaughtered and the meat dried and given back to the Navahos; others were shot and left to rot; still others were shot and partly cremated with gasoline. [In one place, 3,500 goats were shot and left.] To the Navahos this waste was appalling, and the attitude toward their valued resources was incomprehensible. Criticism and opposition, especially, from women owners, was intense" (Aberle 1966). Stock reduction was very much in the air during the last summer of Reichard's stay with Red Point's family as described in *Spider Woman*. Just after *Spider Woman* ends, Navajo families suffered enormous decline, particularly between 1936 and 1940, when the large herds were reduced. Grazing districts were established and permits (with a maximum herd size below subsistence levels) were given out to Navajo families. By 1937, only 8.5 percent of all Navajo livestock owners had herds that could meet family subsistence needs (a flock of 250 for a family of five). The average herd across the reservation was 102 sheep units per family, about 18 to 22 sheep units per capita, well below the subsistence level of 40–50 per capita (Henderson 1989:385). From Reichard's correspondence in 1930, we know that Red Point's extended family owned three very large herds of sheep; they probably lost a large portion of their livelihood during stock reduction (ECP: GR to ECP, 7/6/30).

White education and boarding schools were also making important inroads into Navajo life at this time. Since Reichard traveled to the reservation during the summers, we see little of the impact on the young children in Red Point's family, who may or may not have been in school during the winter months. John Curley (called Tallman in *Spider Woman*), who appears in several chapters, often expresses Anglo views and compares the differences between Navajo belief and the Christian religion. "He was raised Presbyterian, for years has been straddling on the edge of going back to Navajo. He 'done so' last winter by marrying (Navajo way) a woman from Black Mtn. Whom he had never seen. Reverse assimilation! . . . John said his relatives had been coaxing him to marry for a long time. . . . So he finally said they should pick him out a woman with certain qualifications, among which were that he would not avoid his m-in-law. I have run into three cases of it this year, the first." During the wedding described in Chapter 18, "he made a speech at the wedding to this effect and the new groom is not avoiding" (ECP: GR to ECP, 7/9/32). The dropping of mother-in-law avoidance is just one of the many changes that increased education and missionization brought to the Navajo reservation during the 1930s.

Reichard and Navajo Culture

In the first chapters of the book Reichard is absorbed with learning how to weave. Those who wish to understand how Navajo rugs are made will especially want to attend to these chapters (Chapters 3, 5, 6, 7, 9, 10, 12, 13, 14). They are also of interest because they make clear that Navajo learning is quite different from that of white culture. Like most beginning weavers Reichard was instructed to make a rug of stripes. Her second rug, however, was an intricate design with a triangle running toward the center and back toward the edges (see pp. 50, 70–72). In my own experience of learning to weave during the 1960s, I discovered that diagonal lines are much more difficult than the "stair step" patterns typical of Two Grey Hills rugs.

Reichard's teacher, Marie, however, was perfectly willing to follow her pupil's wishes and help Reichard weave the complex design she wanted. Reichard, however, could not figure out how to make a diagonal line just by watching Marie. Navajos learn by watching. The student observes someone doing a task until she has mastered the details and feels she can try it herself. We Anglos want clear instructions. In the case of weaving, we need to be able to count the precise number of warp threads used with a certain color and, above all, to be able to write it all down. Reichard's frustration with her own ability to learn simply just by watching and the ways in which she finally figured out how to achieve a particular woven effect are well described in Chapter 10, pages 72–73.

Reichard, however, clearly enjoyed the challenges of weaving. "I spend many hours a day weaving and the rest working on Navajo. I have never been so intrigued by a job as by this one, for after all gathering genealogies was a bore, second to none I know of except recording texts! The weaving is a foil for the language study. At supper time I suddenly realize I am so tired I can hardly move and it took me two weeks to figger why. Then I realized that wen [*sic*] at my giddiest I have never worked 12 hr. with hardly a break. But it is only a healthy weariness and results are a satisfaction" (ECP: GR to ECP, 7/6/30).

By the end of her first summer, Reichard has worked on three rugs, completely finishing her small third one so that she felt she could weave on her own. She wrote to Parsons, "I had grandiose notions of giving you this one [her first rug] but now I am more humble. You wouldn't have it around the place, and I think I'll hang it in my office as an illustration of the way a rug ought *not* to be made" (ECP: GR to ECP, 7/6/30). A few months later, she felt that it was "advisable to keep the three I made as a learner's exhibit. I probably wouldn't have learned so much had I made fewer mistakes. As it is, I learned a hell of a lot!" (ECP: GR to ECP, 12/30/30).

The account of the details of weaving are broken up by a trip to the well to dye yarn, descriptions of Red Point's sandpainting designs, a trip to a Navajo Council meeting, and a heavy rainstorm in which lightning hit Red Point's sheep herd and a tornado tore out a local diversion dam. At the end of the summer she reported, "The Navajo trip is over and nice it was. I may not know more facts about the Navajo—hardly true!—but at least I understand them a lot better. The only thing I could do to 'belong' more would be to be initiated which means to belong ceremonially. Otherwise I am theirs" (ECP: GR to ECP, 9/13/30.)

Reichard resumed her weaving during the second summer (1931). "We had a blanket in the loom the second day I got here. And altho I wept tears when I took my last one out last year, I was able to weave at once when I arrived this [time]. And so far I do not think the rug is crawling up tight on me! But there is so much to learn! I shan't be happy now until I learn to dye wool in the natural colors. There is quite a revival of that here now and I think I can get a woman to teach me. But you see I am spending most time on the language" (ECP: GR to ECP, 7/11/31). Reichard's progress in weaving, a sheep dip, and other events are briefly described in Chapters 14–17.

Reichard's third summer gives us much more insight into Navajo religion (Chapters 18–25). Much of this section of the book is taken up with her experiences when Red Point performs a Shooting Way Ceremony for his daughter and granddaughter, Marie and Ninaba. Reichard gives us perhaps the most detailed and understandable account of a Navajo ceremony, not only discussing what she saw and heard, but how it relates to Navajo theories of illness and health and how it fits into the context of real lives.

Reichard is ambivalent about the changes coming to the Navajo during the 1930s. On the one hand, she cherishes the traditionalism of "her family" and rails against the damage she sees white society visiting on Navajo culture. On the other, she is active in bringing about change herself. Often she does not recognize her own role in the larger U.S. economy and society that is the vehicle for change. She disparages the

Kinni's-Sons, a family that lives in Thoreau, near Gallup, New Mexico. "These people live near the railroad. They have been exploited for years by white people. They are on the defensive against exploitation, but they really have no defense." The wife seems content to help Reichard learn how to weave double-sided saddle blankets, a tricky, complex process, accepting Reichard's offer for payment. Kinni's-Son, however, feels that Reichard "ought to pay my wife a large sum for having her teach you" since "you will teach the white women to weave so that the Navajo women won't be able to earn money any more" (p. 216). Reichard often failed to see herself as part of the white world and as associated with the system she saw as having such a negative impact on the Navajo. Thus it was much more difficult for her to sympathize with Kinni's-son's point of view (that she might be able to exploit Navajo women) and much easier to identify with Red Point, the traditional Navajo ceremonialist (who also was sympathetic to whites). Reichard expects Kinni's-Son's wife to provide her with grey yarn and then complains when the grey yarn does not match and the white is dirty. Reichard chalks these problems up to lack of standards on the part of Kinni's-Son's wife rather than considering that she might be making impossible demands on a family that is less well off than Red Point's.

Reichard often deplored the uselessness of white boarding school education (which during this period taught girls how to cook, clean, and perform other household chores so they could become domestics in Anglo homes) (see Reichard n.d.b). She criticized the impact of missionaries and the bungling of the BIA bureaucracy. On the other hand, she sought ways in which Navajos could better integrate into the larger U.S. society. She taught Navajo adults to write in their own language and worked with them to translate English medical terms into Navajo.

We can see her ambivalence and her attempt to grapple with Navajo beliefs and understand them on their own terms when Red Point refuses to take a very sick Maria Antonia to the hospital, instead finding a singer to perform a Navajo ceremony over her. "You see we can't possible take her to the hospital. Little-Singer died there yesterday afternoon" (p. 250). She then recounts her reaction.

> I am shocked. I understand perfectly why my grandmother cannot go there. A place where one dies is contaminated, and if anyone goes there, he puts himself in the way of the worst. I know, too, as do they all, although they do not say it, that Little-Singer is the fourth person to die at the hospital within a week. After considering the implications I suggest, "But could the doctor come here to see her?" (p. 250)

The family agrees, but the doctor is not to be found, and Reichard eventually helps the family find an appropriate singer. Here, as in other situations, Reichard tries to find a solution which will not offend Navajo beliefs but will allow family members to utilize some aspect of white society that might prove beneficial.

Reichard's attitudes emerge clearly in her book, and although from the standpoint of the 1990s we might criticize her views, they are there in the text, rather than erased or hidden as was typical in more traditional ethnographic writing.

Navajos in the 1990s

The Navajo life described in *Spider Woman* is that of women who are the grandmothers and great-grandmothers of high school and college-aged Navajo women in the 1990s. Today young girls of Yikadezba's age attend school and will likely graduate from a reservation high school. Many young Navajo women attend Navajo Community College (located in Tsaile with branches in Shiprock and Tuba City) or community colleges and state universities in both New Mexico and Arizona.

Navajo families live in an economy entirely different from that of the 1930s, one dominated by wage work and various forms of third-party payments (railroad retirement, Social Security, AFDC, General Assistance, food stamps). Stock reduction in the 1930s meant that Navajos could no longer live off their sheep herd and their fields. Some wage jobs for men became available in the 1930s when the Civilian Conservation Corps (CCC) hired Navajos on a number of projects. While Navajo women worked in war industries in towns surrounding the reservation, Navajo men were drafted in World War II (some becoming the famous Code Talkers whose Navajo-based code was never cracked by the Japanese). After the war, Navajo men worked for the railroad laying and repairing track, with Navajo families migrating to agricultural areas to pick fruit and harvest vegetables. The Hopi-Navajo Rehabilitation Act of 1950 brought schools, hospitals, and paved roads to the reservation. By the mid-1960s, traditional economic pursuits (sheep herding, weaving, and agriculture) contributed only 14 percent of community income in some areas of the reservation (Lamphere 1977:24). Most Navajos were living off wages, Social Security, welfare, and other sources of cash income. By the 1990s, wage work was even more pervasive, with many Navajos working in the tribal government, hospitals, schools, or the BIA. Local chapters, using money reallocated from the Navajo Nation, were able to hire local men, women, and, during the summer, high school and college students, on work projects or local training projects. On the downside, the Navajo reservation has a very high unemployment rate; many of those eager and qualified for work cannot find jobs. Only 52 percent of the men were in the paid labor force in 1979, while 35.4 percent of the women and 45.55 percent of mothers with children under six had paid employment. In addition, 47.3 percent of families were below the federal poverty level (Navajo Nation 1988:14)

Most Navajo families no longer occupy hoghans. Instead, although they may live in the same dispersed residence groups as their grandmothers and great grandmothers, they are more likely to have a tribally built house or a trailer with a bathroom, running water, electricity, and modern stove and refrigerator. Others live in federally funded "suburbs," clusters of low-cost ranch housing, that have grown up near trading posts and schools. Nevertheless in 1979 more than 53.8 percent of Navajo homes lacked complete plumbing, 76.8 percent lacked central heating (and were probably heated by wood stoves), and 45.8 percent lacked electrical lighting (Navajo Nation 1988:15).

The pickup has replaced the horse and the Navajo horse-drawn wagon as the typical mode of transportation. The trading post has been replaced by small convenience stores, and most Navajos do their major shopping at supermarkets located in off-reservation towns (Farmington, Gallup, Flagstaff) or at large stores on the reservation (in, e.g., Shiprock, Tuba City, and Ft. Defiance). Because many Navajo families have moved to border towns, restaurants, gas stations, and stores are not only patronized by Navajos but employ large numbers of Navajos.

High school students are avid basketball players, wear the latest in fashionable sneakers, t-shirts, and haircuts and are up to date on the most recent rock music. Navajos watch as much TV as other Americans (from large color sets that are inevitably turned on during the day and evening hours) and are just as interested in discussing the latest sports statistics, the O.J. Simpson trial in 1994, or the crash of TWA Flight 800 in 1996.

Many Navajos have converted to Christianity; evangelical adherents (Nazarenes, Pentecostals) and Mormons increased in large numbers after World War II. The Native American Church (the Peyote Religion) is also important on the reservation. Traditional religion is still alive, too. Many

Navajos both attend Native American church ceremonies or Mormon, Catholic, and main-line Protestant services and utilize traditional Navajo ceremonialists (singers, curers, handtremblers, and other diagnosticians) (Aberle 1982, Henderson 1982).

Navajo weaving has changed too. Most women in their thirties and forties do not have time to weave, unless they are in families where weaving has remained a strong tradition. Many young women are not learning to weave at all. Processed wool (spun for both warp and weft by Navajo weavers) and single yarn and multiple-ply yarn (already commercially spun) are used by many weavers, who see them as saving time and labor. According to Hedlund, this continues a long tradition of utilizing Western and commercial products in Navajo weaving (Hedlund 1986). New design ideas and regional styles have become popular, and Navajo women often buy their materials and market their rugs far from their local communities. Navajo weavers are getting higher prices for their rugs; some are able to market their rugs through cooperatives or rug auctions. Since they command such high prices, Navajo rugs are now treated as tapestries and art objects rather than something to grace the floor of a home or office. Several museums have mounted important exhibitions of both historical and contemporary collections (Hedlund 1991a, 1991b).

Aftermath

Gladys Reichard spent the summer of 1934 at Red Point's residence group. She received funding from the Bureau of Indian Affairs for a hoghan school to teach Navajo adults how to write in their own language. In the fall, *Spider Woman* was published, and in the next few years she wrote two additional books about her experiences with Red Point's family: *Navajo Shepherd and Weaver* (1936), a more technical account of how to weave, and *Dezba: Woman of the Desert* (1939) a novel centering on the female head of a Navajo family, a woman much like Maria Antonia.

Miguelito died in October 1937, and his daughter, Atlnaba, died the next spring. Reichard was clearly upset by both deaths. Of her adopted "grandfather" (shichei) she said, "Miguelito's death is a great blow to me, both personally for I admired the old man, and scientifically, for I had not nearly finished working with him." To Roman Hubbell she wrote about the family's second loss, "I am simply speechless about Atlnaba and especially in my feelings for Marie. I don't know why anyone should have to take that much. . . . There is now really no head left in any sense to the family." Marie, her husband and son, and a niece eventually moved to join large family; the head mother in the family belonged to Marie's clan and her husband belonged to Tom's clan.

Within a few years her anthropological mentors Elsie Clews Parsons and Franz Boas also died, Parsons in 1941 and Boas in 1942. With these important personal relationships broken, both on the Navajo reservation and in New York, Reichard went on to publish much more general books on Navajo religion and language. Her short monograph *Prayer: The Compulsive Word* (1944) outlined some of her analysis of Navajo religion as well as the structure of Navajo prayers used during chants or sings. Her magnum opus, *Navaho Religion,* appeared in 1950, and *Navaho Grammar* was published in 1951. Reichard continued to teach at Barnard, and she influenced a number of women graduate students at Columbia who were her Barnard teaching assistants. These included Eleanor Leacock (a well-known feminist anthropologist), Nathalie Woodbury (a Southwestern archaeologist), Kate Peck Kent (who became a specialist in Southwestern prehistoric textiles), and Katharine Bartlett (curator and librarian for the Museum of Northern Arizona). From 1940 on, Reichard spend many of her summers, as well as two sabbaticals, at the Museum of Northern Arizona in Flagstaff. She died there in 1955, of a stroke (Mark 1980: 572).

Although Reichard's contributions to the understanding of Navajo religion, particularly her ability to understand Navajo categories without imposing Western conceptions, are considered by some to be her most important work, *Spider Woman* and *Dezba* remain innovative ethnographic descriptions. Scholars are taking a renewed interest in them because of the information they provide on weaving as a woman's craft, the lives of Navajo women, family interaction, the assimilation of Navajo through schools and missionaries during the 1930s, and the interaction between Anglos and Navajos. These books convey the personal quality of Reichard's relation with the women in Red Point's family and her great regard for Red Point himself. Her connection to him is vividly recounted in a letter to Roman Hubbell on his death.

I am sorta numb still from the shock of your letter which arrived yesterday. Before everything I want you to know how much I appreciate your sitting down and writing me the first thing, and in such detail, too. It marks the end of an epoch with me, really I shall have to start all over psychologically and I am doubtful so far as to how I shall do it . . . But if that is true with me, how much more so with you and all those who came to depend on Miguelito for the things he had to offer. It is too unbelievable and sudden to be able to get a perspective. . . . I don't seem to have any fancy words in which to say it, but it is simply that the experience with Mig's family was an event in my life and if you had not sent me to him, I should have missed all that richness (HP:GR/RH 10/14/36).

Archival Sources of Correspondence

BHP Berard Haile Papers (AZ 132) Box 3a, Folder 5, University
Library, University of Arizona, Tucson
Gladys Reichard to Berard Haile: November 11, 1936.
ECP Elsie Clews Parsons Papers. American Philosophical Society, Philadelphia.

Gladys Reichard to Elsie Clews Parsons, July 6, 1930; September 13, 1930; December 30, 1930; February 24, 1931; July 11, 1931; January 25, 1932; July 9, 1932; February 24, 1937.

HP Hubbell Papers (AZ 375) Special Collections, Main Library University of Arizona, Tucson.

Gladys Reichard to Roman Hubbell: October 14, 1936

1937

References

Aberle, David F.

1966   *Peyote Religion.* Chicago: University of Chicago Press.

1982   "The Future of Navajo Religion" in *Navajo Religion and Culture: Selected Views.* pp. 219–232. Ed. David M. Brugge and Charlotte J. Frisbie. Santa Fe: Museum of New Mexico Press.

Abu-Lughod, Lila

1993   *Writing Women's Worlds.* Berkeley: University of California Press.

Behar, Ruth

1993   *Translated Woman: Crossing the Border with Esperanza's Story.* Boston: Beacon Press.

Boas, Franz

1908   "Decorative Designs of Alaskan Needlecases: A Study in the History of Conventional Designs, Based on Materials in the U.S. National Museum." Proceedings of the U.S. National Museum, vol 34, pp. 321–344.

1966   *Kwakiutl Ethnography.* Edited by Helen Codere. Chicago: University of Chicago Press.

Clifford, James

1988   *The Predicament of Culture.* Cambridge, Mass.: Harvard University Press.

Clifford, James and George Marcus, eds.

1986   *Writing Culture: The Poetics and Politics of Ethnography.* Berkeley: University of California Press.

Hedlund, Ann Lane

1986   "Commercial Materials in Modern Navajo Rugs." *The Textile Museum Journal,* vol 25:83–96.

1991a   "Current Trends in Navajo Weaving." *Focus/Santa Fe.* pp 10–15, July.

1991b   "Then and Now: Contemporary Navajo Perspectives on Weaving." In Eulalie Wierdsma, ed. *Woven from life: Historic Principles and Contemporary Perspectives on Navajo Weaving.* Austin: University of Texas Press.

Henderson, Eric

1982   "Kaibeto Plateau Ceremonialists: 1860–1980." In Brugge and Frisbie: 164–175.

1989   "Navajo Livestock Wealth and the Effects of the Stock Reduction." *Journal of Anthropological Research,* vol.45, no. 4: 379–404.

Lamphere, Louise

1977   *To Run After Them: The Cultural and Social Bases of Coperation in a Navajo Community.* Tucson: University of Arizona Press.

Mark, Joan

1980   "Gladys Reichard, July 17, 1893-July 25, 1955, Anthropologist," *Notable American Women, Vol.4,* ed. Barbara Sicherman, Coral Hurd Green. Cambridge, Mass.: Belknap Press of Harvard University.

Navajo Nation

1988   FAX 1988. Window Rock, Technical Support Department Navajo Nation.

Parezo, Nancy

1983   *Navajo Sandpainting: From Religious Act to Commercial Art.* Tucson: University of Arizona Press.

Reichard, Gladys

1928   *Social Life of the Navajo Indians.* Columbia University Contributions to Anthropology Vol.7. New York: Columbia University Press.

1936   *Navajo Shepherd and Weaver.* New York: J.J. Augustin.

1938   "Grammar of the Coeur d'Alene Language." *Handbook of American Indian Languages* no. 3:517–707. New York: J.J. Augustin.

1939   *Dezba: Woman of the Desert.* New York: J.J. Augustin.

1944   *Prayer: The Compulsive Word.* Monographs of the American Ethnological Society no. 7. New York: J.J. Augustin.

1950   *Navaho Religion: A Study of Symbolism.* 2 vols. New York: Bollingen Foundation.

1951   *Navaho Grammar,* ed. Marian Smith. Publications of the American Ethnological Society no. 21. New York: J.J.

n.d.a   *Another Look at the Navajo.* Ms. on file, Reichard Papers, Museum of Northern Arizona, Flagstaff.

n.d.b   "Assimilation or Extinction?" Ms. on file, Reichard Papers, Museum of Northern Arizona, Flagstaff.

Rosaldo, Renato

1989   *Culture and Truth: The Remaking of Social Analysis.* Boston: Beacon Press.

ACKNOWLEDGMENTS

THE Story of Navajo Weavers and Chanters is self-explanatory as to characters and circumstances. The only distortion of which I am conscious is a slight one of time and sequence. There is no twisting of facts; if there is of interpretation it is because of lack of understanding rather than of the will to understand.

My acknowledgments must be necessarily feeble in proportion to the harvest I have reaped of good will and kindness. The first are due to the Southwest Society, which had enough faith in a dubious undertaking to start me on my way. I thank next the Council for Research in the Social Sciences of Columbia University, which kept me going once I had started.

When I consider the service, spiritual and physical, rendered by the members of the J. L. Hubbell Trading Post, Ganado, Arizona, I am overwhelmed with the inadequacy of my vocabulary. Mr. Roman Hubbell, Old-Mexican's-Son, understood in a flash my somewhat difficult problems, and when he suggested Red-Point's family as the one with which to work he put the stamp of success on my project. He himself is a constant source of stimulation and inspiration as he follows my progress with ever-eager interest and coöperation. The sentiment applies equally to Mr. Lorenzo Hubbell of Oraibi.

My thanks to Mrs. Goodman, Mrs. Parker, Mrs. Hubbell, and their children are of the kind the lone stranger must have mentally accorded to the Good Samaritan when he came to.

The debt I contracted when I accepted the generalized information collected by Mr. Lloyd Ambrose (Mr. Little-Man-with-the-Spectacles) and Mr. Horace Boardman (Mr. Short-Pants) is one which can never be canceled since it is measured in the saving of that most rare and precious commodity, time. Mrs. Laura Armer (White-Haired-White-Woman) made the same sort of contribution. I am indebted to Franc J. Newcomb for the double sand-painting.

Can words express the satisfaction the acquisition of the friendship of a family like Red-Point's can give? I have tried to let *Spider Woman* make my declaration for me.

To Ruth M. Underhill, Charlotte Leavitt Dyer, and Elizabeth Howsare I waft gratitude for constructive criticism of the manuscript, and to Adele Froehlich for "walking happily" amidst the mechanical drudgery necessary to its preparation. There are many others who have helped by their interest and suggestions; I have not forgotten them, nor am I unappreciative.

I cannot sign my name to this and leave out the word "hospitality." I find the Southwest ever hospitable and, in emphasizing my feeling of well-being there, must refer back to the residents of the Southwest previously mentioned as largely responsible for it. This includes all their families and many others which the exigencies of space forbid me naming individually.

GLADYS A. REICHARD

Barnard College, New York City.

TABLE OF CONTENTS

TABLE OF CONTENTS

ILLUSTRATIONS

SPIDER WOMAN

I

WHITE-SANDS

WHITE-SANDS lay silent and motionless in the dead light of mid-afternoon. Here and there a soft, capricious wind stirred up a tiny whirl of dust. A muffled lazy cluck came from a contented huddle of feathers where a hen leisurely gave herself a dust bath. Even the decrepit horde of mongrel dogs was scattered, asleep, or at least indifferent. The few houses with their covering of clay merged into the dull background of the clearing apparently devoid of life. A few yards north of the largest hut was a queer structure. An indeterminate arrangement of odds and ends of sticks and boards from packing boxes was stuck upright in the ground, forming an uncertain circle beginning at the trunk of a gnarled and northward-leaning piñon which served as a roof to this thing. For want of a better name it must be called a shade, because it served as such; but it is strictly individualistic: there was never a structure like it before, it would be impossible to duplicate it. Across the entrance of this affair two boards were laid as a barrier—against what, it is hard to say, for animals could gain ingress at almost any crack. If one crack were too small, a larger one could be found with ease, or the boards could be nosed farther apart at their loose upper ends. The barrier showed, however, that the people who used the shade were elsewhere.

A large dome-shaped hut appeared to be the center of the small settlement. The door was closed but the lock hung loose in the hasp. A cursory glance through the crack above the door showed that it, like the shade, was empty. We opened the door upon a neat silence. There was a broad expanse of carefully swept sand floor, hard and smooth from use, around two sides of which sheepskins, freshly shaken and fluffy, were laid. A large loom occupied the entire height and width of the north side of the house. A blanket five feet wide, about one-quarter finished, of gray, black, white, and tan was strung on it. A small packing case stood on the floor at the right. It contained the worker's yarns, weaving combs and the other small implements of her craft. Her batten was neatly laid between the top cords that fasten the movable part of her loom to the loom proper. All these signs told us of a good weaver who had left her work temporarily.

Carefully closing the door upon the cool silence, we sought further for the inhabitants. At a considerable distance to the south and slightly west is another hut, like the first in all but size, for this one is smaller. It, too, is dome-shaped and blends into the sand background of the clearing. But the door of this one, at the east as was the other, is open, and from its interior comes a dull *thump thump,* the sound of the comb pounding firmly, regularly, and rapidly the yarn which is becoming a Navajo rug. We stand respectfully at the doorway for a time, looking in and allowing our eyes to become accustomed to the dimness of the light, a contrast to the harsh glare from which we came. The woman, sitting on the floor before the loom at the west side continues thumping her comb, as if we did not exist, her way of greeting us respectfully.

This house bulges with life. Bursting sacks of wool hang from its sides. Long, clean, brightly colored skeins of spun yarn hang from the beams and loom posts. The box on the floor at the woman's side has strands of pink and red, orange and green, brown, gray and black yarn fringing its edges. Each one holds itself in readiness to be pulled by its mistress' skilful fingers. A cat rubs our legs, by way of investigative greeting, and returns to her litter of kittens behind the loom. A white dog with a black ear, no larger than a puppy herself, gives a warning yelp notifying us to keep clear of her two pups behind the flour box.

Now Old-Mexican's-Son, the trader, who is introducing me, directs a witty greeting to the woman at the loom. She, for the first time, shows awareness of our presence. We enter. The trader, who is at home in this Indian family, after pushing aside several dogs, uncertainly tolerant, and removing a pile of wool set out for the carding, finds himself a place on a soft sheepskin where he half reclines, lighting his pipe. The woman interrupts her weaving long enough to turn on me a gleaming smile and to indicate a strong low box on which I, being a stranger, may sit. As we talk and smoke, the woman weaves, her swiftly moving fingers causing the blanket to grow visibly. As I watch, I am consumed with envy mingled with admiration, for this is what I have come to learn.

The talk first locates the members of the family. The old mother, whose blanket stands upright in its loom, quiet and unfinished, is hoeing corn about half a mile away. Her husband, Red-Point, the head of this family, is at Ganado, six miles away, directing the irrigation of his fields. The woman, with her lips pursed toward the west, indicates that her sister, Marie, whom we came to see, is at her own home.

Conversation between the trader and the weaver continues, he sometimes interpreting for me, as the afternoon drones on. A lamb bleats at the door, comes in and smells us all, takes a drink from a basin near the entrance, walks over to her mistress for petting. Various goats and sheep, all pets, and dogs stalk in and are chased out by an unconvincing "Su! Su!" A baby, just able to walk, peeps shyly around the doorpost and backs away. Her sister, two years older, somewhat bolder, comes in and settles between her aunt and the trader, not daring to take her position near the strange white woman, to whom she is nevertheless attracted. The trader has learned where everybody is, that Marie will doubtless sell him a sheep, and he now comes to the main business of the day.

Here is a white woman, peculiar in many ways, who wants to learn to weave. As he tells the weaver this, she darts at me a pleased but quizzical look. Furthermore this white woman wants to live right here with the Indians. She wants to have a shade like theirs. She wants a loom anchored to the ground at which she can sit as they sit, on the ground. She wants to learn to weave as Navajo women weave. This particular Navajo woman is interested, but she cannot help being amused. The white woman had shown she liked the weaver from the moment she saw her, the weaver had reciprocated. But, if Marie is to teach her, we must see Marie.

The weaver finishes thumping down the row of yarn she has just laid in along her carefully parted warps, removes her batten, and lays it carefully along the upper cords of her loom. She then winds into its respective ball each thread of the variegated fringe hanging over her wool-box. We all rise, and with a comprehensive "Su! Su!" at the various animals who do not belong in the house, we go out into a different world.

White-Sands has come to life. The sun is on its rapid way to the west. The sand, no longer dull brown, has turned to rose, the piñons and junipers, in mid-afternoon dark dots on the landscape, now cast long purple shadows over the rose-colored earth; shadows draw the scattered objects—trees, houses, corrals, even bunches of grass—into a mellow, home-like whole, a contrast of rose and darkness and over all a golden glow. From the south comes a bleating within a cloud of gold dust. The flocks are coming home. Along the road from the same direction the clatter of wagon wheels and the deliberate tread of horses. The dogs, now an active antagonistic band, make ready to meet the horses with ear-splitting barks. The driver, complacently singing in a high falsetto, patiently urges the horses on.

We go toward Marie's house, but the children—there are now five—indicate that she is at the corral behind her house. Here we find her smiling a shy greeting as she stands among the sheep and goats, animated bunches of wool milling around and around her. Old-Mexican's-Son bargains for his sheep amidst the moving, bleating, belching, coughing flock. In an offhand way he remarks that I am coming here Monday morning to learn to weave (today is Saturday). He wants Tom, who is driving in now with the filled water barrels, to make me a shade by that time, when I will move in. No one denies the trader a wish, much less this Navajo family, whose daughters grew up with him. In a more timidly offhand manner they acquiesce, and we with a "Well, let's go!" start back to the trading post in my new Ford, which now interests dogs, children and grown-ups alike. Monday morning I will begin to learn to weave.

II

ESTABLISHED

UPON my arrival at White-Sands early Monday morning the dogs give me a vociferous and unfriendly welcome. I turn off the motor of Jonathan, my Ford, and wait until Red-Point quiets them. His few decided words cause them to slink in all directions, tails between legs, growling, disgruntled, thwarted. Several women, among them the old mother of the family, stand before the entrance of the shade, holding their hands before their mouths with shyness, ready to duck into the shade at a second's notice. This is not my first experience with the Navajo, and I have already learned to observe the short period of silence required by good manners when coming to a house. This over, I am not obliged to hunt up the family. Marie approaches from her home preceded by her husband, Tom, a lean handsome fellow smiling a welcome.

"We didn't build a shade. There is a storehouse up here. The old man thought it would be a better place for you to live than a shade. At this time of the year there are so many gnats. You can look at it, and if you don't like it we can build you a shade."

So saying, Tom leads off followed by me and the bevy of women and children who have assembled. He leads us to the apparent hole-in-the-ground which is from this time on to be considered mine. It is dug out of the earth about five feet

MY HOUSE

BEN HOLDS SPOT IN FRONT OF MARIA
ANTONIA'S SHADE

MARIE AND ATLNABA RIG THE WARP-FRAME

ATLNABA STRINGS WARP

deep. To enter, we go down a step cut out of the ground, take two paces along a passage and down one more high step. Within, it is cool and comfortable. It has been neatly swept, and in some respects is more desirable than the ordinary Navajo hogan, or house. No one has ever lived in it—it has been used as a storeplace for wool in the winter. It is spacious, about twelve by fifteen feet in size and at least six feet high, and the light, from the large doorway at the east, is good—almost a studio light—at all times of the day.

It takes no time for us to move my possessions, modest as they are, into the storehouse. Tom shoulders the army trunk full of heavy books; Marie gets hold of the blanket roll; her sister, Atlnaba, the first one of the family I had met two days before at her weaving, takes hold of one end of the grub-box, and I of the other. The bustle is short-lived. Within a few minutes my baggage is in place. The trunk makes a good table, but Marie, accustomed to white people's ways, sends a young girl to Red-Point's house for a homemade table. She sends her niece to her own house for a wagon cover which she lends me indefinitely for a carpet. My house is furnished, and we view the prospects for weaving.

I convince them that I really want to learn, and, satisfied that the house suits me and assured that I want to start weaving, the sooner the better, Tom starts off to make the loom-frame. The south side of the house is an ideal place for the simple structure. He has only to measure the space with his eye, get his ax from his own house, and he is off to hew the necessary parts from trees on the place. During the time he is gone we women settle for a talk to get acquainted. While we talk, Marie's mother, Maria Antonia, comes in. She could not come while Tom, her son-in-law, was there, for Navajo women never "see" their sons-in-law. One of the children, with a word and a gesture, has informed her that he is gone for a goodly period of time and she may now come in to satisfy her curiosity.

The women visiting me at this time are my three teachers, Maria Antonia, the old woman who made her daughters famous; Atlnaba, who now with the energy of youth surpasses her mother; and Marie, a self-taught expert and my interpreter. Maria Antonia's smile is not less sweet because toothless. Marie is not less energetic or enduring because comfortably plump. With these exceptions every member of the family, male and female alike, gives a first impression of wiry leanness and of perfect teeth. Herding sheep and riding horseback keep down superfluous fat, constant chewing of freshly killed mutton makes teeth strong and white.

Marie, as interpreter, enumerates the members of the family and tells me their names, those given them by whites and their real Navajo names. She tells me also how old each person is. I, in turn, tell them how old I am, how·many older brothers and sisters I have, how many younger, how I teach girls in winter, visit and learn from Indians in summer, and why I want to learn to weave.

Now a child, playing outside, gives a warning, and Maria Antonia disappears. Within a few minutes Tom comes in again with three freshly cut poles, perhaps four inches in diameter, on his shoulder. He has hacked off the bark but has taken no pains to smooth the surface. On the contrary, he has purposely avoided the smoothness of which his ax is capable, for the rough protuberances will prove useful to us. He brings also a smooth four-by-four stringer about seven feet long. He lays these materials on the floor along the side where the loom is to be. Accepting a proffered cigarette, he squats near the doorway, his weight on his right foot and on the toes of his left, for a short rest.

Red-Point, the patriarch, comes as head of the household to perform his duties of welcome. He admires the coolness and comfort of my house. It is cooler than his and the others because it is underground. For his benefit and Tom's I repeat details of my age, my interests, and my family relationships. Red-Point approves of Tom's choice of posts for the loom, and makes several suggestions about setting them up. He stays only a cigarette interval, saying he must find his horse to go to Ganado. The time is long enough, however, to make me feel thoroughly at home, to convey verbally the feeling which the women only smile, that they are glad to have me here. They are glad I want to learn to weave; they hope they will teach me to weave well.

Our first visit, during which we have become acquainted, has strung along. The sun, slanting diagonally through the narrow wooden ventilator in the center of my roof, shows it is long past noon. The women at last file reluctantly out of my house, leaving me for brief contemplation and realization of my surroundings. My house differs from the Navajo hogan in that it has no smokehole, hence no place for a fire. But even had there been one, I should hardly have used it in the summer. At the crude fireplace of stones a few feet from my door I boil some coffee to supplement my lunch menu of baked beans and cheese. I find an arrangement of army trunk as seat in front of which I place Marie's table quite satisfactory.

As I eat, I examine the details of my house, a matter for which I had little time when entertaining my colorful visitors. The walls and floor are of natural sand hardened by use. As a foundation for the roof, small poles, an inch or two in diameter, are laid with one end on a ridgepole, the other on the ground wall. The even rows of poles form my ceiling. Over the poles soft juniper bark lies, to hold the outer covering of sand packed on when it was wet. The house, though desirably cool, is also snug. Only when the rainy season begins can I tell whether or not it is waterproof. It is early June, and there may be a month before that test will come. As the afternoon wind blows the sand about my house and the flies buzz in the sunshine outside the open door, I consider how lucky I am not to have to depend on a shade, open on four sides, for protection. I consider also the disposition of the contents of my bags, but only briefly, for Tom and Marie are back, ready to erect the loomframe.

It is a simple affair composed of rough poles, a crosspiece fastened to the floor with wedges, and two uprights made firm to the roof at the top with balewire. Tom fits the parts in place, Marie holds them for him as he fastens them. It is not long before the loomframe is not only in place but also firmly supported.

Tom stays only long enough for us to approve and admire the loomframe. I thank him and he departs, for Red-Point has asked him to round up the small herd of cattle for branding, and he has to catch his horse. As soon as Tom is well out of sight and there is no reason to expect his return for some hours, Maria Antonia comes in to help Marie string up my first blanket. Marie has brought warp, a large assortment of string, and two pieces of broomstick, each about two and one-half feet long. Maria Antonia brings in two short heavy logs and sends her granddaughter, Ninaba, for the two slender poles which are leaning against the piñon tree north of my dwelling.

With these miscellaneous-looking materials they proceed to construct a loomframe, or temporary loom. After fixing it horizontally on the floor of the house so that it cannot move, they string the warp, keep alternate strands separate by means of reeds and bind the ends with a kind of braiding. My first effort is to be only modest in size, somewhat over three hands wide and five long. A hand is the distance between the end of the thumb and the end of the middle finger. Since the rug is small, it is relatively easy to string. As Marie winds warp about two poles, her mother sits by, and we talk.

Marie says the hardest part of making a rug is stringing the warp. Some women never learn to do it. Often blankets are so large that they cannot be set up in the house. Then the temporary loom is laid outside on the ground and the tedious stringing is done by several women who consider themselves specialists at it. A woman, though expert, may require help in setting up one only four feet wide by six feet long.

Our hand measures are quite different. We measure off a comparison. It takes six of Marie's to make five of mine. Marie never makes a blanket an exact number of hands long or wide, and she says no other Navajo woman does. She allows an extra inexact measure, slightly less than half a hand.

After the braiding has been put on both ends of the warp, the parts of the temporary loom are untied and put away, and the warp lies a mass of writhing curls which if carefully handled remains orderly.

To an accompaniment of quiet conversation the women perform the succeeding steps of the warp stringing. They fasten the curling mass to sticks. With a clothesline they attach the sticks wound with strings to the loomframe which Tom has erected. They use the stringer which he left on the ground as the top, and fourth side of their frame. It can be moved up or down according to the length of the warp they are using. The roughness he has left in trimming it keeps the rope from slipping.

The warp now stands upright, firmly but loosely fastened. Now with reeds and loops of string Marie makes a "harness" which henceforth will allow us to separate the alternate strands of the warp. This is called a heald or heddle. Every other warp strand is caught up in one of its loops, so that if we pull the reed forward alternate threads will move to the front. A second reed without loops lies behind all the strands which are not caught into the heald loops. By manipulating the heald and rod properly we shall form spaces, called sheds, between the warps through which we can carry our yarn.

All this time I am an interested, if somewhat bewildered, onlooker. The process seems to me very complicated. The hands of these women are so skilful that I despair of ever competing with them in dexterity. They can even talk while they twine and braid and loop. They do not seem to think about what they are doing. But, let one of them make a move out of order, the other laughingly reminds her of her mistake.

It has taken less than two hours to make the loom. For Marie not only strung the warps but also made her loom as she proceeded. Tomorrow we will begin. I can hardly keep my fingers off the loom. I am not overly successful at disguising my eagerness. I know no Navajo would exhibit this kind of enthusiasm, even though she had it. Nevertheless, it pleases Marie as she leaves me with a tolerant smile.

At last I am alone. So many new things, the minutest details of which must be observed, all casually done by Marie and Maria Antonia. I have the idea I must learn them all at once. I know very little Navajo but during the entire day I have kept my ear cocked for words I could understand and have tried to use such simple words as I have picked up. If I elicit a burst of laughter from my visitors, I know from previous experience that I have pronounced the words correctly. If they are not perfect I get a puzzled look of non-comprehension or a correction conscientiously and seriously made. It has all kept me on the *qui vive,* but now I realize I am utterly exhausted. Coffee and tobacco are reviving, as is food. Supper is simple and brief as possible, for I do not want to miss a moment of outdoors at this time of day. I take my bed roll outside my house, lay it on the gentle smooth slope of my housetop, a vantage point from which the whole settlement may be observed.

I have had scant opportunity to become acquainted with the exterior of my dwelling. Leaning against my bed roll, I have leisure to enjoy the panorama. At this, the hour of sunset, the Southwest condenses its charm. The desert addict may not know it, but this hour is the cause of his nostalgia when he is elsewhere—yes, even in a sense when he is here. My eye roves from the rose-colored sand still covered with gray-green grass because of late rains, to the hoar-green sagebrush and over the somewhat lumpy plain abundantly dotted with pine and juniper. It is too early in the season for clouds, and the clear turquoise of the sky blends with pure lemon, gold, and red. To the east, at my right, a piñon and a juniper mingle their branches so closely I am sometimes deluded into thinking the composite is a botanical freak.

There's a gentle tinkling of bells from the south and east. Shouts accompany a collective thud of little feet becoming louder as it slowly approaches. A schoolgirl twirls a rattle, a tin can in which several pebbles have been enclosed, on the end of a string, causing the flock to veer toward the corral. Ninaba's red velvet shirt is a jewel in a wiggling fuzzy white setting. The approaching flock is like a mob of impolite humans. The goats belch and cough; one stops to nibble a likely sage bush; another eats the lower branches of a piñon. Still another finds its way into my house. I think of chasing it out, but I am too comfortable to get up; and anyway there is nothing it can harm. The sheep munch digressively along, slowly as they dare, ever interrupted by their herders; a ewe calls her wandering bleating lamb, lost through curiosity.

Fire gleams through the cracks of the shade made of odds and ends fitted about the piñon tree where Maria Antonia does her summer work. She is out at the woodpile making the chips fly. Her beehive of activity is within calling, but not within talking, distance of me. The smoke of her cedar fire, mingled with the pungent odor of the sage stirred up by the chewing goats, and with the dust of their pawing, is wafted to me on the gentlest and coolest of breezes. Along the old road from the north a rider appears. He is Curley's-Son, Atlnaba's husband, Tom's brother. Tired with the day's farming, he sings a weird song for company as his white horse lopes through the gathering darkness. A dog, tail between legs, in sneaky quiet, makes a foraging tour of my fireplace. The sheep, protesting or conversing ever more quietly, snuggle contentedly into the dust of the corral behind me. I think of Joanna Godden.

Old trite phrases come to me—"witching hour," "peace

that passeth all understanding," a Navajo group I never before fully comprehended:

> *With beauty above me I lie down,*
> *With beauty below me I lie down,*
> *With beauty before me I lie down,*
> *With beauty behind me I lie down,*
> *With beauty all around me I lie down.*

III

TENSION

The place I accidentally chose in my weariness has become my permanent sleeping porch. From it I may look into the Great Dipper all night. Queer how high they hang it out here. Perhaps because they have so little water they do not want anyone to reach it easily; he might spill it. These first nights I spend very little time star-gazing.

The next thing I am aware of is the sun's white light, a warning that he will soon peep over the horizon. This is the time a good Navajo gets up. But I am not a good Navajo, and I wink sleepily at him; he tolerates my blink as I roll over in my comfortable blankets for another hour of sleep. The branches of the freak piñon-juniper keep his rays from my eyes until the indecently late hour of six-thirty.

I am awakened a second time by a goat who wants to know what this new kind of grass is. Goats always want to know things. Dazedly I twirl my blanket strap at her and look about me. Once more long shadows, but these are clear, taut, and energetic, not softly focused and relaxing like the patterns drawn by the setting sun. The sheep have begun their lively munching, the goats their eternal uncomprehending researches. Maria Antonia is at her wood-chopping again after lighting her fire of cedar. Women trail vigorously back and forth from the old mother's shade to their own houses, their full ruffled skirts billowing behind them. The children are teasing the calf, the dogs wait on the outskirts of all this activity for the least sign of a morsel.

I am scarcely through with my morning routine, simple and brief though it is, before Marie is with me. From my lookout on the trunk I have noticed that our warp is not straight. It is noticeably shorter at the left side than at the right. I call it to Marie's attention and she calmly says, yes, she noticed it yesterday before she left. She had measured with a string the distance on the two sides of the temporary frame when she strung it, but she must have made a mistake, or more probably a crosspole slipped before it was quite tight. She sits before the loom and begins at about the middle to pull each warp at top and bottom, working toward the left, until the whole looks more even. Her patience is matched only by my impatience at this delay. At last it is straighter, although even to my crooked eye, not absolutely so.

I have chosen to make first a blanket of stripes using the typical Navajo colors, black, red, white, and gray. Marie begins with black. She makes the start so deftly that I do not learn until we start our next blanket that the first rows are different from the succeeding ones. She pulls the heald with her left hand, flicks the warp with the spread fingertips of her right, inserts a broad smooth stick called the batten, and turns it. She throws her yarn through, pounds it down, and withdraws the batten. Now she presses the heald rod against the loops of the heald and she has a different shed, the alternate warps are forward. A casual flip of the fingers across the warp, and the weft throwing and pounding are repeated.

I at first think this flipping an unnecessary, possibly an æsthetic, gesture like the elaborate motions of a bootblack's flannel. But when I take up the weaving position myself I find it serves a very useful purpose. The texture of the warp changes somewhat from the time it is first strung up to the time the blanket is finished. It is a hard-spun strong yarn, but still capable of much stretching. For this reason the warp must be tightened much more frequently at the beginning of the weaving than after it approaches the center. Furthermore there are wool fibers, so small as not to be easily discernible, which catch one another and prevent the sheds from being completely thrown. The swift light flip of the fingers separates such of these fibers on the forward warps as adhere to those behind. Constant friction of fingers, batten, comb, and yarn wears off these fibers so that as the weaving proceeds to the middle of the loom length, they are gone leaving a smooth tight warp.

Marie weaves about half of the narrow beginning black stripe, then, handing me the comb, tells me to try it myself. It is the moment I have longed for. All those things which are done so easily, so casually by the Navajo women begin to take on unsuspected difficulties when I try them. I have to think of the smallest details as if they were significant. I have for some years prided myself on being able to sit like a Navajo woman with both legs folded back at the right side and with no support for the back. But I now realize that sitting that way for a few minutes and changing posture is a different matter from remaining in the position for several hours with no satisfactory shift. And sitting is not the whole consideration. I am at the same time pounding down the yarn to the floor level and the resultant kink in the shoulder is quickly noticeable, or would be if I were not too interested in the details of my new craft.

I do not even know which way to hold the comb or batten. Marie, laughing at my awkwardness, shows me that the wide part of the batten is the top, the slightly concave side the front. I learn to hold it at the center with thumb at the front, two fingers behind it. This position allows sufficient control in inserting it. I know the principle of the sheds, but knowing and doing are different matters. I quickly learn how to alternate the heald and heald rod, but even now, after I have become proficient at weaving, the arrangement seems somewhat miraculous to me, and in those early days I had to think out each shift.

After I have my shed thrown and my batten in, Marie shows me how to hold the comb. Its tapering handle rests on the bone of the lower thumb joint; the comb is held loosely between the first two and the last two fingers. Since we are weaving stripes which extend across the entire width of the blanket, it is possible to throw the yarn or weft all the way across if it is wound on a reed about twelve to fifteen inches long. This is a crude shuttle. We have one for each color to be laid in stripes. In all other cases we carry the yarn through with the fingers.

After I have got as far as inserting my first weft yarn, I press it down with the batten, as I have seen Navajo women do, or as I thought I had seen them do. "Why do you do that?" says Marie. "I thought that's the way you do," say I meekly. "Never," says Marie emphatically. "Only poor weavers do that. You should pound it down tight with the comb."

I manage to do so, but in my concentration to handle the comb properly I have dropped the batten. It has turned over and I have to figure out its top and front once more. The next time I carefully pull out the batten and hold it in place only to find I have laid down my comb. I fumble for it and get it once more into position. Within a few days during which I not only weave but watch the others for hours on end, I learn by an almost imperceptible motion to shift the comb from the position necessary for pounding to the position of rest.

Theoretically the healds regulate the warp; actually one must be constantly on guard, especially at the beginning of the rug where the warp is rough and stretchy, against picking up a warp or a series of them from the wrong set. A little practice shows me such mistakes as I weave along, and I gradually get a feeling of intimacy for the strands.

I am now beginning to coördinate healds, batten, comb, shedding, inserting the weft and pounding it down. True I occasionally hit my knees with the comb, but my injuries have no interest for me except later in retrospect. In addition to all these matters I am bothered seriously by the heavy double binding strands. They are not a part of the loom, but are tied to the upper and lower sticks after the loom is complete. Nevertheless they are of primary importance. I learn from Marie that the test of a blanket is its edge. If it is bound in evenly it will not pull when the weaving is done, it will exhibit a pleasing purl at the exact center of the rug's thickness, and it will run exactly parallel to the opposite edge its entire length. In other words, the width of the blanket will be uniform throughout.

I must not forget to include these edge strands; I must twist them properly and give an additional twist at proper intervals.

As I throw the lumpy shuttle reeds from right to left and

from left to right, I find that my stripe sags in the middle, in fact sags badly. I have noticed that expert weavers often place additional weft strands at what seem arbitrary places and for short distances. They know that an unevenness of only a thread's width will be a fault. I have allowed mine to become a veritable scallop before Marie suggests my filling it in. Had I been as discerning as she, one row would have done the trick. As it is, I must work with it for several rows and even then the stripe is far from straight. I have also a convex scallop at a different place from the sagging one. I can find no reason for this, but in her matter-of-fact way Marie tightens the warp; and after several rows of filling in, the difficulty is overcome. Once in a while Marie rescues the blanket from my blundering fingers. She tightens the warp, straightens the stripes, corrects the edges.

As I struggle along, learning to control unaccustomed muscles, Marie sits by my side watching carefully lest I make a mistake. We don't talk much, except about the points of the weaving. A child doesn't talk when he is learning to write. Besides, Marie does not "tell" when teaching. She "shows." The Navajo word for "teach" means "show" and is absolutely literal. As the minutes fly, Marie winds the colors on my reeds.

I have come toward the top of my second stripe, a red one, when Maria Antonia comes in. She shows Marie that the left edge is drawing in. Marie takes the comb from me, turns it, and with its sharp point loosens the weft on the left side by pulling it up and spreading the warp with strong horizontal movements which look dangerous to me. I have yet to learn that any blanket worth a continental will survive a greater pressure than this, that all calculations are made on the basis

of this tremendous strain. Another row or so shows that even
this treatment is not sufficiently drastic, and the women see
the rug still drawing in. I myself see nothing to fuss about.
I am to get the shock all at once much later.

Maria Antonia cuts out the sixth warp from the left, elimi-
nates it entirely. I weave on for several rows as she watches.
Marie has shown me how to lay the weft so that it will not
pull in; she has also shown me how to manipulate my comb
with a subtle twist so that the yarn will lie more loosely. But it
is only much later, after I have practised alone considerably,
that I rediscover this subtlety. I hit upon it accidentally and
analyze it; from that time on it is mine. My attempts at laying the yarn loosely are unsuccessful, and now Maria Antonia,
as a last resort, ties a piece of warp yarn firmly into the finished web and hitches it to the left upright of the loomframe.
I have seen many a Navajo at her weaving, but never have
I seen a makeshift like this. The feature most humiliating to
me is that the edge does not look crooked to me, at least not
very crooked.

The argument of the two women and their taking over the
weaving for a few minutes have been an immense relief for
me. I have become almost too stiff to move. They laugh at me
and say, as I draw my legs slowly but lengthily forth from the
folds of my skirt, "You are like a stick."

My hand feels better for the respite also, as does my
shoulder. The comb, being heavy because of the notion this
family has that the batten must not be used for pounding
home the weft, comes down with the cunning torture of a
minor inquisition on the bone of the second thumb joint.
This particular point of the weaver's anatomy receives all the
impact of the weft's reaction. Small wonder it is that many

Navajo use light combs and rely on the batten for beating the weft tight, at least where it is laid straight. I am still feeling too inferior to mention this slight annoyance, but secretly I am pleased to stop for a moment.

I have finished four stripes, a little less than a hand, at the end of this my first day, a black, a red, a white, and a gray one. With standards not very highly developed I am quite pleased with the result of my handiwork as I, eating supper, view it from my trunk. The red stripe lies straighter than the black, the white deviates less than the red. With the gray I have had more trouble than with any, but its upper edge, although not completely satisfactory, is nevertheless acceptable.

I have sampled yarn of every color. The white is the most even, the red next because it is the white which has been dyed. Dyeing apparently packs the fibers, making them firm and even. I suspect that black is always uneven—a suspicion which learning to card later corroborates. The wool of the black sheep has a short staple; it is crimpy, and no amount of hand treatment will make it smooth and regular like the white. The gray I am using is a combination of white and black, blended in carding, and it has a lumpy texture which must continually be counteracted by filling in.

This second evening as I take account of my achievement I can only wonder where the day has gone. My legs are stiff, I have a knot in the muscle of my right shoulder, my hands are cramped, a hangnail on the index finger has been irritated by the warp, my head is weary from concentration. But as I lean against my blanket roll in the magic of the short twilight my fingers itch to do "just *one* more row."

IV

SAND-PAINTINGS

MARIE, arriving early the next morning, finds my hands decorated. I am wearing my favorite blue bandana folded thickly tied around my thumb joint and fastened about my wrist with a square knot I achieved with the aid of my teeth. A neat strip of adhesive around my index finger protects the hangnail, caused by the dryness of the air, from catching into the threads. When Maria Antonia comes in, she laughs quietly but mirthfully into her lap, covering her mouth with her hand. She shows me a thick callus on the bone of her thumb. I respect that scar—it is a monument to the scores of beautiful blankets Maria Antonia has woven. And now I know that I am not alone in my infirmity. The pain on my own blue-bandaged prominence is less poignant; it has become an honorable scar. I shall try to go forward to the callus ideal.

The next two days the adhesive rings advance progressively. If I haven't an index finger hangnail to catch into the warps, I develop one on my middle finger. Obstruct that one, and there is one on the third finger. At its most ornamental stage my right hand has a bandana and three adhesive rings on the first joints. Those of the family who drop in to see my progress—that means the entire family—smile sympathetically with me. Rarely do they laugh at me. I accomplish more each day, the work looks better; I achieve it with greater ease.

MARIE CARDS—

---AND SPINS

MARIE SHOWS HOW TO HOLD BATTEN AND COMB

MARIE PULLS THE HEALD

We stop weaving for several days because there is no more white or gray yarn. Marie and I take time to card, my contribution not adding much to the accumulating pile of fluffiness. The position necessary for carding has my hands cramped in less time than it takes to card a single portion. The next day, however, I can keep at it half an hour. Ninaba and Maria Antònia take their turns with the extra pair of towcards when they come in to visit. I try spinning too when Marie takes to it. It is not a difficult operation although it is not easy to obtain creditable results. Spinning, like bicycle riding, is an art which cannot be taught. It can be "shown"; after that only practise will bring forth a satisfactory result.

Marie tells me—for we have ample opportunity for conversation now—that not all women can spin, even though they are good weavers. They procure their yarn from friends, some of whom specialize in warp yarn, and others in weft. All, doubtless, know how to card, but it is not a favorite diversion. If carding cramps my hands, it is no different with theirs. They are more accustomed, but hands and shoulders become weary, for it is hard work. Besides it is dirty. Contrary to the common notion, wool is not usually cleaned before it is carded. Washing mats it and makes it difficult to card. The carding itself removes a great amount of dirt. Sand and other dirt loosened by the teeth of the towcards fall out of the wool. Before carding, it may be a yellow lumpy matted mass. It comes forth from the cards of an expert in a white fluffy shapely rectangular pad. I like wool in almost any state or form, but it is most attractive at this stage.

I try my little stint of carding and spinning but soon leave Marie to visit the other members of the family, who are doing attractive things. Red-Point is a chanter. That is to say,

[25]

he knows medicine and can sing for days and nights on end the orderly rites which the Navajo believe cure disease, avert bad luck, and bring good. The chants which I think of as charms include singing, administration of herbal medicine, and application of sacred objects to the body. Among the most sacred are the sand-paintings, made at particular times during the chant, by artists allowing colored sands to sift through their fingers in the most incredible and regular manner. The result is an astonishing composition of symbolical figures in the softest shades of black, blue, yellow, white, red, and pink on a pale tan background. The artists themselves need skill, but they need not know the pictures. That is the duty of the chanter who directs them. The art, a beautiful and unusual one, is evanescent. Paintings which take hours to make are, by the rules of the chant, ruined in twenty minutes, removed in less than half an hour after their completion.

For these reasons there is considerable interest on the part of whites to preserve this transitory art. Red-Point, whose fame has spread far, has learned to execute the paintings on paper with tempera. At work he fascinates me even as the weavers. He has a drawing board on which he fastens his paper with thumb tacks. He spreads his colors and brushes on an inverted sheepskin beside him, lays the drawing board on the ground, takes his place before it, legs crossed in front of him, and paints. He is sixty-seven years old, but his hand is steady. The technique is one learned late in life, but his lines are straight and firm. Leisurely and pridefully he works, explaining the figures to me as they grow. He occasionally pauses for a smoke and a rest, and I wonder how he ever gets a painting finished. These people by some subtle alchemy have compounded calmness and competence in a blend whose name is accomplishment. The secret of their formula, I suspect, is that they guard against the impurity of fussiness.

After staying an hour or so with Red-Point I proceed to Atlnaba's house. She has visited me briefly to see how I am coming along, but her own interest has reached a climax. For over a year she has been working on a large tapestry. Contrary to the usual custom whereby women weave the patterns in their heads or in their mind's eye, she is copying as accurately as she can the exact details of a framed sand-painting which stands on the ground resting against the post of her loomframe. It is one of Red-Point's paintings, the Sun's House. She has chosen to use a soft gray background. In the center a large portion consisting of four wide stripes of yellow, green, black, and white represents the Sun's House. Within the yellow stripe are the houses of Sun, Moon, Black Wind, and Yellow Wind, each with a snake as guardian and with a rainbow border. The center portion is surrounded by a rainbow of blue and red, each stripe outlined in white.

At the east a yellow cloud bordered with a red and blue rainbow and set with four sundogs of the same colors represents the house of the Sun People. Five of them show their heads peeping above their house. A similar black cloud at the south represents the Sky People, a blue one at the west the Water People, a pink one at the north the Summer People. These People are all deities of a sort. In addition to the cloud at the north are the Sun and Moon at the right, Black and Yellow Winds at the left. Above each rise yellow, green, black, and white clouds in the form of a triangle. Each series is surmounted by a bird of different plumage. A bird also rests on the head of the center Summer deity, making five birds across the top.

Atlnaba has executed in her weaving every detail of this complicated picture; she has omitted no outline, not a feather of a variegated bird. I watch her today even as I watched her the first day I saw her, with increasing amazement at her dexterity. She has woven the black border from the top down and now has about a thumb-joint length of the background to work in from the bottom. It takes longer to put in this last portion than to do any similar piece of the weaving of the entire blanket. I cannot stay until she has it finished, but it is not because I am bored. The movements of her clever fingers are a source of constant admiration to me, and I am never weary of watching them.

I have waited two days for white and gray yarn. They have not been wasted. I have been "seeing Navajo life," learning Navajo words. I have been to Ganado for towcards and dyes and have taken the teasing my white friends, the traders, consider necessary each time I report to them. I do not weave on the morrow either. Atlnaba finishes her tapestry. I photograph it. I take her, the rug neatly wrapped in unbleached muslin, and such of the family as the Ford will hold to Ganado; Atlnaba and Curley's-Son, Marie, Tom and their two little boys make up what I innocently regard as a capacity load for a small, a very small, touring car.

When we get to Ganado we hear there is a Navajo assembly and exhibition at Kinlichi, seven miles to the northeast. We decide to go along with two carloads of our white friends. We see many people, Navajo and white, play a gambling game with some old Navajo men, and before sundown start for home. Here are two boys, relatives of Tom and Curley's-

SUN'S HOUSE BLANKET

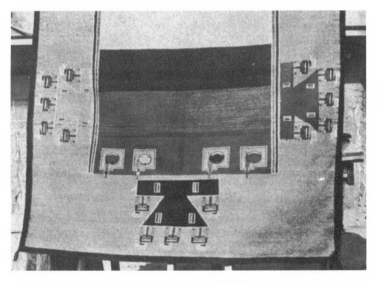

SUN'S HOUSE DETAIL

ATLNABA UNWINDS SKEIN AND WINDS BALL

MARIE'S POSITION OF REST

Son, who have no way of returning. They came in a truck which continued on its way to Gallup. "There is always room for one more," and we take one, our white friends the other. We did our trading at Ganado before we left for the exhibition, and we stop for our goods. We let out our hitch-hiker and take on three sacks of flour, one of potatoes, two watermelons, and a pack of miscellaneous groceries, coffee, sugar, canned tomatoes, and the like. I leave it to the Navajo to get the goods and themselves in, and somehow they do so and never get any legs or skirts in the gears either.

Marie has left the yarn spun and wound into skeins with her mother, who has washed it and dried it. Tomorrow I can get back to my weaving.

V

SYMPATHY

MARIE places the skein of yarn around her knee and moccasined foot, where it fits loosely. She unfastens the end and unwinds the skein into a loose pile on the floor beside her. This additional maneuver is her substitute for the chairback our women find necessary for winding yarn when they cannot get a man to hold it for them. From the loose pile she winds it into a ball, and I am impressed by its shape, so simple it is, yet so unlike ours. Around and around her spread fingers she winds it. After it is about half done she turns it and winds the rest of the yarn at right angles to it. Her ball when finished may be large but it is wound in only two directions, never in a solid ball like ours where the strands cross at all angles of the surface of the sphere.

By this time my habits are becoming established. I still have trouble regulating tension; but I am constantly aware of the fault, and the texture of my fabric is improving. The edges are a greater worry, even to this day. I am fast approaching the center of the rug, and when I reach it we take it down because the weaving has become too high to reach with comfort. After it has advanced somewhat over a foot from the floor, I sit on a blanket folded smaller and consequently higher as time goes on. When the ache in my shoulder becomes too great and the efficiency in pounding weft too little, Marie contributes a strong little box whose three dimensions are all different. By turning this box I can sit at the exact height I need.

But now that I have woven to the middle we loosen the beam cords and let the rug down. This is the hour of my disillusionment. Until now the tightness of the warp and the combined makeshifts of my teachers in loosening the weft have more or less disguised the insidious drawing in of the weft which Marie and her mother clearly saw from the very beginning, and of which I was almost oblivious. The center measures a thumb-joint and a half less than the end we began with. From the first black stripe up to the red one which precedes the wide black center the measurements are versatile, the edge describes a line for which geometry has no definition.

The family are present in a body at this event. They are more sympathetic than amused. They say most first attempts are like that. Marie says some women always weave like that, no matter how long they are at it. Tom says the rug can be buried in damp sand and stretched to a better shape. Red-Point says this one will not be good, the second will also not be good, but the third, *that* will be all right. He says this one has a nice pattern with its different-sized stripes, the wide black one in the middle. It looks like the old dresses the Navajo women used to wear. Why don't they weave patterns like this now, old-fashioned patterns?

I cannot but take heart at all this sympathy and interest. Marie lets the rug down, allowing the web to fall in a large fold behind the loom. Then with a sacking needle she sews the center of the wide black stripe firmly to the cords which fasten the warp to the cloth beam. We are ready to start off anew. If we forget the order or width of the stripes we can refer to the half already finished now lying neat and limp behind the loom.

Once more I am working at floor level. But now in bringing down the heavy comb I hit the weft against the warp instead of my own knees. Occasionally a warp strand tears. Perfect warp never tears. The ideal is probably never reached, but the spinner always has it in mind. Warp as good as Atlnaba's would not tear, however, when strung for such a small rug as this I am making. My warp was made by the old woman who lives near the well, a pitiable creature who comes to visit us occasionally, and whom we see herding sheep when we go to the well. Her chief claim to pity is the fact that she has no relatives—"just that little girl." The little girl is sweet and painfully shy, though as curious as one of the ubiquitous goats she herds. The old woman has lost all her daughters, and her sons, not very responsible, have married and moved elsewhere. Somehow the old woman and her little granddaughter manage to hold on to their flock, now much depleted, and to eke out a meager subsistence. Marie occasionally makes a dress for the child. The two come over to Red-Point's quite often for a square meal.

As she herds, a task allotted by families in better circumstances to the young, the half-blind old woman spins. In return for the many favors our family does her she gives us warp yarn. It is not specially good warp yarn, not particularly bad either; it can easily be used for smaller blankets. It would be very aggravating to have to use it for a large rug because of continual breaking. Her yarn is doubtless like her own life, drab, mediocre, weak. We are, however, grateful for it because warp is not easy to get.

My weaving has not advanced far before a warp strand

tears. Marie simply pieces a portion in, tying a knot at the top of the broken strand. Then, drawing it taut, she firmly holds the lower part of the broken strand as she ties the new piece to the old. Three hands are necessary for this operation, two to tie the knot, one to hold it tight. Since there is not always someone around to hold the strands, the weaver uses her teeth.

Marie of course pieces the first strand that tears to show me. I try to mend the second myself. My efficient friends have always chaffed me about my inability to tie a square knot. Knots have never interested me. Accordingly in my blundering fashion I inexpertly tie a granny in this torn warp of mine. I need only to turn the batten once and it is a loose warp, not torn but slipped. Marie watches not in amusement, however, but with shocked surprise. She shows me how to make a square knot, and now I *must* pay attention and remember. It is of course not difficult to learn.

Marie tells me why my carelessness worries her. She never sees me tie my shoe without a shudder. For the way I tie it is the way the dead wear their knots. They do everything backward—this granny is a backward knot. Therefore doing as they do identifies one with them, and there can be no worse inducement for bad luck. With a reason like this for an incentive it is no wonder I now tie a square knot automatically.

I advance with my weaving to less than half the latter half of the rug. The warp by this time has become stretched and smooth. It is no longer necessary to flip it to separate the strands, or to tighten it. Indeed, it is becoming tighter and tighter as the web advances. And once again a warp tears. The portion of warp left is too short to allow for our piecing it as we did before, when it was possible to tie both ends. We therefore manipulate the long piece of warp differently and have only one knot to disguise with the weft instead of two as we had before.

Placidly I weave now, the primary motions have become automatic and less painful. Marie is with me most of the time. I am no longer biting my tongue in ardent concentration, and she tells me the family impressions. The schoolgirl Angela, who is herding sheep for Red-Point during the vacation, is surprised I have learned even this much. On the day of my arrival she had encouragingly predicted: "She'll never learn to weave. Why, she doesn't even know how to sit down!" Marie tells me this with a gloating air which implies that I have proved her faith in me as well as Maria Antonia's and Atlnaba's.

The day after my arrival at White-Sands, Red-Point gave me a name. He has called me Weaving-Woman. I tell Marie I think it is a nice name. I know very well the Navajo liking for nicknames, especially names that mock at physical shortcomings, and I am pleased to have drawn one so dignified.

I know also that the Navajo do not like to use their "real" names ordinarily. These names are sacred, given at a public ceremony. In old times they were used only when the owner of the name got into "a tight place," that is when he needed supernatural aid. At such a time the mere repetition of his name would help him, give him the idea for a ruse whereby he could entrap his enemy perhaps, or strike the enemy with fear or impotence. To use the name every day or as a means of designation wears out its power.

For this reason a Navajo is "bashful" if asked his name. He is often as "bashful" about his nickname or one given him by whites as he is about his sacred name. Consequently I am surprised to hear Red-Point telling me the names of his children and grandchildren. Evidently the belief is no longer held by him. The sacred names are pretty: Ninaba, Atlnaba, Yikadezba, Djiba. These Red-Point frequently uses in conversation. But I do not wish to use them, in address anyway. I know that the Navajo are more likely to use relationship terms than names. The circle included by any one of these terms is a large one. Any woman belonging to my clan, whether a blood relation or not, if she is of my generation, is my sister.

So it is not difficult for me to give Red-Point the most respectful term befitting his generation and mine. He is my "maternal grandfather"; Maria Antonia, his wife, is my "old mother," that is my "maternal grandmother." But their children, Marie, Atlnaba, and Ben Wilson's wife are my contemporaries and I can hardly call them "mother" or "aunt." In this free-lance sort of relationship one reserves the pleasure of inconsistency and I call them "younger sister." One reason they are interested in my age is to know whether to call me "older" or "younger sister."

This adoption of kin-terms, as matter-of-fact to this family and to their Navajo friends as their ability at weaving or herding, has amusing as well as puzzling implications when whites are concerned. Marie is my younger sister, her husband Tom is my brother-in-law. Their two charming little boys are my sons. Atlnaba and Curley's-Son have the same relationship as Marie and Tom; and their intelligent capable Ninaba, I am proud to call my daughter. Ben Wilson's three little girls who tumble into my house over the high steps of its entrance are also my daughters. The terms for my children are not inconsistent. A woman and all her sisters are called by the same name, "mother," and each one of the group calls her own children and the children of all the others "child." So I, by getting three sisters, secure six delightful children. Marie and I talk over all this. She knows enough of white people to realize how amusing the system is, but she is pleased about it, as are the others.

One day Atlnaba who has many pets underfoot in her own house, tells me the pedigree of Nellie, the little white mother dog we saw on our first visit. She is the "younger sister" of the yellow dog that bites; she has a grandmother and numerous grandchildren, also uncles and aunts. The application of kin-terms to the dogs and other animals is the height of whimsicality—and good practise for me in using kinship terms. I must talk Navajo to Atlnaba; we joke, and such jokes as these are in the range of my capacity and of the appreciation of us both.

The weaving of the first blanket is now so far advanced that I am considering a pattern and colors for my next one. It is to be larger and more pretentious because it will have design. It is on my mind as I criticise this one from the vantage point of my trunk. My grandmother and sisters weave their patterns "out of their heads," but they cannot be expected to weave one "out of my head." So I sketch one with colored crayon in the intervals when I have no visitors, and after several attempts I am satisfied with it. I have drawn it in black, white, and red. But I have been much impressed with the combination of black, white, and green in the center of Atlnaba's sun-house blanket. She has achieved an unexpectedly good shade of green. I decide that, if we can get that shade in our dyeing, I will make the next one black, white, and green. This will allow me to get criticisms from my teachers and visitors at departing from the customary colors.

VI

MARIE LEARNS TO WEAVE

IT IS about this period in my own weaving career that Marie tells me the story of her own struggles in learning. "You have good yarn and good tools," she says, "and we help you all we can. You ought to learn fast. When I learned no one would help me, and I had to teach myself." So saying, she tells me the following story.

When Atlnaba was little, an older sister who was an expert weaver was living. Atlnaba, a mere baby of four, earnestly watched her older sister at her work. Finally, Atlnaba said she wanted to weave too. The elders thought her desire amusing, but Adjiba was lenient and let the baby try to weave on her own blanket. The sister showed the child how to work; she learned remarkably fast. She had no loom of her own at first, but if she made mistakes her sister patiently ravelled the work and rewove it correctly. By the time Atlnaba was five she was a qualified weaver. She made blankets which the trader, making few allowances for an infant prodigy, considered salable and bought as he would from a grown-up.

Marie is only three years younger than Atlnaba, but when she was about six Adjiba died. Atlnaba was now an experienced weaver. Red-Point was proud of her, but the family took her skill pretty much for granted as they did that of her mother. It was about this time that Marie began to yearn to weave. But now she was big enough to herd sheep. In those days, nearly thirty years ago, the flocks were not as large as they are now. There were no highways and dangers were few. Nevertheless someone had to drive the sheep to pasture in the morning, watch them during the day and herd them back to the corrals. Atlnaba was too expert at weaving to be required to do this work. Weaving is sedentary, herding is nomadic. The two activities are incompatible. It is possible to do one or the other, inconvenient to do both.

When Marie begged her mother, who was not indulgent like her older sister, now gone, to teach her to weave, the mother answered that she could not have her weaving spoiled by experimentation, nor did she have time to ravel mistakes. And besides, how could one weave when one had to herd sheep? After being thus ungraciously repulsed Marie was, if possible, even more fascinated by the looms and their equipment. During the time she spent at home she hovered as persistently as a goat about her mother's loom, sitting as near her mother as possible when she was weaving, now before the loom and now behind it when her mother was away from it.

Early in the morning the little girl drove the sheep out of the corral and away to the south. She loved the soft green of the sage through which she drove them, the aromatic fragrance it exuded when trampled by the goats, its poignant redolence when warmed by the sun after a rain. She found her own chewing-gum on the sticky branches of the hardy piñons which, with the gnarled junipers, clumped her pasture land. During the season for piñon nuts she ate them from the time they began to form in their pretty cones, until they were ripe, when she spent hours gathering them.

Sometimes she sat for hours under a juniper tree, still as a cat, but not menacing, watching the birds and listening to their chatter. She knew where two brilliant bluebirds, heralds of the dawn, had their nest. She had watched them build it, had followed the lives of the parents and the fledglings until they were large enough to fly away, when she missed them sorely. The bluebirds' nest was east of Marie's home.

Toward the sunset there was a pair of turtle doves which she knew as intimately as she knew her own baby sister. The well was at the south. On a ledge of the well was a nest of phœbes. Far to the north, in which direction she drove the sheep to water in dry weather, there was a hole in a rock wall. In this hole there was a family of field mice which she could not reach with her hand. But they were not afraid of her, and after the babies were old enough to look the world in the eye they came out and let her pet them.

In July and August there were showers almost every afternoon. Sometimes they were gentle and cooling, the kind her people called female rains. No thunder, no lightning, no wind, just a light curtain of refreshment which the sun had no difficulty in penetrating. When it did, there was a complete rainbow in the sky, or even two. Or there might be showers, long black streamers from sky to distant mountain, which she could see while basking in sunlight herself. Sometimes the sun caught a rain-streamer higher up than the rest and threw the end of a rainbow, a sundog, on the mountain. It was just like the little sun rafts on which the gods of her father's sand-paintings stood. During a female rain Marie did not seek cover but ran about in it, sounding the deepest puddles with her little bare feet.

As the season advanced the rains grew into storms. Male

rains, with wind, thunder, and lightning, gathered their fury. Marie was a good judge of weather, and if she thought a male rain was approaching she tried to get the sheep back to the corral behind her house before the storm broke. But there were days when she drove the flock six miles to water, and on these days a tempest might overtake her. All she could do then was to huddle under her blanket, becoming smaller and smaller in fear and loneliness, until the storm passed by.

During her wanderings, she found pretty, smooth stones brightly colored and oddly shaped. She made a little cache of these which she could always find, the days she drove the flock to the southwest. Wherever she went, she could find sticks with which to build tiny corrals, and plenty of adobe from which she modelled little sheep and goats, even cattle and horses. Yes, there was plenty of entertainment for a shepherd-girl, even for the long hours she was left alone. But the beauties and pleasures of the earth were as naught to the child who wanted to weave.

After a period during which her longing became intense, and after her mother's rebuffs, she determined to learn to weave. If her mother would not show her, she would teach herself. If she could not use her mother's implements, she would make her own. Accordingly she constructed a crude little loom of two uprights and two crosspieces. Her mother and sister used nice smooth broomsticks for their beams. She had only rough, tough sticks which she tried to make as smooth as possible with the knife she secreted in the folds of her skirt.

Her batten, instead of being carefully fashioned of hard oak by her father, was cut from soft pine. In her efforts to make a smooth one she shaved several down so thin she had to discard them and try again. Her best batten caught into the warp and frequently tore it. Her mother had nice combs of all sizes, made of hard wood and smoothed with use. Hers were a hodgepodge of sticks tied together to simulate a comb. They too caught into the warp, pulled at the weft, or became so twisted that she had to stop weaving to make a new comb. They were all too flimsy to become worn by age. But, such as they were, she had her loom and her implements.

The loom, though small, was nevertheless an awkward object to carry about. Each time she brought the sheep home, daily at about noon and sunset, she had to carry it with her, for it was not likely her mother would order her to herd in the same direction twice in succession. She brought the loom each time near to the house and hung it on a tree out of her mother's sight.

Her greatest problem was to get materials. There were large quantities of wool about the place. She was learning to card and spin. But she had no towcards of her own, and she could not take away with her one of the two pairs the family owned. Neither could she, except by stealth, take the fruits of her own labor. Such behavior would excite suspicion. She solved her problem quite simply but with considerable risk. She filched small quantities of the undyed yarn she herself spun, giving her white and gray. Red and black she stole from her mother as she did her warp.

Her own spinning was far from good enough for warp. This was the most difficult to obtain, for her mother, like other women, cherished her warp and always knew quite exactly how much she had. So Marie was able to take only very small amounts each time she made a raid on her mother's warp ball. Her warp when accumulated, though well spun, was consequently full of knots—square knots; she would take no chance with ghosts—because it was a mass of little pieces. The weft yarn, being in short lengths, was not so inconvenient, for weft is constantly and simply pieced throughout the weaving even under ideal circumstances.

It was not long before she could weave stripes, but she wanted to make designs. If her mother or sister were weaving when she was home, she watched intently, trying to see how the designs were made and wherein her own mistakes lay. But the skilful fingers flew so quickly there was no seeing which warp strands were forward or back, or how many forward strands were necessary for this triangle, or how to make the steeper sides of that one.

She was now adept at her thieving. When her mother stopped to cook, she stationed her younger sister before the door of the hogan. She was to warn Marie if their mother returned to the house. After Marie had stolen a supply of yarn, she had time with the pointed end of the comb to push her mother's pattern up, thus loosening it so she could count the stitches. After such a dissection she again tried her own design, but it did not look right. So the next day she crawled behind the loom while her mother was weaving. She seized every opportunity to do this like a puppy nuzzling a sleeping place. But Marie was far from asleep. When her mother asked in astonishment why she sat there, Marie answered that she preferred it as a place to sit. The men all teased her; but after all, if she wanted to sit there, what harm was it? She sat there so that she could count the warps as her mother wove.

So she continued the struggle. Sometimes she became so discouraged she threw the loom away from her in a rage and vowed never to go near it again. But its very crudeness fascinated her; she gathered it up again, and with tears of disappointment tried "just once more." Finally the first of her blankets was finished. Instead of proudly taking it home, she hung it in shame on a tree as far from her hogan as she ever took the sheep. Three of her works of art became the prey of the elements before her mother found out that she could weave.

VII

RESULTS

WHEN I started to weave Maria Antonia had brought a whole armful of reeds of different sizes. We are using two medium-sized ones for healds and four thin ones instead of shuttles. The rest have been lying behind the loom. When the rug is about three-quarters finished I notice it is becoming increasingly difficult to pull the heald forward. Furthermore, the batten often snaps. I am not wary, do not know it is going to play me this trick, and when it snaps from horizontal to vertical it gives my fingers a telling rap. Marie, as usual without saying why, gives me a narrow batten which she has brought with her. This helps a great deal, for the warp is becoming by this time tight indeed, so tight that each operation takes much longer than it did.

It is not long before this batten seems too large, and by this time we have a large assortment of them, for at Maria Antonia's request Ninaba has brought them from Atlnaba's hogan. As the warp gets too tight for the batten we are using we change to the next smaller size. The batten we started the blanket with was two thumbs (two and one-half inches) wide, the one we use last is only the width of two warps (about one-quarter inch). The tightness of the warp, ever growing upon us, makes each operation more difficult. It takes more strength to throw the sheds—and the strain the warps do bear! Occasionally one having become thin as a hair succumbs and we have to piece it, but others, also apparently thin as a hair, seem to have spiderweb strength. Because of the small space through which to operate, it is impossible to use a wound reed for a shuttle. Now I moisten the splintered end of a reed, give the particular weft I am using a twist about it, and carry it like a pushing needle through as far as it will go. Sometimes it goes the entire length, but more frequently the yarn slips off the reed before it has passed quite across the width of the blanket. In such case the yarn must again be coaxed to adhere to the reed, and gently though firmly the combination is thrust through the remaining distance.

We still have about two thumbs' length to go. Marie now takes up her position before the loom. Her hands are working high, and she sits with her legs crossed at the ankles, resting her weight on her knees and toes. *This* is a position of rest. I try it but find I should have no mind left for my weaving if I assumed it. "How do you ever sit that way, Marie?" I exclaim. "They're always laughing at me for doing so," she smiles back.

But now she is weaving from the top instead of from the bottom. When pressing the weft toward the top the comb occasionally slips out of its place and causes her fingers to rub smartly over the binding cords of the warp beam. In my hands it slips oftener.

We finally get the upper weaving straight. It should have been uniformly straight, but the mistakes, so innocent when they occurred and seemingly corrected, have followed us to the end. Marie never did get the length of that warp on the left side quite even with the right. She, given her head, would doubtless have been able to correct it to a degree. But she has had to contend with my continual drawing in of the weft, and we have now a kind of fan spread as we approach the upper left corner. The upper black stripe is a thumb wider at the left than at the right. Marie weaves in the diagonal of the stripe. I have less than two inches still to do. I had planned to finish it today, but I have not learned how tedious are these last two inches.

Next day I am up betimes, at work before Marie comes. I like to try out the work by myself and get very little chance. It is increasingly difficult now to get even the narrowest batten between the sheds. But when Marie comes she tells me to use one of the reeds with a flat end which lies among the bunch her mother laid behind the loom. She selects one that is smooth and concave from use. Its end is not more than one-quarter of an inch wide. She also, ruthlessly it seems to me, pulls the heald rod out from the loops it has been holding, winds up the cord that made the heald loops and puts the ball behind the loom to be used again. It is unbelievable that the thickness of such thin soft yarn could make such a difference, but each millimeter of warp release affords a relief.

With one of the flat-ended reeds I struggle on one warp at a time. The work finally becomes so tight that we can no longer use the flattened reeds, and now Maria Antonia plays her last trump. She has a part of an umbrella rib with an eye in one end, blunt on the opposite end. We thread the yarn in this and use it like a beading needle.

It is now impossible to work across the rug, so we take the yarn back and forth for a distance of only three or four inches. I think the top and bottom are so close that not *an-*

other weft can be inserted. Whereupon Marie comes after me and works in at least five or six more. After each space is packed sufficiently to suit even Marie, she takes the pointed end of the comb and with brisk rapid motions pulls the upper wefts down, the lower ones up until there is no telling where the join comes. I am working on the next three inches to the left.

"Some people are not careful about the way they finish their rugs," she volunteers. "We always make them very tight so you can't tell where they have been finished. They wear better that way."

At last we get it done, and it is late in the afternoon. This weaving is a time-eater.

I am much excited about taking down the rug. We loosen the large cord of the frame beam and the loom collapses. We untie the ends of the edge strands and take the loom from the loomframe.

We have still to unfasten the rug from the upper and lower beams. Marie begins with the lower, I take the upper. I see that she pulls the long strand out from between each two warps which it fastened. If she comes to a knot where it has been patched she carefully unties it. We have untied every knot we have come upon; it would be almost a sacrilege to cut the string because we never waste anything. At last we have the rug loose.

I lay it on the floor. But somehow it doesn't lie. It looks the embodiment of inherent motion, as if it might get up and walk out the door if we do not watch. It is sinuous. A snake has perfect articulation and musculature. This has neither; neither has it line. It is a thing apart, a form without a name.

I am crestfallen. I understand now the struggles of the women early in the genesis of the blanket. I understand how important the edges are. Maria Antonia on her way past the house to the corral stops in. She takes the sacking needle and loosens several edge stitches on each side, thus smoothing out several large gathers. But the rug still does not lie flat. My curiosity about the suggestion Tom previously made about straightening the edges by burying the rug in damp sand is greater than my hopes for its improvement. None of us is proud enough of it to take up the spare lengths of edge warp to form the corner tassels.

I am not like the child, Marie. I have finished my first rug, I must needs show it to my friends. I can always make it a night to go for mail. I wrap up the blanket in a spread flour sack, our substitute for paper, and start rolling off the six miles to the trading-post. I know the blanket is no good; I am disappointed because it is even worse than I expected, but there is a feeling of elation that one is finished. I consider what I have learned rather than the finished product. It is difficult to be downcast in the mellow light of the disappearing sun as it shines on cañon and mesa.

I have no success at achieving a nonchalant attitude as I enter the trading store. At least I restrain myself from showing the blanket to the assembled hangers-on. At last Old-Mexican's-Son is free. As I display the blanket to him privately I ask, "How much will you give me for this?" He answers, "Two bits and a pound of coffee." Arbuckle's, he means. I reply it is worth more than that to me, as I wrap it again in its flour sack.

I take it to show to the women. "My first blanket is done,"

I announce. They are all dying to see it, but as I slowly and tantalizingly unwrap it, I exact the assurance, "Promise me not to laugh." They promise. As the stripes held together by some sort of irregular rhythm appear and start across the room they burst with one accord into a chorus of merriment.

VIII

AT THE WELL

MY WHITE friends, with that thoughtfulness and understanding for which they are known over this entire country, have upon my arrival at Ganado, put a room at my disposal. I may use it as I should my own, come in any day at any hour, stay as long as I like, vacate for weeks if I like. I celebrate the completion of the first blanket by staying overnight, getting caught up on news, examining the new rugs which have come into the trading-post.

I am back at my Navajo home by eight the next morning, and as I lift the rickety door out of its crevice, a sense of emptiness strikes me. The house seems desolate, as if a friendly presence has gone. It must be that this imperfect, unsatisfactory web I have brought into being has taken hold of me during the last week without my knowing it. Not like a dog which has been long and lovingly underfoot, but more like an ugly antique which has stood around since childhood and is at last relegated to the Salvation Army.

During the last few days of weaving the first blanket Marie has repeatedly and interestedly inquired about my next one. What colors shall we use? How big is it to be? I have shown her the design of which she approves, as do the rest of my critics and visitors. She says she has enough warp for the size. But it is only this morning that I learn that her mother,

Atlnaba, Ninaba, and she have been industriously carding and spinning the yarn for the new rug.

I am very emphatic about the dyeing of the green, enough for the entire rug must be dyed at once so we do not get several shades. Yes, of course, but we have enough. We have four skeins, large skeins, of white and four of black. We may dye two white ones green and we shall have to dye the black. "All black must be dyed," says Marie. "The black will become brown if not dyed." "Just like old hair," I remark. "You know white people sometimes keep curls or hair and it always gets lighter." "Just the same," agrees Marie.

Tom comes in as we discuss our needs. He does not laugh at the first blanket although he also does not minimize its faults. "It's pretty good for the first," he remarks as he finishes his cigarette. "When are you going to the well?" "Are we going to the well?" "We usually do the washing and dyeing there because there is more water," he answers placidly. They leave to collect the necessary articles for our work at the well. Marie has arranged with Tom that he need not go to water the sheep because Ruby, the schoolgirl, will drive them over and Marie will help her draw the water. When Maria Antonia finds out Tom is not going she decides to go with us.

When I am ready, shortly after, we forgather about Jonathan, the Ford. There are Maria Antonia, Marie, her little boys, Ben and Dan, Yikadezba, the three-year-old daughter of our youngest sister, a tub, three buckets, the half-dozen skeins of yarn, four empty glass water bottles with carved wooden stoppers wound about with rags, my own canteens, a tow rope, a piece of laundry soap. Marie has the two packages of dye I brought from Ganado. We drive southward two miles along the highway to the well on which the family and others in the vicinity depend for their water supply. It is on the opposite side of a sandy wash. We could of course leave the car on the far side; but we have so many things, and why should we carry them over?

The party turns into something resembling a picnic—but there is no food. Marie asks me in a somewhat startled tone if I have a match. From somewhere I produce just one. It is as good to her as a boxful. She fills two buckets from the well and disappears up the bank of the wash carrying them, is gone for some minutes. Meanwhile her mother and I fasten one end of our rope to the remaining bucket, throw it over the pulley and tie to the other end a rickety dented pail which stands by the well. It is so full of holes it almost empties in the time it takes to pull it up. But on the theory that two buckets are better than one we lower it alternately with the whole one and fill the tub.

Maria Antonia then plunges two of the white skeins, carefully tied at the top so as not to tangle, into the water which the wool soaks up in a brownish yellow way. Standing over the tub with knees unbent she vigorously rubs soap into the wet yarn. After a few minutes of kneading the foamy mass —the water here is pleasantly soft—the wool appears white and clean. She presses out the soapy water, which has become the color of the sand the tub stands on. We draw a few more bucketfuls of water and she rinses the yarn again in the kneading fashion. It emerges creamy white, so fluffy I can hardly believe it is wet, with an inviting wet-woolly odor. Maria Antonia finds the loops which tie the skeins at the top, shakes them several times and hangs them on the wooden supports of the well platform to dry.

As Maria Antonia and I once more begin to draw water

Marie returns announcing that the water for the dyeing is on the fire and will soon be ready. I then help her as she draws more and more water to fill the sheep trough. The flock driven by Ruby appears over the hill. Marie sends Ben and Dan, who have been wading in the trough, out to tell her to keep off the sheep until we have the trough filled. "If they all come up, they drink up the water faster than we can draw it and then some do not get enough," explains Marie.

And now I lower the rope and it jerks up quickly and lightly, no bucket on the end. It wasn't a granny knot this time, just neglect to tie a double knot. But the bucket, our best one of course, is at the bottom of the well. The women merely laugh at my awkwardness as Marie blandly sends the old warp weaver's little girl, who has come up, to her home a quarter of a mile away for a long stiff wire with a hook at one end. We wait until she returns and then have a fishing party. We soon have the bucket out, and in no time the trough is full.

Ruby brings up the sheep, having only with difficulty kept them away. They tumble over, about and around the well platform, sniffing the wool, the water bottles and the soap. "Su! Su!" The goats will eat the soap! The large ewes and mother-goats line up along the trough, so close that the bleating eager lambs and kids cannot get within goat-range as they nose and push into the interstices of the living wool. When the large ones have their fill, the little ones get their turn, hardly able to reach the trough even standing on the tiptoes of their stubby hind legs. Some achieve a jump to the edge of the trough whence they frequently slip into the water as they guzzle it with their parched lips. Funny beings, these

sheep, wiggling, curious, eternally unsatisfied, and stupid,
how stupid! . . .

But Marie quietly turns over the empty bucket to Ruby,
gets the dyes from the front seat of the car and starts off
once more up the bank of the wash. I follow, bearing the two
unwashed skeins of white and the black yarn.

We come to a small fire made of sagebrush and dry weeds
over which the two bucketfuls of water are bubbling. Marie
lifts off one with a stout stick, opens the package of green
dye and casually sprinkles about half of it in. She stirs it with
the stick; it is indeterminately darkish. She adds a little more
dye, carefully folds the end of the package and lays it at
the base of a rabbit bush. She stirs the mixture thoroughly
again and sets it on the fire. She now treats the other pailful
of hot water the same way, using a whole package of black
dye. When they have once more boiled she immerses the white
wool in the green and the black wool in the black dye and
lets them boil for perhaps half an hour.

We have nothing further to do but wait, and as we sit in
the pleasant sunshine and watch I am once more overcome
with the casualness of it all. I have at home repeatedly tried
dyeing; I have always tried to follow written instructions to
the letter; I have invariably achieved only streaked results.
Marie has here done only the most essential things. The wool
has not even been washed; I am soon to find it will not be
rinsed—the dyeing suffices for cleansing and coloring. Verily
Navajo ways are not our ways. Occasionally Marie stirs the
yarn and lifts it to test the color. Too light, not even, she lets
it boil longer.

At last she considers it finished, and after pouring out the
dye and lifting the yarn on sticks she finally cools it enough to

press out; eventually she presses it reasonably dry. We gather our water bottles and canteens, place the white wool now dry in the tub, the wet black in one bucket, the wet green in another. We have our soap, our rope, what remains of the green dye. But now, to my surprise each woman and each child is holding a kid or a lamb and intends to take it home. Marie says they became separated from the flock some days ago and after Ruby had driven our flock off a boy who had found them watered his and gave them back to Maria Antonia.

We are loaded, and I start across the wash in what I think are the usual tracks. I have not been careful to have my motor going in the proper rhythm, I have gone about half a car width east of the usual tracks. The car stops. I start it and try to pull forward with no success. I try reverse and the wheels spin. I run the motor until it sounds more efficient and try both ways again. We do not move. We unload our miscellaneous but not heavy load and look into the situation. It had seemed no different from usual. But I had forgotten that the day before there had been a short though heavy shower. It had refreshed us all, but its effects except for making color more steely sharp had been short-lived. Apparently short-lived!

This seems to be a day of errors. The rain, true, had pretty well obliterated the usual track across the wash, but a little foresight combined with a little Navajo sense would have saved us a great deal of trouble. My slight digression has put the car in dry quicksands just above the old well now covered over. The harder we try to pull out, the women pushing, the deeper we sink in.

Then old Curley, the father of Tom and Atlnaba's husband, rides up. He is a wizened soul with smiling wrinkles about his eyes and mouth. He rides a small wiry bay horse with a cream-colored mane. We ask him to tow us. We tie the rope to the front bumper, he holds it wound twice round the pommel of his saddle, the horse pulls with all his might even as Jonathan pulls with all the power of his lowest gear. The wheels dig deeper into the quicksands. As I jack up the car, putting on the chains, two riders come loping up gayly.

One has a stolid frame, but the usual jolly expression of the Navajo in the face of the unusual. His strawberry roan is heavier than Curley's bay. He announces blithely that he will simply lift the car out of the hole. "Oh, you can never do that," I exclaim. "Why, it is much too heavy!" "But he always wins when we have contests in lifting!" says his companion. "Well, of course you can try," say I dubiously. Curley tells Marie: "You may just as well leave the car and go home. You'll never get it out of there." The strong man answers, "When I get that car out of there I will go home, and not before."

Whereupon he digs his heel into his horse's belly and trots out of sight. In less time than it takes to tell, he reappears dragging three long poles, half overcome with dry rot, in his lasso. He dismounts, unties the rope, lifts a pole above his head, brings it down with telling force and a three-foot piece breaks off. He continues until he has the three poles broken into short lengths. Then he directs Curley and his companion to lift with all their force when he says, "Yego!" and tells us to shove the logs under when they lift. They set their combined strength to the car's right mudguard. "Yego!" and the car rises six inches. Marie and I, almost lying on our stomachs, each get a log under the wheel. We repeat the maneuver on the other side and try the motor. We discover that to pull forward involves climbing a grade, very slight but nevertheless a hindrance where every ounce of traction counts. So I decide to work backward. If we can move three feet, we shall be off the quicky part and on to rough sand.

We gain perhaps six inches, but as soon as the wheels get off the short corrugated road we have made for them they again begin to spin. After repeating the experiment two or three times during each of which we gain the width of the combined logs, I perceive that we must increase the length of our rough surface. I find that quite unnoticed, a piece of heavy canvas lies on the floor of the car. Tub, bottles, and buckets are lifted and the canvas is dragged out. I put it near the logs, just behind the right wheel. The men lift again. Hastily I place my log but first slide the canvas under. Marie pushes her log in next to mine. We get both under the wheel. We have only the three pieces of log under the left wheel. Once more we try the motor. And now the car shows signs of a real will to move backward with the right wheel, but the left holds it back as soon as it has moved off the logs.

I make up my mind to concentrate all efforts on the next try. Curley sees the force of the canvas idea, sees also it is too narrow to do for both wheels and in a trice whips his blanket off his saddle and lays it under the left wheel. We now have logs for both sides and fabrics to extend the rough surface. I ask Curley to let his horse try towing once more, this time tying on to the rear axle to pull the car backward. The strong man realizes we are using all our aces on this play. He ties his lasso also to the rear axle. He lifts the car once more onto its logs. I climb to the wheel, he to his saddle. The men hold the ropes firmly around the pommels. Marie and the strong man's companion push. I, with every gasp of his carburetor, coax Jonathan to his utmost. I slip the clutch and give him the gas, all the gas! The horses strain, the pushers strain. Suddenly we all feel that surprising movement for which each pusher feels that he, and he alone, is responsible. The car is moving, moving—it grips, the horses pick up their feet to get out of the way. With a concerted warwhoop we are out, once more on the firm sand by the real well.

Three feet we had to go. Four hours it took to go it. It has been my custom in the Navajo country, never before having been identified with a family, to pay such men and horses as have helped me out of a "tight place." So I tell these very amiable boys that I have no money with me, but if they come up to the house I will pay them. They mount, once more we load up our children and kids, and start off, this time taking a detour on the well side of the wash, thereby avoiding the crossing. Tired and hungry we arrive home; it is now three o'clock and we have had no dinner. The boys gallop up in no time and I give them each some silver. They are much pleased as they ride off and so am I.

Red-Point rides home singing in the resplendence of the setting sun. As he drinks his evening coffee Marie tells him of our adventure. He is amused; only those happenings are calamities here over which man has no control. But when Marie comes to the end of her tale his amusement turns to indignation. He gulps his last drop of coffee and, followed by Marie, proceeds rapidly to my roof top, where I am as usual absorbing the restful charm of the sunset hour. Red-Point is almost too excited to light the proffered cigarette as he bursts into a perfect tirade against the, in my opinion, very obliging youths who helped us out of our difficulty.

"You wouldn't have had to pay them anything if *I* had been here!" Then he chides Marie for letting me pay them, almost blames her for interpreting my wish to do so. "The very idea of taking money for helping *Navajo* out of trouble!"

This day has been a hard one, think I, as I stretch my back flat on my blankets under the Great Dipper. Muscles are sore and tired, we haven't got much done, but—what a grandfather I have, what an amazing grandfather!

IX

TAKING COUNSEL

RED-POINT was so excited last evening about the Navajo boys taking pay for helping us that he did not think of anything else. Today, as Marie is stringing the new blanket over the temporary frame and as I unwind the yarn from the skein, preparatory to winding the ball, he comes in. He is in his usual mild temper, but cannot refrain from mild remonstrance: "Too bad you paid that money. You wouldn't have had to do it if I had been here." He has come to see my first blanket. As I spread it out I tell him that at Ganado they all laughed at it. Whereupon he leaps to my defense with, "Tell *them* to make one."

Marie strings up the second blanket exactly as we did the first. This one is something over five hands wide by somewhat over six long. She has not enough warp of one kind and uses two kinds, one heavier than the other. When she comes to twining the warp loops with the binding cords I ask her to let me do one end while she does the other. She makes no objection, but when we are finished the warp at my end is at least a hand narrower than that at her end. Patiently she sets herself to the task of pushing each warp loop over a slight distance until the warp at my end is spread over the same length of binding cord as hers. Each person has her own tension. Mine would have been all right if I had twined both ends.

I have begun with stripes because I realize how difficult it is to finish off a blanket with a pattern close to the end. Besides I like stripes. For some reason blankets with borders do not seem to me truly Navajo. I do really know how to make stripes now. I have set my teeth against drawing in the weft and sworn a vow to get a respectable edge. The weft begins to pull in slightly as I finish the first black stripe but this time I detect it and take measures against it immediately. I have learned to lay the weft loosely in a scallop formation and I can now give the subtle twist to the comb which makes the weft fill the spaces between the warps instead of pulling it tight against them, leaving them exposed on the finished web. I know now the signs of tightness in the appearance of the warp and weft and guard against it continuously.

This blanket is much wider than the first one. The distance across the first was just about the distance which can be easily manipulated by one throw of the sheds and one insertion of the batten. If we wove all the way across the second blanket we should have to change our sitting position for every row. We never do this. Instead we work about half of the width, back and forth, forth and back, for a considerable length. Each time we weave to the left we take up one warp less than we used before. When we come back to the right the weft makes a loop over this strand. So the portion of weaving at the right becomes constantly narrower.

When I have woven about half a hand length, I move over to the left side. At the right I now take up one *more* warp strand as I advance, thus fitting my weaving into the exact space left over from the previous weaving. This joining involves no real locking of stitches. When the blanket is taken down, even if it is well woven, a diagonal line will be discernible wherever the weaving has been done this way. It will be made by tiny holes, the result of the meeting of two weft strands looped over two adjoining strands.

It is pleasant to see the loops settle into their places. There is a slight diversion in the monotony of stripes and it is a step I must understand in weaving designs.

Early in the afternoon the concerted barking of the dogs heralds a newcomer. A woman rides up; a baby-board is hung on her saddle. For the rest of the day I am left strangely alone.

It is a rare occasion, and I profit accordingly. There is so much to do that requires concentration, for which there is practically no opportunity. As I work, I reflect how peaceful this family is. Intimate acquaintance with it should, it seems, disclose some inner discord. But there is no evidence of this. The two pairs of young people seem to be really in love with each other; one can see it by the glance in their eyes. The sons-in-law respect the orders of the old man and work steadily at branding, farming, irrigating as he dictates. One or the other hauls water whenever the water barrel becomes empty. True, if worse comes to worst, as sometimes happens, we women eke out the water supply by taking the water kegs and bottles to the well in the car. Once in a while Tom or Curley's-Son hauls in a wagonload of large juniper branches or trunks to replenish the old woman's woodpile. In the short intervals between the main supplies she has no trouble finding wood in the immediate vicinity of the house. Not quite so good perhaps, but quite good enough. Family affairs are well regulated and orderly although there is evidence of none but the roughest sort of daily schedule.

Marie comes later than usual the next morning and she brings sad news:

Yikadezba's-Mother came home unexpectedly yesterday. This is our youngest sister whom I do not know. Hers is the uninhabited hogan of our settlement. She and her husband, Ben Wilson, spend their summer at the top of the mountain where they care for a part of the family's extensive flock. We have a large portion of it at our place, but each year Ben and his wife move to the mountain with the rest. There the grass is long and plentiful even in the driest part of the season. They have their camp in the midst of tall yellow pines, the noblest of all the Southwest trees which grow only at an altitude above seven thousand feet.

Once or twice during the summer Ben and his wife may come back to White-Sands, but there is always some reason for their coming and they come in a wagon with all the household necessities, Ben blithely singing as he drives the heavy, well-fed draft horses. The arrival of Yikadezba's-Mother is unprecedented. Her very appearance alone on horseback presages trouble. The women, the only members of the family who are home, greet her quietly, and without question set mutton stew, coffee, and bread before her after a short period of preparation. Yikadezba's-Mother has not eaten since sunrise, she has ridden twenty-six miles in a much disturbed state of mind, having paused only once long enough to nurse her baby. Nevertheless she daintily picks the morsels of meat from the bone, sips her coffee, deliberately breaks small pieces from the tortilla. Her meal, though eventually a substantial one, is as leisurely and unconcerned as if she had finished a banquet only an hour before.

At last, after small talk and long intervals of silence, the question all have eagerly in mind, but which none would ask, is answered. This morning Ben doubled a rope and beat his wife with it. Marie implies that Yikadezba's-Mother has a bad temper, for, she says, she mistreats her children. "She throws Yikadezba about like a puppy. She beats her too, that is the reason my father and mother keep her here."

Yikadezba is the miniature Navajo who follows the women about, hardly more than able to walk. There is nothing which does not arouse her interest. She wears a modified replica of her mother's dress, a yoke—instead of a blouse—of Irish green velvet to which is attached a much-gathered skirt of large pink and green plaid, ruffled at the bottom. She has tiny red moccasins like her grandfather's with dimes for buttons, but she seldom chooses to wear them. I cannot take a step off my bed without picking up a cactus thorn; Yikadezba runs barefoot all day long and only rarely gets even a sliver in her foot.

Her mischief is the mischief of curiosity. There is so much to investigate, so much to learn. My things are quite different from her mother's or her grandmother's; they must be looked into. But her elders do not think this necessary, and they constantly say, "Leave it alone, get away from there." She does not always listen; then they harden their voices and give a firm catch at the end of the second syllable of the Navajo word which means, "Now I *mean* it." One day she insists on playing with the lock of my trunk, heedless of the warning no matter how emphatically it is said. Then Marie speaks very quietly but at greater length than usual. Whereupon Yikadezba with a start dashes up the high step which forms my threshold as fast as she can go. As she passes the door she catches her skirt on a nail, loosens it, and slaps the door. Marie looks at me with an amused twinkle. "What did you say to her?" I ask. "I told her she was sitting on an ant."

This is the child her mother beats. No one of her mother's family approves of such behavior. Children should not be punished. I get the idea the sympathy is with the husband. But, on the other hand, what are parents for if they cannot protect their daughters? The fact of marriage does not give a husband exclusive rights over his wife. Indeed, it is more likely to put him under obligations to his father-in-law. Therefore Ben has offended not only his wife but her entire family.

In the afternoon Yikadezba's-Mother brings her baby in to visit me. She is handsome, but the open good will so striking on the faces of her relatives I know, is wanting in hers. Her smile, though beautiful and shy, is rare; her more common expression indicates a sober sullenness.

I have expected that Red-Point, perhaps in family conclave, will settle the matter of Yikadezba's-Mother. But I reckon without my hosts. About a week later Marie announces that all the young people and Red-Point are going to Ganado. There is to be the monthly Council Meeting and Ben Wilson's case will be considered and settled.

The United States Government, in its capacity of guardian of the Indians, sees fit to exploit the old Indian custom of "talking it over." But now, instead of "talking it over" with family and clan representatives in a more private way, all subjects, even to the most personal, are aired in a Council which meets as an institution monthly. A judge—at Ganado a Navajo who speaks English—presides. The Navajo of the community attend these meetings well, for they like gatherings and news. There is a particularly large turnout for this one because of two cases, one of interest because of its subject, an accidental killing; the other because of the importance of Red-Point's family.

Each Navajo is dressed in his best. Temperature makes no difference in Navajo styles. The women, no matter how high the thermometer may be, wear brilliantly patterned Pendleton blankets, soft and woolly, some with long fringes. The men, though their knees or elbows may be fringed with wear, never omit their finest four-gallon hats. The judge is wearing a fur cap. Men and women wear all the white shell, coral, and turquoise they can procure, either their own or borrowed from the stay-at-homes. Turquoise-set silver is in evidence as bracelets, rings, and necklaces.

Many of the Navajo come early. They leave horses and wagons in groups about the trading-post. Men and women spend hours in the store, dickering, trading, watching as others trade. They sit in bevies here and there on the ground, where they refresh themselves with canned tomatoes, crackers, and soda pop. The children have tumors of hard candy or chewing gum in their cheeks from the time they arrive until, no longer able to help themselves, they fall asleep. After considerable conversation with one and another the judge makes his way to the large shade where the meetings are held. Leisurely the attendants follow. They talk—the judge, the plaintiff, the defense, the jury. The complainant and the accused speak for themselves. The audience is the jury and will render its decision informally. The talk is quiet, so quiet I cannot hear it, much less understand the Navajo. But it continues. It may take a long time to get started, but once begun it is endless. There are no whites to watch the clock and say, "We'll take an hour out for dinner now," just as they get deep into the discussion.

The meeting lasts for a day and a half this time. I do not stay long, for I do not know the cases, nor do I understand the points. Afterwards the judge tells me about the killing. The summary is as short and matter-of-fact as the argument was tedious and quiet: "Two boys were wrestling in a friendly way, and one broke the other's neck. The meeting decided that the survivor should pay the mother of the dead boy ten dollars."

I get two versions of Ben Wilson's case. The trader has listened to a part of the evidence. Ben contends that his wife has a bad temper. She is jealous of another woman. She said: "Why, that night when he came in he never even came to bed. Just lay down in the dirt inside the door like he was drunk, slept there all night. In the morning he got up dazed just like he was drunk. He must have been with a woman."

The accused, an educated domestic, a girl of sullen, disagreeable disposition, answers that she has more to do than play about with other women's husbands.

At first Yikadezba's-Mother wants a divorce, but when she finds Ben also wants one she becomes less certain. The assembled friends talk and talk and finally come to a settlement. Marie tells me briefly the next day: "They are going back to the mountain and try living together again. But the next time Ben mistreats her they will get a divorce."

The little community council is only a small local model of the Annual Council of the Navajo held at some convenient

[*67*]

point on the Reservation. Red-Point wants to go to this meeting, and I take a load of Navajo to Fort Wingate, where it is held this year.

Most of those attending this gathering come in cars. Very few of the Navajo live in the immediate vicinity of Fort Wingate, and many cars are already parked about the center plaza of the school as we drive up. One decrepit Model T Ford has a well-woven Navajo blanket hanging from the top just behind the front seat. I remark about it, it being the first time I have ever seen Navajo use their own blankets except for saddles. The trader, who knows the family, remarks that it is because the son-in-law drives. His mother-in-law is not self-effacing and willing to stay at home like Maria Antonia. She wants to go along. They have arranged this curtain so that neither sees the other.

The Council lasts two days. It is much more formal than the other; the Navajo tribe is represented by delegates elected from the different divisions of the Reservation who have a vote; the subjects considered are of tribal rather than personal or family interest. This is the time when the Navajo thresh out their troubles, grievances, and wants with the whites. The Commissioner of Indian Affairs and his assistants, the agents of the several jurisdictions, are there. All opinions and discussions are rendered in English as well as Navajo.

The subjects they consider are concessions for oil lands, for cutting timber, the eternal problem of land for the Navajo, schools, sheep dipping to remove disease from the flocks, water supply, conservation of pasturage, and so forth. Theoretically the delegates have talked over the questions with their respective constituencies and vote according to instructions. Actually the decisions are not quite so satisfactory. The

Council is a place where opinions may be aired and where a register of temper may be gained. It is exceedingly interesting though long-winded; the results are usually quite indirect. It affords us a trip, takes up our time, makes us glad to get home.

X

DESIGN

The stripes of my lower border are done, and quite nice they look too. The weft is only slightly tight and corrected after very little pulling in. I have no idea how to lay out the design. It is a simple pattern involving only concentric triangles which extend from the lower stripes to the center, and stripes along the sides. The design is calculated to occupy half the extent of the blanket and to be repeated in reverse for the second half.

Marie sits before the loom. She takes up a handful of warp on each side, seeing to it that each hand has the same number of warps. She drops them and repeats the even counting until she reaches the center warp. At the top of this warp she ties a little piece of weft yarn. She knows it is the middle warp although she does not know how many she has altogether; she has discovered it by balancing each strand on the right with one on the left.

She next measures with a string the length of the blanket, halves the string and with my pencil marks the center of the length. She now tries to fit her design into the space. She is getting a triangular pattern. I know she manipulates the threads regularly, but I am not able to figure out the rhythm. Marie continues to "show" me. I try it myself. Marie sees it is wrong, leans over, and picks up the proper warps through which I should carry the white, the green, the white again, and I go on. For a while it seems to be all right; then soon again she corrects me. I flounder along, blindly really, because I have no way of knowing when I include one more warp with the green to the left, one more with the white. I know of course that after I have done it at the right, I advance one strand to the right at the left side.

By the time "the sun has moved to the middle" we have the beginnings of three large concentric triangles. We stop work to eat. My trunk is the point from which I get my perspective. As I chew the mutton Maria Antonia has given me, it seems to me the triangles are going to be complete long before we reach the center. Their sides are leaning in very fast, their base angles are sharply acute. My drawing calls for a more nearly equiangular triangle.

I hurry my lunch so I can try to work out the advances in the stitches alone. I don't care if the result is bad; I care if I know what I am doing. And I know I don't. Sneakingly and with a guilty feeling I experiment. But Marie has hurried with her lunch also. She is not going to let me ruin *this* blanket. So we continue. If I pick up the wrong strands she shows me the correct ones.

Red-Point is home today. He comes up for a smoke and a talk. He no more than gets settled on the trunk when he notices the pattern. He goes over to the loom and points out what I had remarked to myself. "If you continue this way, the top of the triangle will come here," he tells Marie, indicating with a finger a point nearly a hand below the center. "In her drawing, Weaving-Woman has it at the center." This old sage has plotted too many sand-paintings not to notice the error at a glance. Marie says "Unh!" and we proceed as before.

Marie weaves a great deal on this blanket. Eagerly watching, I feel as she felt when as a little girl she eyed her mother and tried to learn what made the design. She, however, unlike her mother, is not unwilling to help me all she can. She "shows" me patiently each time I need to advance or to withdraw. The only thing she does not allow me is to make mistakes alone. Take them out also if need be, but get understanding I must. However, I finish this day with a feeling of absolute futility. Am I so dull that I cannot grasp this apparently simple point?

The next day we continue to work in the same way. There are moments when I think I have a flash of comprehension; but the flash burns out, and my theory does not hold.

I need supplies and mail, and I spend the night with my white friends. Next day the trader's niece decides to visit me. Cha is a dainty girl who has been brought up with boy cousins. As she dons her corduroy trousers and her blue shirt she declares, "I will be home when my shirt is too dirty to wear." "Or when we need food," I supplement her remark as we drive off.

Arrived at my hogan, Cha takes up a reclining position on the length of my bed roll, where she intends to read a thousand-page volume of detective stories. "You know, Cha, I have been weaving at this design two days, and I don't really understand it yet." Instead of reading her detective stories she watches me. We discuss the problem at length, and all too soon it is noon. With elaborate politeness I share the trunk with Cha, and not thinking much of what we eat we scrutinize and criticise every thread of the blanket. Cha was one of

MY FIRST RUG

MY SECOND

DIVERSION DAM AFTER THE TORNADO

the group who laughed at my first rug, but like Red-Point and the rest, she laughed with me, not at me.

"We are going to reach the top of the triangle long before the center, as Red-Point said," I tell her.

"Yes, and the blanket is cock-eyed," says Cha. "See how much wider the stripes are on the left than on the right."

"You can't imagine how dumb I feel. Here we have been making triangles for nearly two days and we are nearly at the middle, and I don't really understand how to do them. Marie must somehow know how the warps *look,* or she must have some way of telling."

"Why don't you ask her to count?" suggests Cha.

When Marie comes soon after, I tell her she must call off the counts of the warps under which she places the weft as she works. She is amused but willing. As I sit, pencil and pad in hand, she does so. I learn then, much to my surprise, that she takes up an extra strand every fourth row, then relapses to the usual count. The extra warp being taken up at this place advances our diagonal line just as we wish. After Marie has proved to me by repetition that this is the case I try it myself, and it turns out to be the proper solution to my confusion. For some time hereafter we count as we weave.

Red-Point visits us again, greets Cha heartily as "Old-Mexican's-granddaughter-my-granddaughter." He points out once more the faults of my blanket, and we ask Marie why it looks so one-sided. She says it is because the warp on the right side is finer than that on the left, a matter she did not allow for in planning the rug. She should have allowed more warps on the right than on the left in locating her center.

We have advanced far enough to finish the innermost of the concentric triangles, a white one. Almost immediately thereafter Marie begins to finish off the green one, really a triangle made hollow by the white one inside it. I do nothing about the finishing off of the triangles because I do not know how. But I have designed my blanket so that these triangles are blunt instead of coming to a point. Without saying a word Marie works on them. Four of them, green, white, black, and white, get their bluntness by a kind of crown effect very awkward to the eye. After thinking about this matter a long time and discussing its pros and cons Cha and I decide that it cannot be done any other way, or at least any better way.

The mistake is in the designing; the Navajo never do it thus. If they start a triangle, they finish it. We are now working the design in the center, leaving unwoven spaces on both sides. I will fill them in with stripes when Marie stops working on the center. I shall proceed just as I have done in weaving the stripes in two portions. I notice we avoid making our loop joins at the exact completion of a design, the outer boundary of the triangle, for example. I have already noted that other weavers do this also. A woman may work on a particular portion of a design, often the center one first. I can see no reason why she should weave a six-inch space instead of twelve or fifteen inches. But I have never seen one who wove just the design and then filled in. She always weaves a part of the background, so that the almost imperceptible diagonal line, distinguishable by little holes left by two wefts looping over neighboring warps, comes at some place other than where two colors meet.

Marie has now come to the end of our triangles; they are blunted and complete. Since our errors have changed the entire plan of the design, now is the time for me to suggest a change. But I have no suggestion to make. So Marie keeps the two side panels distinct even as I had planned. But she does so by setting off a central white portion by means of straight black lines. I had made no provision in my design for learning how to make straight vertical lines, so here, as in other cases, mistakes teach me more than accuracy.

The vertical lines are easy to keep track of, the only difficult part is regulating the tension. I therefore find the warps spreading unduly as I weave. Although my finished product will be disappointing, I am nevertheless glad that this element of design is introduced. It is an important one, one I must learn sooner or later. I know it now but do not control it very well.

Except for regulating the pull of the vertical line, the weaving has once more settled into a plain stripe web. The expanse of white in the center is growing. It is becoming unpleasing in its extent.

"Don't you think we're getting too much white in the center?" I say to Cha the third day of her visit. She has not gone very far with her stories, for she is as fascinated by the weaving as I am. Although I allow her quiet to read, her eye nevertheless roves from book to loom and reluctantly and briefly back to the book.

She agrees. I keep on weaving in the white space. Cha complains of hunger. I tell her to eat what she can find—there are crackers, the only food we have which does not need cooking or can-opening. We used our last bread for breakfast; crackers even though reinforced by coffee do not really stand by one for the whole afternoon. It is past mid-afternoon and as Cha rises from the blanket roll Marie comes in again. She looks at the rug with an appraising eye.

Cha sinks onto the trunk with a cracker in each hand and begins to examine the rug with Marie. "An awful lot of white in the center, don't you think?" Marie agrees. I suggest, "How do you think a small triangle would look in the center? You know I had one in the drawing."

"We'll try it," says Marie. "There *is* a lot of white."

We continue to study the rug from the distance of less than two yards and I ask Marie, "Do your rugs always get just as you think they will when you start them?"

Smilingly she admits, "Hardly ever."

Her critical attitude as she stands there elicits another question, this one from Cha: "Do you stand off from your blankets and criticise them as they grow too?"

"Always," she says, looking somewhat surprised as if it were a matter of course. "You see the patterns don't always get like I think, or they don't look nice as I plan them. Then I must change them. I almost always change something."

"Well, it's got lots of mistakes," summarizes Cha, "but it's a nice blanket anyhow. I like it."

Marie starts the center triangle and has a few rows woven when Cha announces: "I'm going home for supper. I said I was going to stay until I needed another shirt. I needed one yesterday already, but I said I was going to finish this book before I went. I have watched your old weaving so much I haven't got it done yet."

"We have to go," I agree. "Otherwise we'll starve. But do you realize that that blanket has all the patterns I need learn to make, the broad-based triangle, the vertical line, and the sharper angled triangle? I am not sure I can make those triangles all by myself, but I am sure I can after a little more practice."

"I am sure," she answers.

So saying, we make our sketchy preparations for a return to Ganado.

I come into the hogan the first thing the next morning to find the yarn in a different position from that in which I left it, pulled out of the box and over the floor at random like a string a cat has played with. I observe it the next few days with a suspicious eye. Each morning more of it is pulled out and left tangled. I suspect mice. I tell Marie about it: "You know, when I came in this morning the yarn was pulled out, all over the floor. Do you think I have mice? I have noticed it for several days."

"Yes," says Marie with unusual seriousness, "probably rats. And they'll bite our warp too."

My heart sinks at the thought. We know how to repair tears, but what would the blanket be like if a rat gnawed its way unsystematically through it? The event has evidently been experienced by Marie, who has grave misgivings even with her resourcefulness. "But what shall I do?" I ask, thinking of traps and the impossibility of securing any.

"Cats," answers Marie reassuringly. "I'll bring some up tonight."

"Why," think I, "should my first reaction always be of a complicated mechanical solution instead of a simple natural one?"

As I am reading by the light of my kerosene lamp late in the evening I hear talk and approaching footsteps. I almost never have guests after sunset. Marie and Ruby are coming; each clasps with a firm hand a protesting skinny blackish kitten. "Oh, the cats!" I exclaim, remembering our morning's talk. "But aren't they too small to catch rats? Will they stay with me?"

"Just close your door when you go out. They'll stay all right."

The girls close the door as they leave me. The kittens roam about sniffing. They seem contented enough now they are released. My, but they are thin! I wonder if they ever get anything to eat.

Next morning I forget about them until I open the door. There they are. But now they are roundish in the middle where yesterday they were flat or even curved in; they seem to me to lick their chops contentedly. I offer them a bit of bacon left over from my own breakfast. They scorn it.

They leave me soon after breakfast. Hereafter when I come into the hogan in the morning the wool is as I left it.

XI

RAIN

DURING the first part of my stay the Sun, "our father," has had his will. Each day unhindered he has pushed his way through his own thin white curtain of dawn, passed serenely through the broad blue curtain of daylight, relaxed at the curtain of yellow evening light, and in a parting blaze of glory succumbed to the curtain of darkness.

But at last the Water Sprinklers begin to contend with him. They card cloud puffs of purest white wool. The Sun, joining the contest with mirth, dyes their fluffs, for a time overcoming them, but they gain on him continually. They start with small wisps which hang delicately here and there on the horizon. Then they whisk their towcards harder, and the white wisps rise higher in the sky. At last the Rain gods become drunk with their own effects, and as they card they blow. They send black wind after the white clouds, which chase one another madly across the sky.

I emerge from my hole to retrieve the flour sacks I have hung on my piñon to dry, and to see that the knot of the sack containing the mutton ribs Maria Antonia gave me is tight over its wire strung between the branches. I compress my lips over my teeth as tightly as possible. I make my eyes into the narrowest slits. Even so when I come back to the hogan I am grinding sand between my teeth.

For some days Sun and Water gods play their comedy, the Water People gradually gaining in strength. But we have had so many pseudo-storms we stay inside and forget that the dark edges of the puffs are daily becoming darker and may some day achieve their end.

At last the rainy season is on. I sit in my hogan weaving; the light becomes dimmer; I hear a light patter on the sand roof. Diagonal streaks of water shoot past my door. I rise to experience this wonder. But I first throw my shed for the next row and insert the batten.

"Don't ever leave your stick in when you are not weaving," says Marie. "If you do you will not finish your blanket."

She says it with an expression on her face which I interpret, "So they say, but I don't believe it," but I pull out my batten and lay it on the floor.

We stand before the opening of my house, we see this dry wetness, feel it, breathe it. The first rain is a marvel, all rains are miraculous. We breathe in the dust which rises under the splashing raindrops. It is no longer gritty but earthy and refreshing.

"It is good, altogether good." We say it like a prayer of thankfulness as we return to our work.

This day the Water Sprinkler is not playing with the Sun. He has called on his friend Black Wind, and the two have decided to bless us. And now quite suddenly there is another shower; but this one is heavy. No thunder, no lightning, but rain and wind and more rain. This is the test for our hogans. Rain blows in at the door and makes a puddle on the floor. The puddle grows larger, trickles toward where we sit. We grab up the wagon cover which serves as a carpet.

Rain comes in at the small ventilator in the center of the

roof, splashes on the floor, and spits sand on our blanket. We put the wagon cover over the blanket and wool-box and each finds herself a place to sit away from the puddles. The flock is on the way home, and Ruby drives them as quickly as possible into the corral. The way lies over my hogan. Slim pointed feet on soft sand make numerous perforations which the water, seeking a channel, rejoices to follow. The roof is now like a sieve. Marie puts a blanket around her shoulders, I don my raincoat and hat. The books are in their trunk and papers in their briefcase; I lay a tarpaulin over the trunk. Both Marie and I, by abbreviating ourselves as much as possible, succeed in finding dry spots on which to sit. But we are constantly changing our dry spots as they become fewer and fewer.

At last the rain slows up, and once more we emerge, looking like drenched prairie dogs. The downpour was so ferocious that everyone stayed exactly where he was. Now Tom, his blue shirt sticking to his skin, comes up to inquire smilingly how the house is.

"Not so good," I reply. "The goats went over it after the sand got wet and made lots of holes."

Tom untwists the balewire which fastens the shovel to the rear end of the car and applies himself to the pile of sand which lies about the house, the surplus dug out when it was made. He shovels it in great damp chunks onto the roof, pounds and stamps it down, particularly over the holes and around the ventilator. Then he digs a small trench inside the door. The overflow stands in the trench, the little puddles have disappeared, sunk into the sand of the floor.

Tom and Marie now go to their own house to inspect its soundness. I have a headache and decide to go to Ganado as soon as the water runs off a bit. The ground is wet; I should have to sleep inside the hogan; I will spend the night with the traders. I put on the chains, fasten the shovel, and, after a brief interval, announce my intention and depart.

But this afternoon the sun acknowledges complete defeat. I have not gone half a mile before it begins to rain again. I take the old road which is over a hill and into a dip. I come to a low part of the road, which I have previously hardly noticed. Now it looks like a lake. I stop at the top of the slight incline. The rain pelts down. A wash runs angrily at my side pouring its foaming yellow filth into the newly made lake. It is cold and windy and wet. I know only one thing, that is to wait.

I wait for some minutes. Time has ceased. At last the rain lessens and I test the crossing in the usual Southwest fashion. Take off shoes and stockings and wade it. It is fearfully cold and before I have gone a rod gets deep. I need go no farther. The water is halfway between my knees and hips; it is too much for Jonathan. There is no going forward. The ruts of the road are too deep and too slick for me to turn around in even if the furious wash at my side did not terrify me. I wait longer.

After a while enough water has run off the landscape to allow the car wheels once more to take hold. I back up for nearly a quarter of a mile. At last I can turn out of the ruts and turn around on the nice rough sagebrush.

I arrive back at Red-Point's settlement to find all the family blanketed and wading outside the houses. The rain has ceased, but everything is soaked. This was the test for the houses, and none of them passed it. It rained in, it rained through, it rained under. My relatives are drenched and busy but smiling. Red-Point's house is the worst. The empty bucket and washbasin are swimming about, hitting the loomframe now and again. The few other objects which usually stand on the floor have been hastily stowed in the crevices formed by the overlapping logs of the roof. The blankets and sheepskins are hanging where all good housekeepers put them each morning, over a pole supported by wires hung from the ceiling. The top one inverted has streaks of red clay from the roof, the others are dry.

Marie's house has leaked least, and it would be reasonable to suppose that Maria Antonia and Red-Point could go there for the night. Unthinkable! A respectable woman sleep in the same house as her son-in-law! Sleep in a running stream rather! But Yikadezba's-Mother is not home. Her house has not leaked at all and Red-Point moves in for the night.

After I satisfy my curiosity as to all these arrangements I return to my own house—return to find it completely dry. Tom's patching has made the roof watertight, the door was closed and mine is the most comfortable of all the dwellings.

I am cold. My wading, the wind, the wetting, all have combined to give me a chill. I have no smokehole, but I have some dry wood; and I decide to make a little fire even at the risk of considerable smoke. I am coaxing it along, slowly but successfully, when Tom comes up with a large armful of splintery newly split juniper. "I will make you a fire under the tree," he announces, "so you can cook your supper. It's too bad your house leaked."

"I'm not going to eat any supper because I have a headache," I answer; "but I am cold, so I am building a fire in here. You needn't worry about the house. You can see it is better than your own."

"The smoke will make your headache worse," he protests. "I don't think it will smoke much now. But if it does I will put it out."

He goes, leaving me the dry wood.

I lay my bed as far from the door and ventilator as the space allows. I have never slept inside before. The only drawback the house has, noticeable chiefly in the quiet of the night, is the activity of a big black beetle which burrows in the wall, allowing sand to run down the sides. I hear it, snap on my flashlight, see nothing. I hear a tsuk! tsuk! tsuk! above me, see nothing. This is the noise of a wood-borer—"Wood-he-eats," the Navajo call him. He spends his time boring holes in the ceiling logs and shedding rivulets of sawdust or sand.

But with an aching head and back tired from weaving and driving Jonathan in the slime, I do not long remain conscious of these busy insects, which never come near me anyway, except rarely when they drop from the ceiling.

The next thing I know, the sun, high in the sky, is casting streaks of gold on my floor, filtering through cracks of my crazy door. I am warm all over and rested. But I hear loud snicking sounds just outside. Those wood-borers never before made that much noise. I get up and peep over the door, trying to locate one at work. To my amazement there is a huge crackling fire of juniper. Not a fire such as I make myself of scattered sage and broken branches, but one gay, sputtering, flaming, of heavy chopped cedar sticks. Do the Navajo have fairies, gnomes? They have Toms.

We are prepared for rain now. Our houses are all patched, our goods well stowed, no unused oddments lying about, our covers—tarps, ponchos, sheepskins, blankets—within easy reach. Once more I sit weaving, with Marie chattering amiably, somewhat sleepily at my side.

"Do white women ever sleep in the daytime?" she asks.

"Why—uh—uh! Why, yes, sometimes we do when we are tired."

"The Navajo women never!" she remarks, suddenly lifting her head with a look of surprise. "It's raining again." And that look of satisfaction typical of the Navajo when they are pleased, settles on her face.

We continue our weaving placidly although the storm is gaining in velocity. This is a male rain with wind, thunder, and lightning, sharp lightning. I have learned to lay my door over the supports of the entry when it rains. Quite satisfactory to keep the house dry, but it cuts off most of our light. So we cover the weaving and just sit, as small as we can make ourselves, and look at each other. Suddenly there comes a cry from Maria Antonia's house, a startled cry of fear. The settlement is galvanized into action. Marie darts up, I thrust the army blanket at her. She rushes out while I put on my rain things.

I try to go out but the rain sends me back. There is no going between drops, no walking between puddles. The settlement has become a single puddle in which shoes slip and slide. I see my relatives running about barefoot. The women have hastily thrown on their blankets, but their ruffled skirts drip water. Tom and Curley's-Son have been shovelling to divert the water from the houses, and they are soaked. No one has time to watch Yikadezba even if he wants to, and she is enjoying a thorough drenching.

Marie comes back to me in no time. "You must go to

Ganado and get the old man," she says excitedly, "the sheep have been struck by lightning."

Tom comes in. "We must go at once," he says.

"Yes," I answer. "We will go, but we'll get there quicker if we wait until it stops raining. You put the chains on for me and see that we have the shovel, ax, and tow rope."

This is an almost superfluous remark for, even in the brightest weather, Jonathan has a shovel, ax, and tow rope, just as he has headlights or tires. But at this uncertain season the shovel may be resting against the door of my house, the tow rope may have been used for our dyeing activities. Better to check up for an emergency.

We huddle for twenty minutes in my hogan until the rain becomes lighter. As we wait I ask about the sheep. "Were any killed?"

"We don't know. It looks as if three or four were maybe."

"Where were they?"

"Just off there." Tom and Marie point with pursed lips to a spot directly in front of Maria Antonia's hogan, where many white dots are still moving among the dark piñons.

"But why don't you know? Didn't you go over to see?"

"Ruby ran right back to tell us."

"Didn't you go out?"

Their answers are vague and indefinite. The fact remains that no one went over to see. No one even drove the surviving sheep in. That is why they must have Red-Point at once. Until he comes and, with a prayer, releases the survivors from further harm, they are as afflicted as the possible dead. This is one of the few occasions upon which I have seen Navajo in a hurry. There is need for great speed. Jonathan will help. But he will go faster if we wait a little.

Tom and I get started. We make the half-mile from our houses to the highway easily, the road is of hard sand. The highway is new, it has ditches on both sides for drainage. We slither along, now toward the ditch at the right, now Jonathan prefers that at the left. But he wants to go into *some* ditch. Tom is good with a shovel, but I try to save him by guiding Jonathan and curbing his desire for leaving the road. We proceed a mile and suddenly find the car holding the road. The tracks are only damp and in a few more rods we are on a perfectly dry road.

Red-Point is at the dam. For weeks he has been bossing a gang of Navajo with teams at repairing the ditches and flume. Today they are reinforcing the spillway. We approach within a half-mile of the place they are working and again run into deep mud. We leave the Ford in a sizable puddle and proceed by foot.

Red-Point and his gang are a sorry-looking lot. Rain spills from their four-gallon hats. Their coats are soggy, wrinkled, and shapeless. They are barefoot, having hung shoes and moccasins under the wagons to keep them dry. They have worked hard ever since the rainy season began, repairing the spillway. A twenty-minute shower washed it out entirely. But, as the water runs down over their faces like copious tears, to a man they smile characteristically as they point to the results of their work. They shrug their shoulders fatalistically as they say, "Hola!"

All are duly excited by our news. Red-Point has his horse, so cannot go back with us. But he arrives at White-Sands very soon after we do. For the rest of the evening all is quiet. The sons-in-law have gone off to cut trees and branches to build a new corral. Red-Point goes out to the sheep, taking with him several little pouches of pollen and medicine from his large medicine bundle. He goes to pray and to remove the dead sheep to the cañon. The women wait.

When he returns, the women drive back the rest of the flock. They may once more go near the sheep. The lightning striking into the flock as it did, had contaminated all within its range. Red-Point had freed the survivors from the immediate taint by his sung prayers, by sprinkling pollen, and by removing the dead. The remainder of the flock must be kept in a corral by themselves until he removes the permanent results of the catastrophe. By the time the sheep return the boys have made the new corral. They have left the branches on the trees and have laid them so the flock can eat them during their eight-day incarceration. For four days during which they will be treated for their ill luck, they must remain, for four days more they stay in order that the medicine may take effect.

Next day Marie tells me nine animals were lost, one of her own goats, a lamb and sheep belonging to Maria Antonia, and six sheep of Atlnaba's. This morning another of Atlnaba's lambs died. "They" have been sent for sheep medicine. I have to this day never been able to find out exactly who "they" are. When Red-Point wants herbs which must be gathered at a distance, he sends "them," evidently messengers, probably relatives, he is able to call upon at a moment's notice.

Red-Point, tired and coughing, comes in for a cigarette and visit. He says: "Nine were lost. When I got there they were all swollen up. But if I had got there sooner I could have sung and brought them back to life again. It is too late when they are swollen up. It's too bad I wasn't home."

I remark to Marie—my remark carries no weight—that

they had their singer in two hours after the sheep were struck. "The Navajo don't usually get a singer that quickly, do they?"

"No," she agrees, but her faith and her father's have not been shaken by a jot or a tittle.

We weave only for short periods today because Marie must go help Red-Point or Atlnaba and I must go with her to see the short ceremonies and all that they do. They do not mind my tagging along; they are only surprised that I want to.

In the intervals when I am alone I continue my marvelling at my grandfather and at his firm belief in himself. It is more than conceit, it is over and above that. It is absolute faith in the efficacy of the sing. He knows it perfectly. If then he performs it without a mistake, why should it not be powerful, even sufficient to bring life to that which is dead?

But I, with my un-Navajo type of mind, say to myself: "Ordinarily it takes, with good luck even, half a day for a man to find his horse. He then rides perhaps half a day or longer to the home of the singer he wants to hire. If he is in luck the singer is home and it takes only half a day to wrangle *his* horse and another half-day for the two to ride back. Two days is then about the minimum time when a medicine man may be expected. Two hours is about the greatest speed they might achieve. And yet Red-Point is sure he could have brought the sheep to life—if he had been here sooner. . . ."

A dull day, a hot day, a still day. Even in the morning the sun does not shine, nor does he ever peep between clouds causing them to part and scuttle away. An ominous silence lies over us all. The air is heavy and dead. The sounds of humans and animals are startling even in their appropriateness. It has been unusually hot and oppressive for a week, but today it seems as if threat, of what I am not certain, must culminate in action. It is one of those days when something dire seems about to happen, a time during which one holds his breath and crosses his fingers. Life seems to be running along smoothly. One thinks of the possible calamities on the principle that it is the unexpected that happens. If then we expect something awful, it at least won't be that something.

For some reason I am restless today and for some other reason I have no visitors, not even Marie. My weaving does not hold me, and I tire quickly of learning my Navajo language, a pursuit that usually interests me for hours, more hours than there ever are. With a conscience guilty at reading in the daytime I open a book. It is not interesting, nor are the magazines I have. I must be tired; I will try to sleep, even if Navajo women never do. But there is a fly on my nose— its buzzing sounds like a saw in the tense silence. I will go outside. But there is no wind and the flies are worse than they are inside. Besides, ants crawl vigorously over tarpaulin and over me. I go back in. I think I am hungry and eat some crackers. I repeat my list of entertainments. Those hours which usually flit so fast I cannot see them, now drag interminably.

The silence is broken at last. I go out. This is no ordinary sandstorm. As I watch the clouds I am the only living thing between the fury of the sky and the earth it rages over. From the southwest thick clouds, black as night but not in a solid curtain, roll up, gather fierceness, and in anger pass madly over White-Sands. They contain, I see easily, every possibility for destruction. They pass over us so swiftly that they are not able to drop on us any of their contents. They race madly to the northeast. There they meet all their own kind and others too; all unite to become the embodiment of cataclysm. Black puffy wind clouds, smooth black thunderclouds, gray rain clouds, yellow, hail-bearing masses. They knot up in the northeast, snarl and snap and finally, releasing their accumulated frenzy, vent it on the earth. Wind, male rain, thunder, lightning, hail.

I, from my roof-top, view it all, seeing only the general calamity, unaware of details. As suddenly as the storm gathered, earth and sky relax about me. The air is cool and fresh; sounds take on their usual matter-of-factness; the earth is sweetly fragrant. A smooth black cloud lies long and horizontally an arm's length above the western horizon. At last the sun triumphs; he breaks forth under the cloud in a red-gold glow, grinning so broadly the eye cannot bear him. But the presence of the cloud has let him turn our little world, which seems to me immense, to copper.

I am the only reality. The herdboy, whom I have always heartily disliked, has turned into a statue of living bronze. The thought passes fleetingly through my mind, "Why, Paul is really exceedingly handsome!" The sheep grazing near by are fluffy fulvid beings, no longer stupid and impolite, but something existing only in the imagination of a super-being.

A moment of superb insubstantiality, and we are back to the comprehensible, a well-run, prosperous Navajo family driving sheep into corrals, cedar fire crackling in the fireplace, mutton boiling, children teasing, dogs barking.

Next day we learn the results of the tornado and take a trip to survey the havoc. It has raised the water level of the large reservoir near Ganado, empty all summer, five feet. But it has ripped out entirely the diversion dam which controlled the ditches. The place where it stood used to look like a smooth lake. It has now become a wide forty-foot cañon. Concrete piers are torn completely away, their mass dumped in the side of the wash at intervals half a mile down. The traders tell me the waves rose as high as the telephone poles in front of their place. In the sixty years of their experience they remember nothing like this. Poor old blind Tonto, the twelve-year-old son who led him through life, and his little grandson were drowned just outside their hogan. No one knows how many sheep were lost.

We continue our pilgrimage in the bright mellow sunshine. We drive toward the storm belt, come to a halt nine miles southeast of Ganado where the chief sights are to be seen. Cutting an eight-mile swath the storm has denuded every tree of branches, leaves, and cones. This is a year for piñon nuts. Within this belt every tree has become a spiked trunk.

At the right of the road is a pile of hailstones, packed as if in an icehouse five feet high. I had never believed the tales of "hailstones big as hen's eggs," but these were larger than walnuts five days after the storm. The wall they made melted gradually for three weeks afterward.

We walk a short distance to our left. There we see how the wash brought down stone slabs twenty-eight feet long, uprooted trees three feet in diameter. The débris brought down forms a natural dam so that the wash which formerly ran west by north has now been turned and runs nearly directly south. As we gaze on it and contemplate what we saw at the diversion dam, we realize in a feeble way how the Grand Canyon could have been possible. These last days have shown me wonders my senses almost repudiate. They are uncanny but as actual as this lacerated earth itself.

My friends add their observations of nature's freakishness to mine. After the world turned to bronze the moon came up. But some rain lingered between it and the clear western sky. The moon reflected its quiet rays through the light rain streamers of the night, causing a white rainbow. It happened to fit perfectly over a well defined little hill, and the effect was of a great empty white stadium.

A few days later in the course of our conversation Red-Point remarks casually: "It's awful dry. We need rain."

XII

UNDERSTANDING

IN SPITE of rain, changes of the earth's surface, rites of restoration, and other interruptions, the green blanket has been steadily advancing toward the top. A number of warps have torn—they are the thin ones of the old warp weaver; the heavier evenly twisted ones of Maria Antonia are sound. Marie helps me a lot with the stripe weaving. I know that now, and do not need practice. Suddenly a question of my old grandmother brings too vividly to mind a matter I have refused to dwell upon, "When are you going home?"

There are indeed few days of my stay left. Maria Antonia says she will be lonesome after I leave. She is a dear old soul. Shyly she steals up to my house for a short visit whenever I am home and the rest of the family gather together. If one of her sons-in-law is home she may be left alone. She and I make good conversation. I have taught her to teach me the three most important principal parts of the Navajo verbs. There may be ten or twelve, unpredictable and different in form, but for the present I am doing with the simplest forms. I get them by making sentences with past and future adverbs.

Maria Antonia tells me about her ailments, which are many. They are the chief reason why her large pretentious rugs remain static for days, even weeks on end. She tells me too about the sings she has had for illness, shows me the tiny charm, a small cowry shell strung with a turquoise bead, that she wears on her hair string and another like it which she has tied to a string on her belt. Many a time has her husband sung over the members of his family. But if they need some power other than he possesses he does not hesitate to call in another singer who has that power.

I know my grandmother has had gallstones because when we were at Fort Wingate the Mission doctor, coming a day later, reported to Red-Point that Maria Antonia had been very ill. He had gone to see her and had diagnosed her disease. He would not operate, he told us, even if he thought it advisable, because Maria Antonia has a bad heart condition. There would be a reason he does not reckon on, namely, that Red-Point would not let him. "We must return at once," decided Red-Point. The need for a sing is the touchstone with which to speed up and excite a Navajo. But we persuaded him to wait until after the Council meeting, because the doctor said the immediate attack was over. We returned two days later to find Maria Antonia apparently as we had left her.

As soon as her pain passes by, she thinks she is well again, but is rarely without headache and stiffness. This is the frail old woman who swings an ax vehemently at her woodpile in the setting sun. The one who wakens me at sunrise by the snapping of a dead juniper branch she is wrenching from a stump. Lazily I watch her assemble a pile of wood and say to myself: "Poor old thing! Somebody ought to do that heavy work for her."

And then, to my shame, I find my own woodpile replenished. Maria Antonia has dropped an armful on it as she bustled by.

It doesn't seem right, and yet I believe she would be grievously hurt if she became too feeble to do the things she wants to do. The flesh may be weak, but the spirit is as vivacious as in the days long past when she was as productive as Atlnaba. She grieves not to be able to weave more steadily, but her back hurts her and she does not see as well as formerly.

Maria Antonia is the one who rose first to my defense on the day a visitor criticised her for my presence. "My mother is awfully mad," said Marie the day after.

"Why?" I must naturally ask.

"Because that man who was here yesterday said we ought not to teach you how to weave. It made her awful mad, and she said she guessed she would teach you if she wanted to."

As we sit on the side of my house like two crones at their smoking, she tells me about herself and her family. And her heart will feel sad after I am gone.

Now that my time is becoming shorter I have more visitors than usual. Maria Antonia comes oftener and stays longer. Atlnaba has strung up a small blanket half of which she finishes the first day. When Marie asks her what she is going to do with it, she answers, "I am making it for a present for a friend." But with no large rug on her own loom she has time to spend with us. As I stiffen up after a few hours of weaving, she and Marie take my place and like magic the web advances.

One day they all come and bring three visitors. They are Silversmith's two wives, who are sisters, and his grown daughter. They are dressed in their company best, and all, but especially the daughter, are weighed down with silver, bracelets, rings, necklaces, earrings. I have often noticed that Marie and Atlnaba fasten the collars of their velvet shirts with safety pins stuck at a precise angle, but I thought it was because they had no other pins. Silversmith's daughter has the straight front piece of her shirt and the sleeves from wrist to elbow highly decorated. Altogether she has perhaps three dozen or more of the lovely ridged silver buttons the Navajo make. Between each two, placed with the greatest nicety, a medium-sized safety pin is fixed.

The number of persons in my hogan is large now, for the children have come too; Ben has brought a lamb and Yikadezba a puppy. But somehow the house does not seem full. As each new visitor comes in, she folds her numerous skirts neatly and compactly around her as with one movement she sits, lighting like a bird which has drawn in its feathers.

The visitors are of course weavers and they discuss in friendly fashion the blanket I am making. My family proudly present me as Exhibit A. They laugh, as tolerantly as the rest of my friends, at my first blanket. Somehow I am not as ashamed of it as I was, for the green one stands on the loom, even and respectable, with faults not of weaving but only of design.

There is the pleasant hubbub of conversation, often breaking into quiet jolly laughter, the *thump thump* of the comb on the warp, the scurrying of the children in and out, out and in the hogan. Suddenly Ben gives a cry of surprise and, as if electrified, all the women spring up and out of the house. I do not wish to lose my place and insert the batten into the shed before I go out. It is a strange hawk soaring high in the sky; we do not see that kind often here. We all come right back, and as I take up my place ready once more to weave, I notice the batten has been pulled out of the warp and lies on the floor.

About this time in my career another marvel happens. I find myself no longer counting the rows or the warps which are or should be forward to make my triangles. Suddenly I *know* which ones they are. It seems so simple, the way they look, different on four rows, and the differences regularly repeated. How could I ever have been so confused as I was in those first days, after we had put in the design? It seems incredible that anyone could be so stupid.

The time has grown so short I am forced to consider it, even as does Maria Antonia; and even as she, I count the remaining days with heaviness of heart. True, when I leave here I am going to Europe; but I should love to follow the train of thought I have just begun to get and to allow unaccustomed muscles really to become hardened. I shall miss the friendliness and kindness of this White-Sands plain, a spirit which pervades it from the white light of pre-dawn even to and through the darkness.

As I ponder the shortness of my stay I get pangs of conscience. Here I came out to learn to weave. Have I learned? What an object that first blanket is! The second green one is excellent, but who wove it? Marie did more than half altogether. If I leave like this I shall not be able to say honestly of any piece, "*I* made this." It will take an age to finish off the green one, and I know how. It is merely a struggle with tightness, tedious but not new.

When Marie comes in on Friday I say to her: "Do you think we could get this done by tomorrow, if you help me a lot? I would then have three days left. I should like to have you string up a tiny blanket for me, just two hands long and one wide, and I want to weave every stitch of it myself. I think if I work hard I can get it all done in the three days I have left."

Marie is more pleased than usual. She sets to work with a will, and together we push battens, reeds, and umbrella ribs, and together we pull on heald and heald rod. Saturday we take down the green rug, finished. It shows no disposition to move away from us when we put it on the floor. There are mistakes in the pattern but the web is good. Even the edges are good. Marie has seen to that. We criticise it once more as, with the sacking needle, Marie fastens in the surplus of the edge strands to form tassels at the corners. The blanket may not be as we intended, but it is good. We know it, and everybody who knows blankets agrees with us. But I cannot say it is mine.

XIII

SELF-RELIANCE

MY LITTLE rug is strung up and well along. It is over two hands long, not quite two wide. It has a white background and not very much design. This piece is so small that it begins to get tight before it is one-quarter done. I use smaller battens and release every millimeter of tautness. I have no particular difficulties with it except tightness and the need for speed.

On Monday, Marie says, "Silversmith is having a sing for his daughter tonight."

"What kind is it?"

"The girl's sing. Last week he came over to ask my father how old she is. My father says she is fifteen, so they are having it."

"How far is it to his place?" I inquire guardedly.

"About fourteen miles toward Water-in-Ground."

"Shall we go?"

"Yes."

"I guess I can get this done on Tuesday anyway," I remark. "We'll be back early in the morning."

Marie agrees.

I have a dress like those the Navajo women wear, but I have never worn it. I have waited for an auspicious occasion. Today I tell Marie I have it. "Would you like to see it?"

"Yes," she says eagerly.

So I take it from the depths of the trunk. A black blouse of fine velvet lined with red calico like the skirt, which is ten yards around its ruffle and modest at that. Marie loves the feel of the velvet. She and her relatives always have velvet shirts, but the velvet is cotton-backed and does not have as much of a sheen.

"Shall I wear it tonight?" I ask, knowing there will be no whites at the sing.

"Oh, yes!" she assents, looking pleased.

We are all ready just about dark, I in my black and red dress and with a red cap and sweater. Marie and Tom, their little sons Ben and Dan, Atlnaba and Curley's-Son, all done out in their best blankets, wearing their jewelry. Even the little boys have small four-gallon hats—about two-gallons, I should say.

The sing is actually only about fourteen miles from our place, and we arrive about eight-thirty. There are only a few people there when we arrive. A well-made shade under which the women are cooking has an excellent fireplace with a large fire.

We are cordially welcomed by Silversmith's family. My sisters sit down at the back of the shade, the hostess brings me a kitchen chair. Marie and Atlnaba smile at the thought that I need it, but I sit on it for a while to be polite. As we wait and watch the extensive cooking operations, various Navajo filter in. The young men shake hands somewhat bashfully, then stand about outside the shade. Women enter quietly and sit in the semicircle with us.

I am as usual fascinated by the cooking activities. The women have many irons in the fire, and all are watched, none is neglected. Ribs are broiling on grates bent with use to fit the places they have occupied during their existence.

Silversmith's older wife, shielding her eyes and face by holding her hand a short distance from her face, is tending the boiling. Several bucketfuls of a corn and mutton stew are bubbling on a pile of hot coals. The woman finds the water for the coffee is boiling. She lifts it off the fire, measures out coffee in the palm of her hand for the five coffee pots standing before her, fills each with the boiling water. Then with her stick she skilfully separates more embers from the blazing fire and arranges them about the coffee pots. When she is through she turns the ribs.

Another woman, bronze in the flickering firelight, is mixing dough, which she pats into flat flabby round shapes and bakes in a frying pan. Beside her a pile of tortillas, nicely browned, stands on a clean flour sack. This woman's sister is shaping her dough in the same way; but she has a Dutch oven full of sizzling fat into which she gently lowers the limp round portions of dough. Each time she puts one in, the fat sputters and spits, the dough bubbles up in irregular spots. Soon she turns it to display a blistered golden surface; a delicious form of breadstuff is the result. The yeast-raised bread has already been baked in the adobe ovens of Spanish shape, and the round loaves sit in rows covered with flour sacks on a shelf above our heads. Meat hangs on the various posts of the shade, high enough to be safe from the numerous marauding dogs. Tonight at least they will get their fill when this large crowd of people throws out bones and scraps.

About one hundred yards to the left looking past the cooking fire, there is a wide bed of glowing coals. Now and then a man devotes a short time to splitting some of the wood from a pile house-high near it. The fire is over a pit in which an enormous sweet cake is baking. This is the *pièce de résistance* of the occasion, corresponding to a birthday or a wedding cake. The fire will be kept blazing all night.

Like a mighty huddled, uneven, opalescent mirror a large flock of sheep reflect the light of both fires at my right. A herdboy sits before them, occasionally driving them a little nearer to the shade, or scattering them a little farther away. From a hogan at the left come sounds of the laughter of the men. The girl whose party this is, sits demurely wrapped in her blanket at the center of the west side of the hogan. She looks modestly at the floor while the guests enjoy themselves eating, smoking, and gossiping.

Just before midnight we all go into the hogan where the girl is. It is a small house and one wonders how it can possibly hold all these people. But they all have the faculty of fitting themselves and their clothes into a minimum space, just as they do in hunting the only six-inch space of dryness in a hogan during a rain.

A chorus of young men accompanies the singer. They sing as they beat time with the rattles. There is a cedar fire in a sordid stovepipe and galvanized tin arrangement which furnishes heat without light. The cedar smoke combines with the perspiration of the tightly huddled audience to produce a typically Navajo odor. We pay our respects to the girl and her family by withstanding the warmth, the close air, the smoke, the monotonous singing. It is a perfect soporific to which we must not yield, for the purpose of the sing is to keep a vigil. Anyone may go to sleep, but he should not do so inside the hogan. A little after one, there is a pause to allow the chorus a short rest before they start off on a new group of songs. I pass about a package of cigarettes, gratefully accepted by the women around me. Marie keeps nudging me, "What time is it?" I hold out until two. Marie says she is going to stay.

I go to the car. There I find Tom and Ben wrapped in Tom's blanket on the back seat, Dan spread out with my blanket over him on the front. I haven't the heart to wake them, and I saunter up to the shade. I will lie near the fire. But I no more than show signs of retiring than one of Silversmith's wives hunts two soft sheepskins, shakes them out and smilingly lays them down for me. No mattress ever felt so good. I am just dozing off when she comes again with a woman's blanket which she lays over me. Exactly the way they put their children to bed. I am too sleepy and too much touched by her thoughtfulness, her version of hospitality, to think more than dreamily of the implications. I drift into a sound sleep.

I am aroused at dawn by a general bustle and by the changed and energetic character of the songs. The chorus has started with the dawn songs. I get up. The magic and the glow have faded. The fires are low. The air is cold, the sheep are uncivil balls of milling white, even the colorful clothes of the guests have become dulled. The sun is only a promise; his rays are long, faint, and cold.

Young fellows stand on both sides of the entrance to the hogan, some of the women collect in bevies farther away. Two continue to watch the cooking. One group of women has gone over to the pit and is engaged in uncovering the sweet cake with cunning fingers so that no sand gets into it.

We stand shivering for some minutes. Then the girl rushes

out and tries to run toward the east. She is partially blind and
the race the boys have with her is pathetic. But they let her
win. After they return, all gather about the sweet cake. This
is the reward of all participants. The singer and his aides are
served first, then we each get a generous piece served on a
clean brittle corn husk. It is rather soft and soggy, saccharine
to my taste, thus early in the morning. We pull off bits of
the confection delicately as we sit about the renewed cooking
fire. That which we cannot eat we tie up and take along to
be criticised by the stay-at-homes.

The sun has not even become warm when we drive up before Red-Point's house. We have only one passenger more
than we took, one of Tom's aunts who wants to visit us a
few days. We are not guests, but we pause for a time while
the dogs settle down and Marie looks into the house to locate
her mother. She reports favorably, and the husbands go into
the hogan to eat with their father-in-law. I proceed to my
own ablutions and breakfast, thence to weaving my little
white blanket. Today is my last chance and I should be much
humiliated to require Marie to finish it when I have vowed
that not one stitch shall be hers.

I am left alone for several hours. I suppose the others are
sleeping. I could do nicely with a nap myself, but I will not
be defeated. I am not very efficient. I make no major mistakes
but the batten frequently snaps down from its horizontal
position and that when my fingers are between the sheds. It
makes me grumble the things I say when a hammer goes
wrong in driving a nail. I find there are two reasons for its
snapping, one that the warp is tight, a circumstance not to be
overcome. The second is that the batten is at an angle which

will not allow it to accommodate itself to the tight warp. One can learn to change this angle so that it does not snap very often.

By noon I am not nearly as far as I ought to be, and I notice the blanket is getting narrower toward the top. Soon after, Marie and her mother and her aunt come in.

"Did you sleep?" I ask her.

"No. I lay down, but every time I nearly went to sleep I began to cry; so I got up again."

"Why was that?" I ask innocently.

"I feel lonesome when I think of you going away."

"Well, I am going to miss you all too. But I hope I shall come back next year. How does your mother like the cake?"

"We don't think it is very good. It ought not to be soggy like that in the middle. My mother is the only one who knows how to make it real good."

"They used to chew the sprouted wheat for it, didn't they?"

"Yes, my mother can remember that; but never in my time. Instead my mother boils sugar in water and makes a syrup which she mixes with the dough made of sprouted corn. This was made of sprouted wheat and the sugar was just sprinkled over the top. Everybody says my mother's tastes better than anybody's."

"I think the sing was kind of tame. Not nearly as good as I have seen," I remark by way of summary.

"Yes, it was. You know it's always like that with those people. They always do things that way."

"Did you stay in the hogan all night?"

"Yes, and even the singer and all the people went to sleep right in there."

"Isn't that terrible! The girl will not have good luck, will she?"

"It is not a good way. She is pitiful anyway. Not very strong, and she can hardly see."

As we talk one of the educated Navajo boys who acts as an interpreter comes in with a geologist. They are prospecting for coal. Although our conversation is indeed pleasant I am on pins and needles, for I *must* get that blanket done. I get impatient about it. I have never been so tired and kept on weaving. I have never before been pinched for time. I think, "If I could only be left alone to do it!" but I have company more steadily this afternoon than ever.

I think it strange that Atlnaba has not come. Marie says she is busy finishing her little rug. At length she appears with it as I am forcing in my last stitches. I am the friend for whom she was weaving it.

The sun sinks low and finally they all leave me. After all there are chores to do. I work until after six, when I take down the little web. It is not sinuous like the first, but neither is it uniform like the second. The upper end is three-quarters of a thumb joint narrower than the lower. At a number of places the warp shows—a sure sign that the weaving is too tight. But a new fault appears. On the back of the piece, which ought to look the same as the front, there are peculiar lumps, loops made by setting the weft too *loose*.

I am glad to be alone as I endeavor to keep my disappointment from dissolving in tears.

I have, by my lateness, missed much of my favorite hour on this my final day with it. But the last minutes of the sunset hour have somewhat dispelled my disappointment when I hear the chug of a motor. The trader has brought Cha. They bring my mail. They say they do not think the third blanket bad. They comfort me on having made it all by myself. "It is so little I don't know what you could use it for," says Cha.

"You could fold it up and it would make a nice handbag," suggests the trader. "The wide part could be the flap, and you could fasten it with a silver Navajo button. The designs fit perfectly for that too."

The idea is a good one. I have always held it in reserve as a symbol of the comfort it gave me. My friends, both white and Indian, have the faculty of spreading balm on the wounds of my discouragement.

Next day the whole family helps me pack Jonathan. Red-Point and the women embrace me in the Navajo way, arm around the waist and bowed head of one lying on the other's shoulder for a second or two. Then I start off as quickly as possible, not looking back.

XIV

CRITICISM

THE next summer I arrive at Ganado to learn that Marie and Tom have gone to Los Angeles, but Red-Point and his family want me to come there. Atlnaba and Maria Antonia will be my teachers. I arrive at White-Sands and receive a welcome the cordiality of which cannot be dulled by shyness. Everything must be just as it was last summer. Maria Antonia bids Ninaba go for a wagon cover but I stop her; I have one of my own this year.

Last year in leaving my pleasant house I felt a pang I was too ashamed to mention at leaving the poker I had used all summer. It was only a stick of a convenient size and shape, strong enough to carry a full coffee-pot, having a fork at the proper distance from the end, just one of those things. I am pleasantly surprised then to find the same poker lying with its point to the fireplace when I reappear.

I wanted to weave last summer; it is understood I shall want to weave again this. I have given the next rug long and serious thought and have concluded to try once more to make what we set out to do last summer. I have modified the design so as to conform to the technique. I will do it in the conventional colors, black, white, and red.

This time Atlnaba strings up the warp, her own spinning. There will be little trouble with this tearing. She notes the design, changes somewhat the proportions of this one. The green was more than five hands wide by more than six long. This is very little less than four by little less than six. There can be no doubt that these proportions are better for the hourglass design we intend to use.

Strangely no complications enter into this weaving. The warps of the different sheds do not stick together. My hand does not hurt from the continual thumping. Even when the design begins to grow after we lay in a series of narrow stripes, the warp strands seem to know their places. I make mistakes, of course, but find them at once and know, too, how to correct them. The finished web is far from perfect. Atlnaba has tried to catch my errors and has succeeded in bringing wandering strands back to their places.

With Marie and Tom gone, the ranch is short-handed, and Atlnaba must put her mind and effort into duties she was free from last year. She has two large rugs strung up in her small hogan, a sand-painting one and an ordinary one with red background. Besides bearing an additional burden of labor, she does not feel very well, and her own weaving hardly progresses. For these reasons and because I do not need her so much as previously, she often leaves me to work by myself. My blanket when finished has therefore inaccuracies which one of Atlnaba's would not have, but they are what "make it look handmade."

As I advance about halfway to the center it seems to me the combination of black, white, and red is too hard, too glaringly clean. I ask Atlnaba if she has some gray yarn and she gives me a ball of a beautiful dark gray mixture. When she sees that I have introduced it into my side stripes, she is

MY FOURTH RUG WITH PATTERN PLANNED FOR THE SECOND

A GOOD EDGE

SHEEP

HUSKING BEE

pleased. She feels with me that the pattern is softened and thereby improved.

The mistake Marie and I made in the hourglass of the green blanket left too much space at each side of the center to be filled in with stripes. But I could have improved the effect had I made the stripes wider. Somehow the narrowness of the stripes detracts from the dignity of the design. This is only a minor lesson the green rug has taught me, and in setting the side stripes of my new rug I guard against changing the colors too often.

We need not wait until the blanket is finished to see that the changed proportions—longer and narrower—the accurate placing of the pattern, the introduction of the soft dark gray, and the widening of the side stripes combine to make a vast improvement.

My delight in weaving has now a quiet satisfied character. The matter-of-fact attitude of my family has communicated itself to me. I let Atlnaba take a turn at the weaving just as her mother might and have no qualms of conscience. When I complained of not being able to see the edge pulling in, one of my white friends suggested that I tie a string from the cloth beam to the top of the loom so that I could constantly measure the distance of the web from a fixed point. I have done this, and it adds materially to my perspective. Maria Antonia and Atlnaba consider it a good idea.

We have visitors again this year. Many of them are women who were here last year. One day Maria Antonia brings Tom's aunt, the one we brought with us from the girl's sing last summer, to visit while Atlnaba is with me. We are discussing the pattern. Atlnaba has suggested that a small gray triangle within the innermost white one of the concentric triangle combination would be nice. And still another good pattern would be a step motive within the red triangle running in toward the center white one and breaking up the rather large white space. We tell the newcomers of these ideas, and they approve. Tom's aunt says she would outline each of the triangles in a contrasting color, the red with black, the black with red.

I should like any of the modifications. None would be difficult. The outlining means additional work, but is very typical of Navajo weaving. When Atlnaba made the small blanket with the comb pattern for me, she picked up and dropped thirty different weft threads in weaving a single row across the middle. A good weaver of course never considers how much work a pattern is. She sees it as a finished whole and exerts herself to accomplish the ideal.

This summer a number of interesting blankets are brought to the trader. There is a revival, under the encouragement of trade, of the blankets made of vegetal dyes. I happen in at the trading-post one day when an expert at this type of weave brings in her blanket. It is a soft harmonious combination of dark gray, black, white, a yellowish green and two shades of rose, the color of the sand cliffs. The effect is indescribable and impossible of reproduction.

The trader and I sink to the floor at the sides of the spread rug, the weaver lights at the end. She tells us what each dye is made of. The plants whose roots, leaves, stems, or blossoms furnish the materials are scarce nowadays and it requires a great deal of labor to gather enough to dye sufficient yarn. As we talk over the details several other women come in, sit as lightly as the first, and unobtrusively add their information.

The trader pulls out other blankets dyed with natural colors as the talk goes on. Each one brings forth some bit of new knowledge or an opinion on texture or pattern.

The so-called vegetable dye fabrics may legitimately be termed blankets. The kind I have been weaving, the most ordinary type, might better be called rugs. For they are tight and firm in texture and therefore somewhat stiff and hard, at least when new. They become softer and more pliable with wear. The constant wear of tramping feet brings out all latent flexibility.

But the vegetal dye blankets are in a class by themselves. They have a style which is theirs alone. From their very inception they are delightfully yielding. The warp of their foundation is coarser than the one we use. The strands are separated by heavier twining yarn, which causes them to stand farther apart than those to which we are accustomed. The weft yarn is thicker but more loosely spun.

I return from the interview with the conviction that what I have learned is a mere drop in the bucket compared to what there is to know. Not only must I learn the plants and minerals used in the dyes, but also where to find them and the long tedious processes of concoction. Nevertheless I shall never be content until I have sometime made a blanket of this type.

Another of our visitors is a schoolgirl who in spite of her education is interested in weaving. She has been back at her home long enough to take it up intensively again. I have James' *Indian Blankets and Their Makers* with its many colored illustrations. She and Atlnaba leaf it over by the hour until I think the whole book will disintegrate. They happen upon a photograph of Atlnaba taken when she was only five. She was then called "The Little Weaver."

They criticise the designs in the book. They like the old-fashioned ones best. The girl likes one so well she sketches it to take home with her. But they have no tolerance for quaintness as such. If an old design is badly placed or irregularly executed, they condemn it as heartily as they do mine. Age does not excuse bad technique to them.

Much is said about keeping designs open so that the weaver "does not weave her spirit in." The idea is still believed by some women. Atlnaba makes many rugs with borders. The tapestry of the Sun's House has a black border. But at the upper right-hand corner she has run one gray thread across the border to serve as a "path." The little red-background rug she made for me also has a black border, but it is unbroken.

From the discussion and criticisms of my guests this day I gather that many designs with openings, especially those which are irregular are really due to miscalculations and ill-adjustments. They may be later rationalized as "sacred." One figure is, because of its age and texture, a beautiful piece; these modern weavers have nothing but scorn for it. The separate motives are not woven regularly, nor are they well spaced. My critics and teachers refuse to make a rationalization for "holiness." They continue with their remarks, leafing the pages over and over and back again to begin once more.

XV

DAN

OUR family has a lurking worry. Marie writes us faithfully
from Los Angeles. Everything is going well with her and Tom
on the white man's ranch. But there is an unreasonable cause
for her unhappiness. She is homesick for Dan. She and Tom
went under an agreement to stay a year at least. In each letter there is an appeal for Dan, and finally Marie writes the
trader that unless he sends Dan to her she will not stay.

Dan is seven and small for his age. He is bright-eyed and
smiling, observant, curious, and original. We never go anywhere that he does not have a hundred "Looks," "Whys," and
"Hows," many of which are laughingly suppressed, others of
which are patiently answered. He is the miniature old man
who on festive occasions wears a suit like his father's best and
always his broad sombrero. He makes uncounted games out
of sticks and stones, tin cans and pieces of string, ever new
and thrilling.

His brother, Ben, whom I should name "Pretty Boy," is
nine. He is Dan's faithful satellite and antithesis. His second teeth are gleaming white and sound. Dan's first set
are still with him but they are decayed, showing only disintegrated stumps. Ben lacks vivacity, originality, and endurance. He is content to stay quietly with his grandmother
when Dan rides off with Tom and Curley's-Son to round up

the cattle or horses. I asked Marie why Ben does not ride, and she said sorrowfully but also intolerantly: "Oh, he can't stand it. When he was only three months old something happened to him, I guess to his back. He is all right now, but he can't stand anything. Ruby was taking care of him. We don't know to this day what happened. She cried for two days but she would never tell us. My father sang for three months that time and he got better but he is not strong, not like other boys." I can see nothing whatever abnormal about Ben. He is charming and quiet, shy of course, but so is Dan. However, Dan's sense of inquiry soon rises above his shyness, and he must become acquainted in order to learn "why" and "how." Ben is satisfied if Dan finds out. And he cannot stand the strenuous contest with nature which keeps his grandfather, father, and uncle lean. So he is his grandmother's boy, and his mother does not yearn for him.

Red-Point is much disturbed by Marie's request. He does not like to refuse a request to any of his family if he can grant it. But this one makes him ponder, and as long as possible he staves off his decision. For the truth of the matter is, he cannot bear to think of White-Sands without Dan. He misses Marie and Tom sorely. True, Marie has been away from home for many years, but those days are always the best when all the members of the family are home. Dan has never been away in his short seven years. When his mother is gone Atlnaba and his grandmother take care of him. Red-Point must choose between his own desire and Marie's.

At last her ultimatum decides him. He has been saying: "Marie wants Dan, but I do not want to send him alone. We have been waiting for someone to take him." This has been a good excuse for procrastination, although of course many persons have gone from Gallup to Los Angeles in the last three months.

It has come to the time for the Gallup Ceremonial, to which we are all going. Red-Point has trained Ninaba to dance to his own accompaniment of song, drumming, and calling of figures. He has finally made up his mind to send Dan to his mother. Dan, characteristically, wants to go.

We journey to Gallup with our usual capacity load. The week of the Ceremonial is the gayest of the year for Gallup. The streets, oft-times dull and lifeless, are teeming with life and color. There are Indians from near and far, and Mexicans in their colorful shawls; but the majority of the visitors are Navajo. A team of dancers from any pueblo is large if it numbers more than twenty. The Navajo are present in thousands. They come by car, by horseback, and by wagon. Covered wagons driven by smiling Navajo, beside each of whom sits a demure woman with a baby, contain all that is necessary for a day or a protracted stay. The older children peep brightly out of the rear curtain. Within the body are hay for the horses, cooking utensils of the simplest sort, and perhaps some blankets the woman hopes to sell or display. They may be her own or those of her relatives or neighbors. The horses drone along, and suddenly Gallup is a Navajo town.

Dan has never been to Gallup before, nor has Ninaba. They are two of the many, but they come with Atlnaba and their grandfather in my car. If I were not there, Red-Point would find some other car to go in. Possibly the trader would take him. If there were no other way Curley's-Son would drive his wagon the sixty miles from his home to Gallup. We meet and pass many teams, riders, and cars. To the horsemen we shout a greeting. Sometimes we stop and talk quietly with a rider we know. What is the Ceremonial for if not to visit? The visiting may begin on the road. The Navajo drivers of wagons and autos turn out of our way far sooner than necessary, farther out than anyone would expect. Their horses are not skittish; they just turn out.

Arrived in Gallup, Dan tags about after Red-Point and Ninaba. Red-Point is known far and wide, and he has much to talk over and to attend to. An artist wants Ninaba to sit for her. Red-Point arranges the matter. He finds out the arrangements for his own performance and is insistent about promptness. At the Ceremonial grounds hundreds of Navajo blankets are shown in the exhibition hall. There too are the best specimens of other Navajo crafts. Women card, spin, and weave, a man hammers at his anvil making silver, another group sifts colored sand through practised fingers to show the white folk how sand-paintings are made.

The hall is small, the exhibitions are numerous. Whites rub elbows with Indians, meeting now a friend from New York, now one from California, and again Navajo from remote parts of the Reservation not seen for years. Good nature and gossip are rife, jokes are made and readily exchanged. Dan is almost crushed in the crowd milling about as aimlessly as sheep in a corral, but Atlnaba and Ninaba protect him and he does not murmur.

Now the hall is closed for the afternoon sports, and all move out, the whites to the huge grand stand, the Indians to the large place reserved for them in a central circle surrounded by the race track. The dazzling crowd is even more interesting than the entertainment.

There have been too many new things and they have moved too fast for Dan to get out many questions. Then the high spot of the day for him is reached. The Navajo horsemen are showing off. Racing, bronco busting, relays, roping, contests of all sorts. He sees men win and lose. He sees them as cheerful about losing as about winning, for the Navajo have been good losers ever since legendary times. To them it is the game that counts, not the score.

The sports are followed by a few dances. Most of them are deferred until night, when huge fires will serve equally for footlights and stage setting. But Dan is not interested so much in the dances. Even if he were, there is a limit to the excitement a hardy little soul can bear, and he drops asleep, his head on Atlnaba's indulgent lap.

At evening Old-Mexican's-Son announces abruptly as usual that he knows someone who is going to Los Angeles next morning and he has bought a ticket for Dan. His grandfather accompanies him to the station and, although he is anxious to go, he makes no attempt to hide his sobs as he bids farewell to Atlnaba and Ninaba. They sit quietly as unbidden tears well over protesting eyelids. Atlnaba turns her face aside as she surreptitiously wipes away the flood with the back of her hand.

At the station Red-Point and Dan, accompanied by the trader, look for the white lady who has promised to look after Dan, but she has decided to wait over a few days. So, properly tagged, Dan is put into the hands of the kindly conductor. At first, he forgets his sorrow in the newness of everything. He sits on the edge of his seat marvelling at the landscape which flies past far faster than it ever did when he beat his willing horse into a gallop. But it is not long before he knows loneliness. It comes over him like a pall. Here are many people, all interested in him, fussing over him. He likes their candy and oranges, but he does not understand any-thing they say. Twenty-four hours is a long time for a little boy to sit still and meditate on his own smallness. His grief is too deep for tears, and besides he is not a baby like Ben.

The conductor looks after him, and some of the time goes by in sleep. The sight of his mother and father after an eter-nity of strangeness once more opens the floodgates, and they all weep in concert.

XVI

SHEEP DIPPING

I AM surprised one day to see my grandmother dressed up just as if she were going away. She usually looks quite shabby. Ordinarily she wears a shirt so much washed that it is difficult to realize it has ever been velvet. Her elbows may show through the fabric, or the sleeves may crawl halfway up her forearm from frequent cutting off of worn cuffs. Her twelve-yard skirt is faded too. Its width is efficient for driving sheep. When she lifts the side of her skirt, it undulates in a determined way, catches the attention of one sheep's eye, and the flock goes forward. The skirt's fullness also has advantages when its wearer sits on the ground. It not only furnishes protection from sand and prickers, but also caters to Navajo prudery. There are of course disadvantages, not the least of which is the tendency to catch on the prickly bushes of the little-watered plateau. Maria Antonia's skirts usually have at least one three-cornered gash, and often more than one.

She wears her shabby clothes not as one who has no better, but rather as a city person in the country who says, "I always look like this out here." Today she looks quite as well as Marie or Atlnaba on the way to a sing. They have been telling me that it is time for the sheep dipping; but this is the first time in two summers that my grandmother has gone away from home, and it comes upon me unexpectedly. They pack up all their necessities, cookpots, food, hay, children, in the wagon, and Atlnaba takes the reins. Her husband is riding his horse to the dip; Ruby and the herdboy drive the sheep.

I ask her how long they will be gone. She is not sure if it will be two or three days. It will depend on how many flocks are ahead of theirs and how fast the sheep are dipped. I promise to come to see the dipping next day. As they drive off, I set about the activities for which I need concentration. In no time the sun is far past the "middle," and in a few minutes— so it seems to me—he is nearly down. I have decided to pass the night with the traders.

The rainy season is not quite over although it has nearly spent itself. I drive leisurely along five miles of roller-coaster highway, down and up, down and up again as I drink in the grandeur of the sunset. I come to the "big hill," around and over which the road twines narrowly. From its summit I see at my left a deep purple cañon, green at the bottom with irrigated fields. At my right the sun is setting across a wide valley, the shadows replaced by roseate gold interrupted by the white resplendence of chalk cliffs. As if all this were not sufficient, a light female rain like that which falls constantly over the home of the Corn gods, drops between me and the sun. I gasp in my inability to comprehend the sight fully as I turn my head forty-five degrees to behold a complete rainbow and behind it the thinnest slice of a new moon.

At the sheep dip all is action. A number of saddled horses tethered to a small piñon stand in a circle. At a short distance a shade has been erected. From one of its posts hangs a sheep, just slaughtered, which a woman vigorously skins. Not far from her feet another woman sitting on the ground is cleaning the intestines. Farther away a woman and a young girl are tending a small cedar fire from which rise wisps of white smoke like the gentlest of the clouds thrown off the towcards of the Wind gods. Near the sharp edge of the wash a girl, shawl over head, stands before a resting flock, awaiting its turn at the chute.

A smell of live sheep mixes with the odor of cedar smoke as we advance into the thick of the activities. Several hundred bleating, baaing sheep and goats, wondering and frightened, mill about in the corral from which a narrow chute leads to the dipping trough. Men and boys stand thick on the sides of the chute with prods in their hands, urging the reluctant animals toward the jumping-off platform. A young man tries to keep his balance on this platform, slimy with the yellow sulphur solution splashed up from the trough, at the same time that he forces the animals into the uninviting mixture directly beneath. Only about one beast in a dozen goes into it voluntarily and he must grasp each by head or wool and push his own weight against its determined resistance. It is the hardest kind of work.

One after another the balking creatures slip, jump, or are pushed into the trough with a splash which speckles all within its radius. The liquid is so deep that even the largest animals must swim. They are dipped for prevention and curing of scabies. Since the head is one seat of infection, the tenders must see to it that even the heads are immersed at least once. Close along both sides of the long narrow trough stand Navajo women, young and old, and young men all with long forked sticks. They see to it that the animals are thoroughly doused, but with the sticks they hold up the heads of the lambs and flustered ewes as they frantically strike out and make for the other end of the run. There one of the men in charge of the dip counts them as they emerge into a roomy corral. Bedraggled and injured-looking, each runs up the incline. They are discouraged and surprised as they shake themselves in a yellow huddle in a corner of the corral. For several weeks travellers on the Reservation will ask, "Why do all the sheep look so yellow?" instead of remarking as usual, "Why do Navajo sheep always look so white? All the sheep I've ever seen have looked brown and dirty."

Those who tend the trough have not worn their best clothes. They know only too well what a disagreeable task they confront.

The mothers-in-law, for once the better dressed, are somewhere in the background butchering and cooking. Dipping is a job heartily despised by all, but it is a necessity. If the dipping is done faithfully twice each year, at an interval of ten days there is a good chance it may soon be unnecessary. It requires skill as well as strength and endurance because if the sheep breathe or drink any of the fluid or get much in their eyes they may die. Nevertheless the liquid must saturate the wool of the head. To surprise the sheep by ducking it suddenly under with the prod, then to see that it instantly bobs up is the trick.

I drive home alone after watching the entire procedure. Another day without interruptions. As I come up to the main hogan, that of Red-Point, I see the lock fastened in the door. I walk a few paces to Maria Antonia's cooking shade. Not a pup or even a kitten is in sight. Two chickens cluck outside the barrier although they can easily squeeze in if they like.

The rest of the day is incredibly short, but quiet, too quiet.

The sun, by its death bringing the earth to life, lures me out-side. I expect at any moment the bark of an oncoming dog, hence I have not gone to Ganado. But there is not a sound. The glow is with me, it brings the sage and sand into a gentle radiance, but there are no woolly pelts to reflect its splendor, no scarlet shirts to cast it back into itself. A bluebird chirps to his mate in the branches of my piñon, a turtledove cries mournfully near Maria Antonia's shade.

I still expect my family back, and after dark lay out my bed under the Great Dipper. Silence meets my expectation of munching, bleating, crying, companionable sounds. Not even the dull comforting sounds of noses pushing against close-lying woolly bodies as they crowd into the dust.

This is limbo. A perfect place where for me the gods are not. I am not lonesome, I am only alone. They must be here but I have not yet earned the right to say:

Holy Young Woman sought the gods and found them
On the summits of the clouds; she sought the gods
*   and found them.*
Truly with my sacrifice she sought the gods and found
*   them.*
Somebody doubts it, so I have heard.

It is quiet, too quiet. . . .

XVII

HOUSE GUARDIAN

Two days later as I thump one thread upon another, Red-Point comes in. This is a day devoted to much needed rest for all the family. They had to stay at the sheep dip longer than two days. They returned the afternoon of the third day, and the ranch came to life again. Red-Point sinks on the floor with the trunk a prop for his back. I know from his posture that he is going to stay for a visit. He is usually in a hurry, has to catch a horse, go to Ganado, or start off in another direction for a sing. But the day after a long strain like the dipping is a day of light activity, and the men at least will sleep part of it away.

"The sheep are dipped at last," begins Red-Point as he lights the inevitable cigarette. "It was lots of work. We have all our own. Ben Wilson brought those he has on the mountain, and I have to take care of Marie's, Tom's, Dan's, and Ben's. There are lots."

"How many do you have?" I ask.

He tells me a large number which I figure out to be 1,063. Red-Point is the best of my Navajo teachers. I understand him better than anyone else. His gestures are more than vivid, his speech is distinct and classical. He does not use, as do many of the young people who speak English, a syllable or two instead of a whole word. From learning chant lore, from singing it, and from teaching he has developed the habit of clear enunciation.

He tells me I must write a letter to Marie telling her about the dipping. I promise to do so. I ask if he lost any of the sheep, and with satisfaction he answers: "No. It is difficult to do the dipping properly, but here at Ganado we know how now. Not many were lost, none of ours. They don't use that tobacco any more, it was no good. This yellow stuff is better, but we have to be careful." He refers to the sulphur solution they are trying this year instead of the nicotine previously used.

Usually when Red-Point visits me I stop weaving, because I have to concentrate on listening and I cannot see his helpful gestures with my back toward him as it must be when I am weaving. But today I weave as he talks, stopping only occasionally to look around for a cue. Atlnaba and Maria Antonia come in with the little children, Yikadezba's two little sisters. They no more than get nicely settled each with a child on her lap, than the answer to a question of Red-Point elicits a general stir. They have told him Ruby is at the hogan. They call Ben, who is playing outside. He goes for Ruby. Red-Point will not be satisfied until he has reported to Marie the status of the dipping.

Soon Ruby comes in. Red-Point extracts from her a soiled, crumpled scrap of paper which he hands to me. It is the receipt, $10.63 paid in sheep, one cent apiece for the dipping. It states also what part was the portion of Marie and Tom. He wants me to write about this. He gives a long sentence to Ruby in Navajo, I translate it mentally and wait. After a long time Ruby says a few words. I then say, "And he said so-and-so also, did he not?" "Iss," answers Ruby as though the word was torn from her very being.

In this efficient fashion the entire letter is constructed. It is easier, I vow, to learn Navajo than to depend on English with Ruby as interpreter. I feel like shaking her, unjustly of course because she almost certainly does not understand me. She should because she has been in school for many years. But she does not understand really, and her defense is dumb stolidity or worse yet, upon occasion, silly giggling. On this occasion I have no difficulty in following Red-Point, for I know the details of the situation. But in an emergency, or when we are in a hurry, Ruby exasperates me even more than she does Red-Point, who mutters to her, "You have no sense."

Besides the main topic of the day he wants me to tell Marie that he has made arrangements to improve his flock by having the ewes served by some pedigreed rams the Government secured for the purpose. He says too: "Tell her we have hired the young man, as she told us, to herd the sheep. We are doing just as she said. So far everything is all right. The sheep are all right, the cattle are all right, the children are all right, we are all all right. The corn is high. We'll have lots this year. Tomorrow I will go and dig it out again. Three times it has been buried with sand because of the rains. It was lots of work to dig it out, but it is good.

"Tell her we need her and Tom here because we have lots of work. It costs lots, too, to pay the herdboy. But we are paying him as she told us. We are getting along all right. Tell her to make Tom save his money. Don't let him drink, but save up the money so they can help us all out. Tell her we are sending the wool she asked for and a big ball of warp. And tell her to write to us."

All these things I write as faithfully as I can. Then I add a little note of my own explaining to Marie that the translation of her father's sentiments is to be charged to Ruby and me, and if there is that which she cannot understand to fill in between the lines herself or ask me. I continue, adding my version of life at White-Sands. Marie will be glad to get our letter, and she will reply promptly but, like many white people I know, will ignore the questions we especially want answered.

As soon as he is through with this effort Red-Point gradually slips down along his spine until he is resting against the trunk with the edge of his shoulders. He props one foot on the opposite knee, his accustomed position for relaxation. During his dictation the children have clambered over him. He has quieted them if they started to talk, but now he babbles pettingly at them and occasionally breaks out singing a lullaby he composed for Yikadezba. A child nestles in the crook of each of his arms. Ben is sitting for a moment quietly beside his grandmother, playing with his puppy, Spot. Ninaba has come in during our writing, and she sits near her grandfather. Red-Point looks about with a happy contented expression on his face. Sweeping the circle of children with his hand he remarks, "My daughters have been very good to me —to give me these grandchildren."

My blankets no longer have "news value." I am working on another now. The last one is a success. There were no disagreeable surprises when we took it down and we carefully fixed the corner tassels. Atlnaba wove quite a lot of it; but I have a feeling of confidence now, and I am not conscience-stricken about her share. I had hoped to be able to make my next blanket of wool dyed with vegetal dye. But that is impracticable, so we are introducing a small amount of red instead of rose or yellow as I had wished to do.

The pattern is an adaptation from a simple old-fashioned rug. The weaving seems easy. Above all it proceeds in a matter-of-fact way. One of my principal ideals is to attain the nonchalance of the Navajo about weaving. The goal means the acme of skill. I have not set my teeth over a vow or anything of the sort. I have said to Atlnaba: "I am going to put up another blanket. But if I do not get it finished I will take it home rolled up on the sticks and finish it there." So I need not hurry. If we are interrupted by visitors or a sing or a celebration it will make no difference.

I have nevertheless resolved to do as much of the weaving as possible and have told Atlnaba to allow me to make mistakes. She has smilingly acquiesced. I have her lay out the design when we come to it because I have no experience, hence no judgment about the space. Atlnaba weaves in about an inch, laying out the center, but that short space suffices for the trail blazing which I need. I advance the diamond pattern by using small rectangles. When watching up the terraced rectangles I am likely to forget my stripes. I have no trouble with coördinating materials and implements and muscles now, but I realize the need for coördinating vision, the vision of the complete design and its individual stripe components.

The blanket nears completion as my stay nears its end. I have only plain white space to do. Atlnaba thinks it too near to leave unfinished. I am not particularly interested in finishing off and I allow her to weave the last, most tedious two inches.

We need have no doubts about this one. It is a beautiful conception (not my own), the idea is carried out, not perfectly but reasonably well. When the rug is thrown on the floor it stays there. It is worth its corner tassels.

One day when he is about five months old, as I innocently make eyes and faces at the latest baby of Yikadezba's-Mother, he suddenly laughs aloud. He had smiled before, often, but this was a real laugh, "out loud," his doting aunt says. Then I am told that he who makes a baby laugh aloud the first time is supposed to give him a present. "Anything" will do. During the swift-flying days of my stay with them I have eaten with Red-Point's family occasionally, particularly when a sheep has just been killed. This time I will give a feast, have a mutton killed in the baby's honor, and I will invite my white friends, the traders, too. The meal is of Navajo simplicity, mutton, bread, coffee, and by way of luxury jam, honey, and peaches.

The hour is sunset, the table a tarpaulin spread on the ground, the appetizers good nature, good talk, and good will. We send a plateful of food down to Maria Antonia who remains at her house because Curley's-Son is present with Atlnaba. In the course of our conversation Red-Point picks up the poker over which I have become sentimental.

"This is one of the very first things the Navajo ever had," he explains. "A poker should never be destroyed. It should always be kept with the point to the fire. If one moves away from home, he should lay it up high somewhere with its point to the fire where it will not be disturbed. There's a song about it which I know. Nobody else knows that song now. That is so the persons who live there will come back safe."

My goods are packed, the women help me load the car.

The house is empty, except for the inanimate loomframe.
Maria Antonia and I look about to be sure I have forgotten
nothing. Red-Point comes in. There seems to be nothing more.
I go out to the fire and bring in my poker, as good as the first
day I picked it up a raw unmannered stick, or even better
now than on that day, for its point is hard and tempered and
it has the earmarks of a beautiful old tool. I hand it to Red-
Point and ceremonially he points it to the fire, then singing
his song, lays it carefully at the top of the hogan, its point on
the ridgepole toward the fire, its handle on the western wall
of the house.

XVIII

WEDDING

AT THE beginning of my third summer with Red-Point's family, I arrive with a white visitor; one who had never seen a Navajo before is staying for one night only. As we pull up to the trading-post, Old-Mexican's-Son greets us. "There's going to be a wedding tonight. Do you want to go? Ask John Tallman about it." "Do I want to go? I have been on this Reservation six summers and have never seen one." John is one of my interpreters, the judge at Ganado, an important man. We ask him about it. He wants to go to the wedding; we can start about nine.

We start at the appointed time. The wedding hogan is only about seven miles from Ganado. The roads are dry and good, the moon is full and bright, it takes us no time to get there. The settlement is typical. There are several hogans, in one of which the bride sits. We are ushered into this house, in which there are only a few people. One of my friends and his wife and children come in to eat with us. John explains afterward that they came in because, since we are not clan relatives, the family did not want us to feel strange as we might if we ate alone.

The crowd outside is large, well dressed, and jolly. We are served graciously and eat leisurely; my friend does not eat much. Very soon after we finish eating, we are told to go into the house where the wedding is to take place. At the back of the fire a little to the north the groom is sitting. His relatives occupy a position near him north of the center and the rest of the space north of the fire is filled with women among whom we sit. The bride's relatives sit south of the center at the back of the hogan; men visitors occupy the rest of the southern semicircle.

Soon the bride enters carrying a small bucket of sugar and a cup. Her close relatives, each bearing some kind of food in large quantity, follow her. As they enter we fold ourselves smaller because the circle in the center of the house must be enlarged for the participants. The bride takes her place at the right of the groom; the food is placed before them. Then from a pail of water each of the betrothed dips a cup. The bride pours hers over the groom's hands. He washes them and pours water over hers. This continues alternately until both cups are empty. Up to this time the audience has been quiet, much like a Quaker meeting.

Now John interpolates in his quiet bantering voice: "Use lots of water. He's a good water-hauler. From now on you'll never have to skimp on water." This remark relieves the seriousness. Everyone laughs and quiet talk begins.

A basket of ceremonial gruel is now set before the young people. On it an old man of unimpeachable character has made a cross by sprinkling yellow pollen from east to west, south to north and around in a sunwise direction. The girl's family chose this old man in a conference at which the good and bad points of his character were aired.

Beside the basket is a dish of canned tomatoes which John afterward tells us is a substitute for jam made of yucca fruit. After she washes her groom's hands, and he hers, the girl with her two first fingers takes a mouthful of the stiff mush from the east side of the basket, then two fingerfuls of the canned tomatoes. Her groom imitates her exactly, as he does when she takes her next portions from the south, west, and north sides of the basket and finally from the center. I cannot tell how they manage the tomatoes; I only know they do so without trailing a drop.

After sampling it thus ceremonially the bridal pair eat all the mush in the basket and the relatives of both girl and boy fall to and feast on the many dishes of bread, mutton (boiled and roasted), tomatoes, and coffee which they brought with them into the hogan. They eat slowly and long; their capacity matches the lavishness of the repast.

The feast is followed by several speeches which John interprets to us on the way home about midnight: "In old times they used to talk to the newly-weds all night. Tonight there were not so many speeches. One was a little 'rough.'" As John settles back in the rear seat I mutter to my friend, my voice protected by the noise of Jonathan's motor, "Advice about sex behavior, I suppose."

John again leans forward as I ask, "What did you say?"

"I said that a man and his wife are like two streams running together for the common good. You may haul water and wood for a woman, but if there is no love in your heart for her she knows it and does not appreciate it anyway. It is the little attentions with love which make for happiness.

"Now I wish to bring up the mother-in-law question. I for one, basing my judgment on sense and reason, setting religion and ceremony aside, feel the girl's mother would get along better if she could 'see' her son-in-law. There always comes a time when the old lady needs help and kindness. These her son-in-law stands ever ready to give. But he can be much more helpful to her if he does not have to dodge away every time she comes in sight. Therefore, it would be wiser for you, young man, to agree with your mother-in-law not to avoid her, but to give her all possible aid and respect without doing that."

We then ask, "Did the mother agree to let her son-in-law see her?"

"Yes," said John.

One of the winter items of gossip which my white friends wrote me was that John had married. He had been a widower for eight years or longer, a period unusually long for a Navajo to remain single. John occupies an anomalous place among his people. Because his father deserted John's mother and her children when they were very young, he was raised by the Presbyterian Mission. His upbringing was that of a white institution, but it took place in the midst of his own people.

I have worked many hours on the Navajo language with John. His teaching me is interspersed with numerous questions. What is the difference between religion, philosophy, and anthropology? (Anthropology must be explained because that is what I call what I am doing, and anyway John loves big words.) What do you mean by a totem? What are other Indians like? Our reciprocal lessons show me that he is wavering in his allegiance to white teaching; by thinking, he is trying to find a satisfactory way out of the quicksands of belief and doubt.

During the many years of close contact with whites he was observing his own people and aiming to make smooth the understanding between the two incompatible points of view, his mind has been actively at work. He notices, for example, that the Christians preach love to all their fellows while at the same time they persecute some of them, not always Indians either. One thing he finds incomprehensible is that some whites feast while others near by starve. As long as Navajo have a crust of bread and a cup of thin broth, they will divide it at least among their relatives. He finds also that promises to an Indian stand little chance of becoming fact. Above all, he is impressed with the intolerance of these whites toward "sin." True, some Navajo are incorrigible. John believes a kindly example and the sound advice of the old men can do more for these than imprisonment or preaching.

Above all he questions religion. Old men of his tribe, like Red-Point, perform cures and care for their sick. It is their religion which does so. The white people tell the Indian children never to go to a sing; it is wicked to do so. They make them learn long pages of Scripture and prayers, yet these things do not cure; it is difficult to see what use they are. John understands thoroughly the function of the hospital and doctors. When he is ill he wishes to be treated there. But repeated failures of the whites and frequent successes of the medicine-men—above all, the character of the chanters— have made him doubtful as to whether Christianity is the better part. Can it be that the "philosophy" of the Navajo old man is more desirable than the sanctity of the whites, hardly ever noticeable in practise? So dubious has he become, indeed, that he has decided to live more like the Indians.

John's marriage is one answer to his questionings. As we roll along the moonlit road I ask him, "Is your wife an old-fashioned Navajo?"

"Very," he answers. "She's from Black Mountain."

"How did you ever come to get her?"

"I was married like Jacob. I didn't know the girl I was to marry. You see, my relatives didn't think it was good, my not being married for such a long time. They kept at me, urging and advising me to get a wife. So at last I said to them: 'Well, pick me out a good girl and I'll marry her. She must be industrious, good-tempered, and quiet. And I don't want one who dances. But, above all, her mother must not mind if I see her.' I couldn't dodge behind a tree or blanket every time I see her coming," continues John. "Why, I'd be too embarrassed!

"Well, they found a girl that seemed suitable, and her mother said she wouldn't mind. Her family is a very good one."

"Were you married the Navajo way?"

"Yes, just like tonight. But my wedding was kinda funny. They asked me to make a speech myself."

"Who usually speaks?"

"Well, they pick those who make good speeches, and that is why they asked me to speak even if it was my own wedding."

"What did you say?"

"My speech was very much like the one I made tonight. I spoke especially about my mother-in-law, gave them the reasons why I didn't want to get out of her way. I said I thought I could help her more in this way."

I have another white guest, and we decide to go to Polacca, a Hopi village, for the Fourth of July. They are going to have races. I ask John to go with us. He suggests that we go by way of Salaine because we have a matter to attend to there. "If we go that way, we can stop and see my wife. Maybe she will go with us."

John is a perfect guide. He knows every grain of sand in the road; he gives little but excellent advice about routes. The road is dry and hard now; it may be non-existent by the time we return although the Rain gods have not yet hung a tiny signal of carded wool in the sky. John has been on trying trips with me before. When a wash roars past, he can tell whether or not Jonathan will make it. But his experience and judgment are even more useful when the water in a small wash slinks deceitfully and innocently along. "Better wait," he says. "There are often quicksands here."

I wait until he gives the word. Meanwhile he busies himself with shovel or ax and with sounding with his bare feet. As the water runs more feebly and becomes ever more shallow, he not only announces the very first moment when success is probable, but warns me even about the point where the quicksands are likely to be and exerts himself casually to get the car over this spot. I have come through many a wash with not a quarter of an inch or a jot of horsepower to spare, but I have never been stuck when I took his advice.

However, we have nothing in the way of road or motor troubles on this holiday. As we drive along to Salaine John tells me to turn west over a track to me indiscernible. After bumping about four miles over sagebrush and hummocks we arrive at a settlement of three hogans. The absence of sheep and dogs, the brooding quiet in the glaring sunlight, and finally as we come up to the first hogan, the lock in the hasp, show us there is nobody home. John is neither surprised nor disappointed. After he has made his observations he directs me again, and less than a mile from the settlement, which is on a flat, we come to a thickly wooded slope, the foothills of Black Mountain. Here in well-built shades made of piñon and juniper boughs, scarce distinguishable from the trees, John's wife's family are making their summer home.

The slope with Black Mountain behind it at the west, near enough to make convenient its resources of grass, water, and wood, commands a view of the Chinlee Valley. The Chinlee Valley is formidable beyond words to the stranger. It is so huge that man is of no account upon its surface. As we drive along the main highway for forty miles, there is space on either side, interminable distance unbroken by anything save color that makes me gasp with unbelief, color awe-inspiring, but devoid of all that is friendly or hopeful. No trees, no water, no houses, just earth gashed by cañons, and sky. I have the feeling of walking on a high trestle over a roaring torrent; I am afraid to go back and more afraid to go forward. So it seems, too, from the hogan of John's father-in-law.

The distance of less than a mile achieves one more of the miracles of the Southwest. At the summer camp the trees extend a hospitality which gives the views on both sides perspective; they shelter and welcome, as they bring the vast panorama into a comfortable reality which for some moments I had lost in the uncanniness of space. The people who choose them for a shelter are like a hand stretched to me as I walk over the abyss.

This family is an example of the "wildest" of the Navajo. The air of self-sufficiency makes them so. "Wild" because their dependence on the white man is at a minimum. They visit a trading store perhaps once a month or even less frequently. When there they buy only staples, flour, sugar, and coffee, occasionally some velvet and dress goods. They do not loiter long. Many of the women's rugs are colored with dyes made from plants found on the slopes of Black Mountain. They usually wear their silver and turquoise instead of pawning it. We are greeted by John's father-in-law, a tall, straight, lean, handsome man whose poise no situation could disturb.

John looks in three or four of the camps for his wife and finally disappears for about fifteen minutes. Then he comes back to us as we sit talking with his father-in-law. We continue our talk for some twenty minutes. I ask John if his wife is going with us, and he says he doesn't know. "After I found her I had a nice little visit with her, and then suddenly she ran off."

Finally we decide she is not going, and all reëmbark. Jonathan's motor is even started when a little boy comes to John and diffidently communicates the fact that Molly, his wife, is going with us. She is dressing, we must wait. John beams with pride as we linger. After nearly half an hour Molly comes toward us overcome by shyness so poignant as to be painful even to us. Her sister's son, a half-grown boy, is with her. She has to sit pretty close to John in the restricted quarters of our rear seat, never too roomy, and filled as it is with part of our camping outfit. She does not talk even to the boy for hours.

We transact our business at Salaine, drive through the valley at the northern end of Black Mountain and turn south once more along its western edge. As the mesas cast long soft shadows, John, at my request, picks our camp some ten miles from Polacca. He knows where there is a delightful spring. We pull uphill toward it until deep sand impedes our progress. We are so near a fine camp that we stop here and carry our belongings to a large rock not far from a medium-sized pine.

John has made us a splendid fire, and he and the boy have assembled a large pile of wood. Carrying all the empty canteens, they go exploring for the spring. As my friend and I prepare our simple but ample supper, Molly sits by at the edge of the flickering firelight and watches. The virulence of her affliction has so far abated as to allow us an occasional brief smile implying just a shade of trust. As the setting begins to take on the polish of perfection I am unpleasantly reminded of a large anthill near the rock which is serving as our table. A red ant bites me on the ankle. Now I know why "sitting on an ant" is a bogy to Yikadezba. All ants are uncomfortable, not all bite, but any ant *might* be a red ant. Its bite does not sting for a moment unmercifully. It hurts, pains, and settles down into an ache which rivals toothache and lasts for several hours. I overcome the unpleasantness by rubbing and considerable grumbling.

As our fire strengthens and our coffee cheers, several Navajo come within hearing distance, where they stop and sit. By this time John has returned and we are ready to eat. "Do we feed those Navajo? Navajo always feed Navajo, do they not?" "Sometimes we ask them, and sometimes we don't," answers John. "This time we don't."

He goes over and talks to them briefly, returning with the report: "The one man lives in that hogan there"—pursing his lips toward a fire about two hundred and fifty yards distant. "He wanted to know if we were stuck in the sand or something. I said, 'No, we are camping for the night.' Then he told me if we need water there is a good spring where I already found it, and he says they have lots of water at the well down at their hogan."

"A hand on a high trestle," think I, as we settle comfortably to our coffee.

When John replenishes the fire, he notices a piñon stump about ten feet high a short way from it. With his foot he shoves the glowing embers to its base, reinforces the fuel supply and we soon have a flaming pillar of warmth.

As we settle comfortably with cigarettes I have a feeling that this is adventure. A full stomach, quenched thirst, the warmth and brightness of the burning stump, the cool softness of the air, the friendliness of the man who lives in the hogan, the presence of a friend too overcome to speak her joy, John's beaming face, even the smiling timidity of Molly— it cannot be that these simple components can define such a will-o'-the-wisp! Yet for me they do!

The next day we attend the rodeo at Polacca. It is very tame. We agree to return home early as John remarks: "The Hopi are no horsemen. They do not travel enough. Burros are their speed."

My friend answers: "Yes, and a half-hour between events. It is too hot to wait for them."

Arriving at Ganado, we relate to our white friends our impressions of John's wife. Two days later they tell me, "John's wife has gone home."

XIX

SHOOTING CHANT

MY BEHAVIOR this third summer hardly indicates my interest in weaving. I have been at White-Sands three weeks and have not set up a blanket. There are visitors. Then the Navajo Council meets at Fort Wingate, and I attend. I am delayed at Gallup, and I take another trip.

At the Gallup Ceremonial last year I met again two traders who had befriended me during my early travels in the Navajo country, Mr. Short-Pants and Mr. Little-Man-with-the-Spectacles. I thought I had learned much about weaving, but their exhibition and erudition taught me I am far from finished. They were showing small looms with blankets half woven, each illustrating a different weave. Among them were beautiful but simple effects achieved by skilful manipulation of the warps. These traders invited me to come to their post and learn these weaves.

I am just about to start on my new and interesting quest when word comes that Red-Point is going to have a nine-day sing. The letter from my white friend says "for Marie." I am a bit worried, for when I left her Marie seemed to be in perfect health. A sing means usually one thing, that someone is ill. I hasten back to White-Sands. Red-Point is going to perform the Shooting Chant, the major chant for which he is most famous. I have already seen the forty-seven sand-

paintings, any of which he may choose for a given performance, and I have the long myth on which the chant is founded.
It had been written some years ago but never published, from
the narration of Blue-Eyes, Red-Point's principal teacher. I
have heard much about the chant, I have never seen it, nor do
I understand it. In all my experience in the Navajo country
I have never followed a chant through.

The very first night of my stay at White-Sands the family
visits me. The sing is quite the most important affair in their
minds. All efforts are being centered around it. I tell them I
shall be glad to do any errands they may require with the car.
Red-Point says there is one medicine they must get from a
long distance, and it must be fresh when they use it. Perhaps I can get that when the time comes.

"I told Old-Mexican's-Son that if he brings any white
people to this sing, each will have to pay a dollar. So I want
you to put up signs. Old-Mexican's-Son can come himself for
nothing, of course. He is just like my own son. White people
make us pay for everything, and they ought to pay, too. Now
you, you are just like my own child. That is different. I am
going to tell you about everything. You must watch and get
everything just right. One morning I start before sunrise, and
I will wake you up."

When I reiterate my desire to help, he says, "You don't
help the Singer, just the patients, Marie and Ninaba."

After he goes out, Marie and I plan what I am to get for
her. She needs many yards of calico. I have three ten-yard
lengths and give her those. She will need also a great deal of
flour. Finally we get around to the question that interests me
most. For a long time Marie has had headache and pains in
her legs. When she was in Los Angeles last year her employer

took her to the hospital. The doctor pulled a tooth and said she ought to have them all out. I shudder at the very thought. So did the friendly white woman, but Marie grew no better.

One night while I was away, she felt so ill she did not sleep at all. Whereupon Red-Point decided to have the sing at once.

"Usually they think about it a long time. They get some-one to tell which sing they ought to have. We don't need to do that because my father knows this is the right one. You see when I was at school at the Mission, it was struck by lightning. That is why I am sick. The Shooting Chant is the cure for diseases caused by lightning, snakes, and arrows. Since there is no doubt, my father says we will begin right away. It will last nine days. Ninaba will be with me because she often has headache, too."

Red-Point and Maria Antonia spend several days getting their large well-built hogan ready. "I am going to use my best and largest paintings," he says, "so we have to have lots of room."

My casual visits to his house have not sufficed to make me realize how much there is in it. It is a rich man's home. There are trunks and suitcases filled with valuables, cloth by the yard, velvet, baskets and other objects of bulk, not to speak of surplus food, particularly flour, sugar, and coffee. There are many things which have supernatural power; some large and bulky like the elaborately painted, wound, and feathered prayersticks he will set up around the sand-paintings; others tiny but important, like the bits of precious stones, abalone, whiteshell, redshell, jet and turquoise, and the diminutive sacks of buckskin which contain sanctified pollen. These and many other things are the tangible symbols of Red-Point's profession as a chanter. As such, they are tied up in a bulky and orderly bundle which hangs from the ceiling logs of the hogan. And since he knows many chants he has many of these bundles. All but the one he is using are moved to the vacant house which belongs to Ben Wilson's wife.

Jewelry and beads are left hanging on their nails because they will be used. They furnish the only touch of color. Bundles of dried herbs, which always give Red-Point's house a faint and pleasant odor of having been sprinkled with incense, are also removed. Maria Antonia takes down her loom and lays it with the unfinished blanket attached across the larger supports of her rickety shade. She moves her cooking utensils to Marie's hogan.

In front of his own house Tom is erecting a large shade of piñon posts and juniper branches. Here Maria Antonia will have her headquarters during the sing, here the food will be prepared and from here dispensed. In my uncertainty as to which interest to choose, Tom erecting the shade, or Red-Point working in his hogan, I vacillate between the two. Tom's work proceeds rapidly as he digs a hole for a post here and prunes another log there. Red-Point's house has been emptied; it now looks huge where it was only large before. It is clean from sweeping and sprinkling; an earthy smell combined with the fragrance of crushed herbs pervades it, for Red-Point has settled down to preparing the medicine for the morrow and the following three days. He has larger or smaller quantities of plants lying beside him. There are more of the branches of Douglas spruce than of any other kind. He sits with his feet crossed tailor-fashion, as he does when he paints on paper, his chopping block placed before him. As he talks, he chops the medicine fine with his ax, which he holds close to the blade. "I don't usually have to do this tedious chopping," he explains. "The patient has someone to do it. But since we do not have many to help us, and as the boys are all busy, I am doing it this time."

He tells me the name of each of the fifteen plants he uses and gives me a sample of each, explains also where it grows. He uses the entire plant of one of the mints. One called "thunder-plant" is fragrant; one of the sages he calls "frog-food"; a red pentstemon is "humming-bird's food"; there is one called "bat's food." Some are shrubs or twigs from trees such as red willow, scrub oak, and chokecherry. A water plant "on-top-of-water-it-spreads" must be secured from a spring. Red-Point chops a hard dry root, "the-vomit-of-Enemy-Slayer," and adds only a small quantity to the mixture. Most of them are found near by, but he must go far afield for a few. A still smaller number are rare indeed, and he uses only a little from the pouches in which he carefully hoards it. They all smell pleasant, some are pungent. When, after three hours' steady labor, he spreads the combined bits of greenness out widely on a blanket, it is a pleasing mass indeed. He leaves it to dry for the afternoon as he peers about in hope of dinner.

I am unwinding my legs preparatory to getting my own, when Maria Antonia comes in and asks if I won't stay and eat ceremonial gruel with them. I will. She soon brings in a clean cloth which she spreads on the ground. On it she sets a bowl of thick corn-smelling mush. There is, too, a bowl of mutton cut up in fine pieces with much strong broth, piping-hot, a basket of fresh tortillas, and the indispensable coffee. The mush is made of coarsely ground blue corn to which juniper ashes have been added. "Without the ashes," Red-Point explains, "it would be like tortillas without baking powder."

It has no salt; but the stew has plenty, and I find the combination delicious. My family seasons food much better than other Navajo I have eaten with. The women are eating the special treat in Maria Antonia's shade. After Red-Point and I are well started, Tom joins us, tired after his labor.

The first "day" of the chant begins at nine o'clock this "night." All ceremonial days are counted from sunset to sunset. There is a short rite in the large hogan. One of its main purposes is to purify the house and call the blessings of the gods. Curley's-Son, after Red-Point's instructions, takes down the dried sprigs of scrub oak which lie between the rafters of the house at the east, west, south, and north. He lays them near the door, then places fresh sprigs in their stead. He sprinkles the one over the door with white cornmeal as he murmurs, "The east pole, the pole I first leaned against." He moves to the west and strews the meal, "The west pole, the second against which I leaned." At the south he says, "In the sand I leaned against it," and at the north, "My home is covered with vari-colored goods."

The prayer and rite are for the purification of the patients and the house. By "the sand" he means the outermost earth cover of the hogan; by the "vari-colored goods," the soft bark which holds the sand in place. He continues the house blessing by throwing the meal in a sunwise direction with the words, "The floor of my house is of vari-colored stones." This refers to the first hogan that was ever made, which had four floors, one above another, of whiteshell, turquoise, abalone, and jet.

The house blessing continues:

May the house be beautiful within.
May the house be beautiful at the back.
May the house be beautiful at the center for the fireplace.
May the house be beautiful near the door where the metate
* rests.*
May the crosspieces of the doorposts be beautiful.
At the doorway of my house where Pollen Boy stands may it
* be beautiful.*
At the doorway of my house where Cornfly Girl stands may
* it be beautiful.*
Surrounding my house where talking gods are standing may
* it be beautiful.*
Surrounding my house where house gods are standing may it
* be beautiful.*
Surrounding my house where plants are may it be beautiful.
Surrounding my house where trees are may it be beautiful.
Surrounding my house where stones are may it be beautiful.
Surrounding my house where Mountain Woman is may it be
* beautiful.*
Surrounding my house where Water Woman is may it be
* beautiful.*
Surrounding my house where bluebirds are may it be beauti-
* ful.*
Surrounding my house where blue swallows are may it be
* beautiful.*
Surrounding my house where spotted yellow birds are may it
* be beautiful.*
Surrounding my house where robins are may it be beautiful.
At Pelado Peak may it be beautiful.
At Mt. Taylor may it be beautiful.
At Mountain-of-Variegated-Beads may it be beautiful.
At San Francisco Peak may it be beautiful.
At Black Mountain may it be beautiful.

At San Juan Mountain may it be beautiful.
At Whirling Mountain may it be beautiful.
At Spruce Butte may it be beautiful.
At Rain Mountain may it be beautiful.
At Corn Mountain may it be beautiful.
At Pollen Mountain may it be beautiful.
At Cornfly Mountain may it be beautiful.
At Old-Age-Walking and on the Trail-of-Beauty may it be
    beautiful.

After Red-Point gives him more pollen and instructions, he takes out the old dried herbs, strews them with pollen, and deposits them in a tree.

By this time the family, except, of course, Maria Antonia (she will not come since Curley's-Son and Tom are Red-Point's helpers) and the two patients, are in the house, the women on the right of the entrance or fire, that is, at the north, the men at the left. I have decided when in doubt to imitate Atlnaba. There is a space at the back center of the hogan where a blanket is laid for Marie and Ninaba to sit on. As they walk solemnly in at the south side of the fire, Ben and Dan begin to giggle uncontrollably and contagiously. Ninaba bites her lip and Marie has difficulty in subduing her mirth. It takes very little to set her off, as I have often found. We as audience are not out of place if we smile, joke, or even laugh heartily, but it is not proper for those-sung-over to sit giggling incontinently.

(The next day Marie tells me that Dan whispered to Ben, "Everybody is so busy getting his moccasins ready, I am going to make little moccasins for the pussy to wear to the sing," referring to the kitten which was crawling over them.

She tells me this with pride in her eye at Dan's "cuteness"; but at the time he said it, Red-Point with a word, not harshly but nevertheless firmly given, tried to quiet the boys. A word was not sufficient and they remained out of order, constantly tempting their mother until Tom took them out and gave them a talking-to.)

During this time Red-Point is taking a number of objects from his bundle which he lays carefully in one of the ceremonial baskets at his side. Tom and his brother tie herbal medicines to these prayersticks as Red-Point sings the proper songs to the accompaniment of a rattle, also from the bundle, made of buffalo hide. They make an altar by laying a blanket and on it placing the prayer-bundles properly tied. Two thickly folded pieces of new calico are placed behind them, and Marie and Ninaba are told to undress.

They leave all their clothing except their skirts on the blanket where they are sitting and take their places on the calico, their bare feet stretched out straight before them. Red-Point now performs many acts, all of which must be in a particular order. Tom and his brother have tied the bundles with a special knot. Red-Point blows medicine mixed with water over the patients, then takes each bundle and presses it firmly from hips to soles of feet, along the arms from shoulder to palm, at two sides of chest and back, at back of neck, at forehead and back of head, as well as at both sides, and finally at the top of the head. With each movement he makes a *blu-blu-blu* sound with his thick protruding lips.

After this he pulls the string of each bundle and draws one over the soles of the feet, the palms, chest and head. Finally he marks each patient with another kind of liquid medicine, and they bathe their bodies with it. Tom brings two coals which he blows into a glow, Red-Point puts a little plant powder on them. The patients breathe in the smoke and rub it over their bodies. The pressing and ravelling are done to take away fever. The burning of the incense is the Amen or doxology to each rite in a Navajo chant. Since this one is to continue for nine days, tonight's performance is short and we retire at about eleven-thirty.

For the entire duration of the sing and four nights after it, all connected with it intimately, that is, patients, Chanter, and helpers, must observe absolute sexual continence. For this reason the patient or patients sleep in the ceremonial hogan with the Chanter. If there is only one woman patient, a helper not her husband sleeps there, too, to act as a chaperon. Self-restraint is not the only reason for the custom. It may be necessary to begin rituals before the first peep of dawn on some of the days, and the Chanter must have his patients where he can wake them at a moment's notice.

XX

COMMUNION OF SUFFERING

I AM up betimes the next morning—I do not want to miss anything. The sun is still only a promise when the men go out for wood. They bring a pile into the hogan and call the patients, who sit in their usual place at the middle point of the back of the house, facing directly east, behind the fire. Red-Point takes a fire drill of wood from his bundle. Curley's-Son brings a bundle of juniper bark, and by rapidly twirling the drill in the hole of the fireboard creates a spark. Only a faint wisp of smoke indicates its presence; but Red-Point blows vigorously though steadily upon the shredded bark which serves as tinder, and soon a lively flame is burning. Curley's-Son, holding it carefully, moves the ignited mass in the ceremonial cross from east to west and from south to north, then lays it under the pile of wood awaiting it at the fireplace, and a good fire results.

Now the women are dismissed as the men prepare for work. A little before nine we, the audience, are called again. The hogan has once more changed its appearance. Everything is swept and in order. I am warned as I step inside the door and behold at my feet four small snakes made in sand, as if one were crawling into the fire from each direction. We women walk around the south side of the fire with its paintings to our places at the north side, I following Atlnaba. Behind the fire but far enough away to leave a trail is a charming bit of mosaic done in sand. It is like the black cloud of Atlnaba's gray sand-painting blanket, except that it has a variation of the border.

Ordinarily a frame surrounds the cloud. It is composed of wide red and blue stripes, each outlined entirely in white. Tom calls my attention to the fact that this one has the red inside, the blue outside. "There are two branches of this sing," he explains. "Usually the red is outside and the blue in, but since this is to do away with evil caused by lightning the blue must be outside. It will be that way all the way through this sing. If it were sung to bring blessing and ward off evil the red would be outside. This black cloud has the Sky People on it. They are the gods for today."

Everyone familiar with Navajo sand-paintings knows that the outline frame of white, red, and blue represents a rainbow frame or garland, but I had never before heard that the red and blue could be reversed. I notice then that the small light rafts, short stubby versions of the frame upon the cloud, have the blue outside. I am to find that the colors will be used thus consistently every time these elements appear in the chant hereafter.

As I hastily note a few details of this sort, Red-Point is arranging four sticks about an inch in diameter and three feet long. He spits on each one, sticks one end into the fire, and lays it at the side of one of the snakes, always observing the order of direction. He spits again to east, west, south, north, and around, then sprinkles pollen over the Sky People at the west of the house, along the canes and their accompanying snakes, and finally up and down.

He had already sent Curley's-Son to call Marie and Ninaba,

and they come in. But now to my dismay he orders me out. I do not know if I am to be left out permanently or only temporarily, and my chagrin overpowers my hopes as I loiter alone like a naughty child outside at the back of the hogan. Almost at once, to my relief, Tom hunts me up, explaining apologetically: "The old man says you could come in all right, but he don't think you want to. You see, they are all going to undress."

"But I don't mind that as long as there are no white people," I protest. "Your women all do it—why can't I?"

"They are going to take the medicine too, but you can take just a little and use the rest to bathe yourself," he prompts as we edge toward the door.

Inside, the participants have made ready. There are no gay blankets or soft sheepskins for patients, Chanter, or guests. Marie and Ninaba, naked except for their skirts, and with hair unbound, sit on the ground behind the painting of the Sky People. The women whom I now join sit, stripped as are the patients, on the bare floor at the north. Tom has no red headband across his forehead to bind in his short hair; Curley's-Son and Red-Point, as well as the few men visitors, have removed their hair strings and let down their hair. They wear only a gee-string.

The fire is now reasonably hot. The men who are officiating, Tom and Curley's-Son chiefly, replenish it frequently from the large piles of wood on each side of the door. At the side of the fire stands a large old-fashioned soot-blackened Navajo pot in which some concoction is boiling vigorously. As soon as the fire had been ceremonially lighted with the fire drill, Red-Point had put on water to boil in a bucket. Then he had thrown a generous portion of the herbs he had so patiently chopped yesterday into the pot and added the hot water. Since then he has carefully watched it so that it keeps boiling but does not bubble over. The surplus water stands ready and hot with a few coals under it.

Each woman, I find, has brought with her a small enamel pan and a sackful of clean sand which she has deposited on the ground before her. The Chanter's assistants arrange everything for the patients. They set a basket on the middle of the cloud and at the side of each patient arrange a pile of sand which they scoop out in the form of a basin. Around it Red-Point places four hoops of cottonwood which he has cut and painted to resemble white snakes. I find myself totally unprepared. But Atlnaba helps me out. She calls to little Ben outside to bring a pan and tells Tom to bring me some sand.

By this time I realize that I am to witness the administration of the emetic which is indispensable for purification. We must make ourselves acceptable to the gods we shall invite. We have cleaned the hogan, purified it with new herbs, invoked the gods by sprinkling pollen with a prayer. We have washed our hair with soapweed, we must now cleanse our bodies inside and out. Red-Point finishes off the final preparatory detail as he places an eagle feather against each side of the basket, one for Ninaba and one for Marie.

All is now in readiness for Tom has brought in a large bucket full of cold water. Ruby waits outside for orders to get more. We form into a procession around the fire, lining up north of the east snake while Red-Point sings. At a particular accented word in the song we cross the east snake right foot forward, stop and wait for the next accented word when we cross the south snake left foot forward, repeating likewise for west and north snakes, and the whole circuit four times.

We have already gone around the fire this way once upon entering, and we do so once more at the end of the rite. Atlnaba has brought Yikadezba and Djiba, her sister. Djiba can walk, but only uncertainly, so Atlnaba carries her. But Red-Point directs Yikadezba just as he does us. For some unexplained reason she has tied a long string to her big toe. Most earnestly she tries to do as she is told but does not know right from left and succeeds in consistently getting the "wrong foot forward" at the same time taking exaggerated strides in her attempts to do exactly right. All burst into loud laughs as they watch her and egg her on.

Red-Point now takes the cane lying beside the black snake at the east, pokes its end into the fire, then presses it to the soles of his feet, along his legs, hands, arms, chest, back, and head, singing the while. He repeats the performance, pressing it to the same parts of Marie's body, then Ninaba's. Once more he goes through with it using the cane belonging to the white snake of the south, first on himself, then on the patients. When he gets to the cane belonging to the blue snake of the west, Atlnaba begins to treat herself with the one Red-Point has replaced at the east. She presses the end which is covered with ashes firmly and repeatedly to her ankles and wrists. She has rheumatism, and this will make it better. Her husband and Tom use the poker cure also but in a more general way as Red-Point uses it for his patients.

Latterly the fire has become hotter and as we proceed with the pokers the men heap more and more of the dry crackling wood upon it. Red-Point takes down the sack of drying mixed herbs and puts a handful in the patients' basket and a portion into the dish standing on the floor before each of the audience. He then pours over each portion some of the brew from the sacred pot. Curley's-Son follows with the bucket of cold water and fills each pan until the medicine is lukewarm. After the liquid settles Red-Point strains the solid parts off from the top of the basket through a brush he has placed near it during the preparation. Handled with care this brush made of fine pliant sticks makes an excellent strainer. After the patients' medicine is clear Red-Point passes the brush around and we each strain our medicine and rub the herbs over parts of our bodies.

Over the ceremonial basket Red-Point sifts a cross of white pollen as he murmurs a prayer. He treats each of our dishes to the same blessing and follows it with one of yellow. The patients stir their supply with the eagle feathers, we stir ours with our index fingers. Each of the audience arranges his sand before him to form a basin as Red-Point settles into his usual place at the southwest point of the hogan and starts singing. After repeating the burden of his song several times, he stresses a word as he accentuates the lilt of his rattle and Marie and Ninaba stoop and drink of the concoction in the basket directly with their lips. We have been told to wait. They take four long draughts and sit waiting miserably. By this time the sweat is dripping from us all, running in streams down our faces and in tickling trickles down our backs. It feels like flies, but the heat and smoke have driven them to the crevices between the house logs of the roof as far removed as possible from the fire. We have no such refuge.

The four drinks of the emetic should cause the patients to vomit but Marie never vomits even when she is ill. They sip some more of the greenish-yellow medicine and now we may drink also. Thinking to myself, "When in Rome do as the Romans do," I bow to the inevitable. The medicine has a bitter taste quite in keeping with its bilious color. I have often encountered more disagreeable tastes in our own medicines. Marie and Ninaba continue conscientiously their struggles with it, resorting to the feathers for aid, and after long minutes succeed but only with strain on Marie's part. I know she has not eaten anything and has a severe headache.

Atlnaba no more than swallows the stuff when up it comes in the most satisfactory manner. She takes more, and if ever there was internal purification, she is pure. Her husband is as conscientious about it; but Tom finds work to do, wood to be put on fire, water to be poured in basins, anything to keep him away from his own medicine. He does as he advised me, takes just a little, uses the rest to bathe.

By now the fire has risen and the hogan is suffocating. Even Atlnaba, my own model of endurance and the object of my constant admiration, pulls back to the remotest circumference of the house after covering over her sand basin neatly with the surplus from the outside edges. As she wipes the perspiration from her face, it registers complete misery. Marie and Ninaba look wretched, too, and as my eye wanders about the circle I see the same drawn expression on the faces of all but Red-Point. He is as active and as cheerful as always, pleased because all is being done thoroughly and well. I enjoy a certain exultation because, although I am not inwardly pure, I have not moved from my original place even when the fire reached its height.

At last there remain only small bits of wood for the fire and small amounts of medicine in each bowl. Marie and Ninaba stand up and rub the remainder over all parts of their bodies; the entire audience follows their cue. The liquid has a clean refreshing feel, but the sticks and leaves which have settled to the bottom adhere to our bodies, which, even if dripping, are clean. Red-Point shakes a few ashes from the end of a poker into Marie's and Ninaba's basins of sand and Curley's-Son covers them over with fresh sand making them little mounds. We all shake ashes into our own basins before covering them. Under the big piles of wood there were two neat sets of small regularly arranged and evenly shaped sticks. These are now laid on the fire, one set from east to west, the other crossing it. The flames die down, only the hot coals remain. Red-Point jumps over the fire; reversing his customary direction, he starts at the west and jumps to the east and back, then from north to south and back. Curley's-Son and Tom imitate him exactly. Red-Point tells the audience to go outside.

We sit facing the door while Tom and Curley's-Son gather up the sand of the paintings and take it out for deposit. As we wait, the agonized expression gradually gives place to smiles, and we rub the drying leaves off our backs, arms, and legs. Never did sun and wind feel so good, never was a breath of fresh air so delightful. After the few minutes which have sufficed to dry us off, we come into the house again. The fire is tame once more, only a glowing bed of coals with the four pokers in their cross formation. The air is comfortably cool and has a slight pleasant fragrance.

Once more we take our places and wait, as Curley's-Son and Tom sprinkle the coals with water and move them back and forth with a poker in each hand until all the fire is gone. They gather the remains into a gunny sack and deposit them outside. Soon after they return, we place the sand which formed our receptacles on the sacks and pieces of old cloth in which it was brought in. Then forming a procession we march in single file to a place near an anthill about one hundred yards northeast of the hogan where lie also the lifeless remains of the once vehement fire. Here we deposit our sand.

As we return from performing this office we sit near the patients at the rear of the hogan. Near us stands a basket filled with clear water on which bits of dried herbs are floating. Red-Point takes a large bunch of eagle feathers, dips the tips into this medicine which smells like sweet grass, and gives us and the house a generous sprinkling. It is a cool refreshing shower. We breathe the smoke of the purifying incense placed on the coals of benediction and dress.

Marie goes off to her own house, her head aching too violently for her to want food. I go in the opposite direction to mine, marvelling on the way: "There is a communion of suffering, as well as a communion of Saints? Certainly I have never before felt this sort of oneness with other individuals. Can I ever make anyone understand how utterly inoffensive and unobjectionable this barbaric-sounding rite appears?"

I despair but I do not think it matters. I am a part of this activity and feel exhilarated at the turn the affair has taken. Tomorrow I shall be casually accepted.

XXI

THE GODS INVITED

THE house has been blessed, the inmates have suffered together to purify themselves. Already the materials for the sacrifices have been considered and are in readiness. All is prepared for the gods. A little after one Tom calls me. I enter the house to behold a pleasant scene. Red-Point reclines on his pile of sheepskins, physically relaxed, nevertheless keeping a watchful eye on the work of Tom and Curley's-Son. At a point south by west of the hogan they sit on a blanket on which is spread a multitude of dainty and fascinating objects: accurately cut, even pieces of reed, smooth flat stones which serve as palettes for the small quantities of white, blue, black, red, and yellow natural pigments, brushes of yucca fiber, bunches of fluffy gay-colored feathers, a pile of vari-colored stones, each one almost microscopic, a cup of water, a penknife, a piece of rock crystal.

Under Red-Point's directions his sons-in-law have cut from the reed the prayersticks which, after the proper treatment, will convey to the Snakes our desire to have them present during the following days. They helped to bring on Marie's ailment, they have power to cure it. There are two double prayersticks, each about six inches long, eight small ones, only about three inches long. They have been cut so there is a node in the middle making two compartments. Tom and his brother handle these objects delicately as they sketch with the tiny brushes the same designs which were used for the morning's sand-paintings near the fire, a black snake with white border, a white snake with black border, a blue snake with yellow border, a yellow snake with blue border. Tom is more skilful at this kind of work than his brother. Neither of them needs to remember the patterns or position of the figures; Red-Point tells them before they begin. If they make mistakes they must correct them. If they leave them, the supernaturals will punish Red-Point, for he is responsible. He becomes impatient only if the helpers are stupid or inefficient.

Occasionally as they work Red-Point sits up, grasps his rattle, and sings a short song. As he waits and rests, he hums a tune, allowing no false move to elude him. Tom finishes painting and, as Curley's-Son continues, places pieces of cotton cloth, yellow with age, in a row on the blanket. Then from the open sack of precious stones he chooses one of each kind beloved by the gods, turquoise, whiteshell, redstone, abalone, and lays one on each cloth. Along with each in punctilious order he places one wing feather and one tail feather of a wild canary, three feathers from the bluebird's tail, one feather of eagle down, one of turkey down, a hair from a turkey's beard, and a bit of cotton thread ceremonially spun and torn.

Curley's-Son is still painting. Red-Point sets out an open sack of yellow pollen. Tom makes little balls of bluebird feathers, which he sprinkles with the yellow pollen. By this time his brother has finished painting the reeds. Tom lays them on the cloths according to Red-Point's instructions while Curley's-Son removes the surplus paints, pieces of reed and all implements they had been using. Tom puts the bits of precious stone into one end of each decorated reed and inserts the blue feather ball as a stopper, taking care to lay the reed back on its cloth in the stipulated position. Curley's-Son, after depositing the unused materials outside at the places ordained, calls Marie and Ninaba.

My heart goes out to Marie. The excitement, the fasting, the emetic, have combined to make the headache she has from a severe cold almost unbearable. I can see she can hardly sit up. I know from experience she would feel as badly if she lay down. The only boon she could ask would be to be left undisturbed; this will under no circumstances be granted her, either today or at any time for the next eight days. She and Ninaba take their places near the prayersticks. Red-Point takes from his bundle a small case of yellow bone, smooth with age. From its hollow he pulls a tiny brush which he hands to Marie. She dips it in water, then in the yellow pollen and runs it lightly (really only symbolically) over each prayerstick and the articles accompanying it. Ninaba, as usual, imitates everything she does.

When Red-Point has placed the tiny brush in the little bone case, and it in its diminutive sack and laid it away, Tom hands Marie the crystal. Then he holds one of the offerings before her. She lifts the crystal to the smokehole of the house, where it symbolically catches the sunlight, and with it "lights" the prayerstick. Ninaba does the same. Tom dips a finger lightly into the cup of water and conveys a drop to the opening of the prayerstick, which he then seals by placing pollen on it. After all are sealed the encircling cloths are folded; then Red-Point piles the prayer-bundles in regular order and gives one pile into Marie's, the other into Ninaba's hand. Curley's-Son stands ready with an old blanket which is in constant use in this chant.

Red-Point takes his place facing Marie and Ninaba and leads the prayer which they repeat like a litany. The prayer is long, it must be spoken without error, no word may be left out, none should be repeated. In order to concentrate, Red-Point closes his eyes, Marie and Ninaba cast theirs down. Marie does not know the prayer but she repeats it accurately. Ninaba falls behind, catches her breath. As Red-Point hastens on with it she loses some phrases here and there. A stillness and solemnity encompass the hogan, the moment is altogether sacred.

> *At Sky-Reaching-Butte,*
> *At House-Made-of-Darkness,*
> *Black pollen with which he conceals his body,*
> *Black-Horned-Rattler, young chief, your sacrifice I*
> *   have made,*
> *Your smoke I have prepared.*
> *This day I have become your child,*
> *This day your grandchild I have become.*

> *Watch over me.*
> *Hold your hand before me in protection.*
> *Stand before me and arise as my protector.*
> *Do my commands as I do your bidding.*
> *Let no harm befall me from the air as I breathe,*
> *From the rain as it falls, from the Thunders as*
> *   they strike,*
> *From below the plants, from the trees under which*
> *   water flows.*
> *Dewdrops and pollen may I enjoy.*
> *With these may it be beautiful before me.*

With these may it be beautiful behind me.
All is beautiful again, all is restored in beauty.[1]

Dewdrops and pollen may I enjoy.
May I be restored again in beauty.
May my body be light, may my body be cooled.
As I formerly was, so may I now go.
May it be beautiful for me
From the Far-Reaching-Butte
At the House-Made-of-Darkness,
At the House-Made-of-Dawn,
At the House-Made-of-Blue-Sky,
At the House-Made-of-Yellow-Evening-Light.
May happiness be mine again, I say.
This day may it be beautiful behind me,
May it be beautiful before me,
May it be beautiful below me,
May it be beautiful above me,
May it be beautiful all around me.

With white corn pollen, my mouth speaks no evil.
Big-Fly's voice is made my voice, I say.
I have become Old-Age-Travelling and the Trail-of-
Beauty, I say.

All is beauty again,
All is beauty again,
All is beauty again,
All is beauty again.

[1] "Beauty, beautiful" are only my choice of the English words, all unsatisfactory, which might be used in rendering the Navajo word which means "beauty, goodness, success, comfort, good luck, desirability, good will, blessing, good health, happiness," in fact, all qualities and virtues which man desires and cultivates.

At the end of the prayer, which includes many repetitions of the stanzas, Curley's-Son takes the sacrifices out and deposits them where the black-, white-, blue-, and yellow-horned rattler chiefs and maidens must see them. Since we made and planted them properly, the Horned-Rattlers cannot refuse our invitation. They will be present at our sing.

XXII

THE HOLY TWINS

AT THE very beginning the Navajo lived in several worlds under this one. They were beings not like man, in some of the underworlds not even like animals. But they had consciousness, even moral ideals, and because of the adultery of one of the beings with the chief's wife, got into trouble and were forced by flood waters to the next world above. Even after they reached this one, they endured a long series of wanderings before they became humans.

Two women lived alone and except for them the earth was inhabited by monsters. They were Changing-Woman, who is the Earth Mother, and her companion, Salt-Woman. Life was very difficult for them. They had only wild seeds and fruits upon which to live. Not only were the foods scarce and far-scattered, but they grew in places infested by monsters. Monster-Evil lay in hot springs; Horned-Monster lived at a place called Blue Lake and faced in all directions, so that it was impossible to approach him without being seen. Kicking-Off-Rocks was an ogre who lived between two bluffs—his queue had grown into a crevice in the rocks. When people went through the narrow pass between the rocks he would kick them down to his children, who waited below to devour them.

Throwing-Against-Rocks was a monster who with his

wife lay in wait for the unwary to undo them by crushing them against the rocks on which they lived. There was a bear who tracked and killed all humans; Eye-Killers stared people to death, Walking-Stone followed a person slowly, but inevitably caught up with him and cut him up; the Night and Day were at odds with each other for it had not been decided how Light and Darkness should be divided. There was a creek as narrow as a man's finger which spread when anyone tried to jump across it, and drowned him. There was a patch of reeds like knives, and when a person tried to pass through it the blades all had at him and destroyed him. These were only a few of the major evils that prevented the world from being inhabited.

Changing-Woman lived in the midst of them all, safe but unhappy. As she gathered her scanty food, she thought and thought about what she could do to rid the world of the dread monsters. The thought became a passion with her, and she tried a great many things but in vain. Vaguely she thought if she could bear a child he might have power to overcome the difficulties so that humans could people the earth. There were no men, and she knew none of the facts of procreation. As she wandered in agony of spirit and in tautness of body, she offered herself to the dripping water in a vain attempt to conceive.

One day, as she continued her quest for knowledge and fulfilment, she heard a loud noise. She looked up and beheld a young man so bright her eyes could not endure the sight. He was the Sun. He took pity on Changing-Woman, taught her sex intercourse, impregnated her with his holiness. When they lay together two children were conceived in her womb, one of the dripping water and one of the Sun.

In four days the children moved within her, in four more she was in labor. Through all of the ninth night she suffered, hoping to be delivered. At dawn black clouds covered the sky. When it was light, lightning struck in four directions and the first child was born; somewhat carelessly he was dropped. Because of that he is very dangerous, for he was born to kill monsters and is therefore named Enemy-Slayer. The second child was born easily when it thundered gently. He is called Child-of-the-Water. The infants were hidden under six covers, darkness was below, above it was blue sky, then came blue horizon light, yellow evening light, mirage, and heat.

When Changing-Woman went out for food, Bear-Man and Rattler-Man, her guardians, fed the boys. Bear-Man fed them with mountain pollen and mountain dew, Rattler-Man with earth pollen and earth dew. These foods were so powerful that they made the boys weak at times. Nevertheless they walked in four days, in four days more they were grown and Talking-God came to instruct them. He gave them an arrow which was henceforth to be the symbol of the Shooting Chant.

Soon after Talking-God had given the arrow to the twins they began to wonder who their father was. Three times they asked their mother as they lay under their six covers at night, three times she scolded them and told them to sleep. The fourth time they asked her she said: "Far away your father lives. Every imaginable danger lies between here and his home. So don't talk about it. Go to sleep."

Then the boys realized that the first thing they needed to go to their father was a song. They soon heard a nice song and thought their mother was singing it, but found it was really the curtain of darkness. The next morning very early

Talking-God woke them and instructed them how to go to their father. He dressed Enemy-Slayer in white: white buckskin shoes he put on his feet, white leggings on his legs, and a white shirt on his body. He dressed Second-born with the same garments, but of variegated color. He strung out a rainbow and motioned them to step on it. He had put white, black, blue, sparkling, and yellow medicines on it, but he did not tell the boys of this. Sometime after sunrise the rainbow dropped to the ground and the young men started out afoot.

They came to the house of Spider Woman, who killed people with four strong webs. Second-born blew black, white, blue, and yellow flint from his mouth at the webs. Spider Woman then became frightened and begged them to desist. Wind sat on the shoulder of Child-of-the-Water and guided him. He allowed the woman to beg until he had secured a bow of mountain mahogany with a yellow tail-feathered arrow and his brother a bow with a black tail-feathered arrow. Thus they not only escaped the snare set by Spider Woman and her companion Mocking-Bird-Woman, but secured a life token for future use.

When they came to the Spreading-Creek they pretended to jump three times and it spread but did not capture them. Measuring-Worm, who had a long rainbow—theirs was only a short one—helped them across, and they rewarded him with a song.

They came to mountains which clapped together, but passed through the opening between them by arranging the bows and arrows Spider Woman had given them so as to keep the mountains apart until they were safe and had picked up their weapons.

When they came to the Knife-Reeds they all ran up with a

sizzling sound, but Fire-God helped them when they insisted on going through. He burned the reeds with a spark from his fire drill. A few did not burn. They are used today as the paper upon which one writes. That means they are used for prayersticks, made holy by adding precious stones and laying aside as an offering; thus they are made to carry messages to the Holy Ones.

Wind carried them over Sliding-Sand-Dune, which entrapped mortals by sliding. They then crossed a red, a glittering, an abalone, a whiteshell, and a turquoise mountain; these were harmless. These were the Sun's mountains, and not far from the blue one stood their father's house. When they arrived about noon and tried to enter, they found four doorkeepers, Wind, Thunder, Rattler, and Bear; Wind blew them back. The Wind that sat on the shoulder whispered the names of the doorkeepers, and by mentioning them the twins quieted down their owners and were allowed to pass.

In the main room a very stout woman sat. She was the wife of the Sun. As the boys were examining the house the Sun suddenly appeared, and as his wife was uncertain of his temper, she hid them. Nevertheless he knew they were there and questioned her. Finally she answered angrily: "I thought you said you did not do anything as you go about! But here your children have come."

The boys, hearing the argument from their hiding place, took out the life feathers Spider Woman had given them. When the Sun found them he dragged them out and attacked them with four trumpets he had made of turquoise, whiteshell, abalone, and redstone. Any one of these by folding on itself could have crushed them; but when it touched the life feather it drew back leaving them unharmed. Similarly the life tokens saved them from the poison of the Sphinx-Worm which the Sun called forth.

He next gave them a freezing test, took away all their clothes, and left them to sleep on a small rocky island. Beaver-Man and Otter-Man lent them their skins, and the boys returned unharmed. When the Sun saw this he ordered a sweatbath for them. Instead of tough stones to be put into the water to make steam he ordered agate which would fly to pieces and destroy those who were bathing. Talking-God came in, dug a little hole in the wall and covered it with four layers of whiteshell. When the boys went into the sweathouse they hid in the hole.

After the noise caused by the agate exploding when the Sun poured water on it had subsided, he looked in, asking, "Are you warmed up now?" There sat the boys. These tests convinced the Sun that they were really his children. Then he instructed them about the sweathouse: "When in future the people arrive, do not imitate it because you do not keep it sacred. If something evil should happen on account of it, who would remedy it?"

For that reason the Shooting Chant, although there is sweating, does not use the sweathouse.

After being convinced that the heroes were his children the Sun began to ask them what they came for.

"Well, my children, why did you come? For the red horse perhaps?"

"No, that is not what we came for."

"For the black horse did you come?"

"No, not for the black horse."

"For the blue horse then?"

"No, not for the blue one."

"Perhaps the white horse?"

"No, not for that."

"The gray?"

"No, not the gray."

"The speckled horse then?"

"No."

"The red-maned horse?"

"No."

"The spotted horse?"

"No."

"The white-maned horse?"

"No, not that either."

"Well, what did you come for then?" And he asked them about the white, black, spotted, and red sheep, and the sheep with thin-bladed horns which was the one he most cherished. But it was none of these. He then offered the mule which changed to mirage, and then all his precious stones, turquoise, whiteshell, red beads, and abalone.

No, it was none of them.

"Well, children, what did you come for? Is it dark clouds with male rain counted in, dark mist, female rain, or the mirage which turns into a gray-bellied burro?"

"No."

"Well, I have enumerated all these things and it is none of them. What then did you really come for?"

"Yes, father, all those things are valuable and hard to come by where we live. We should much like to have them, but they are not what we came for. We came about these monsters, the Monster-Evil, Horned-Monster, Kicking-Off-Rocks, Throwing-Against-Rocks, Tracking-Bear, Eye-Killers, and the others. They eat up all people and they cannot flourish on earth," said First-born.

"Obsidian armor, shoes, clothes, headdress—these are what we have come for, as well as the flash-lightning arrow," said Second-born.

At these words the Sun was overcome. He could not speak, but bowed his head and remained thus for some time. When he finally looked up, there were tears in his eyes. Then he wiped away the tears, took a long breath, and blew *whu! whu!* four times. Then he spoke. "I suppose it can't be helped. But those are my children just as you are. Nevertheless let it be done."

Two suits of obsidian, moccasins, leggings, shirt, and hat, were laid down for them. Near them a dark zigzag lightning arrow for First-born, a blue flash-lightning arrow for his brother. Then the Sun made an agate into the shape of a man and placed it inside his son. "That song with which you were fed is the food of the agate man I have placed standing up inside you," he said. "The mush you ate from the east side of the basket stands inside you as the legs of the man, that from the west side is his head, that from the north his left hand, that from the south, his right. What you ate from the center is the heart. When I sang, 'The pollen of Old-Age-Travelling he eats,' I meant his thought would be standing in you. When I said, 'The dark cloud its dew, Old-Age-Travelling, its dew,' I was making his intestines. Not a thing is missing, complete he stands up in you. Thus I made it."

He stood a turquoise in the shape of a man inside his second son and fashioned it completely. Then he pressed parts of his own body to those of his sons to keep the protectors in place.

"You will conquer the enemies with those things I placed inside you. That is why I did it. Although the flint armor is good, that which stands inside you will conquer the fierce monsters which now exist and even those which may come into being in the future."

The twins were now invincible within and without, and the Sun, enveloping all three in a dark cloud, aided them in overcoming their first enemy. From that time on they went about the world, always into places forbidden by their mother, encountering monsters. With the aid of the powers the Sun gave them, and the advice Wind, Big-Fly, and Talking-God whispered in their ears, they overcame most of them. Whenever an evil was subdued, they cut off a portion of its body for a trophy to take to their mother. If an animal helped them, they allowed it to select a part of the evil for good luck. Never did they themselves do a harm without correcting it.

Two streams of the blood of Monster-Evil flowed thickly and swiftly over the land when he was cut. Black Wind told them, "If the bloody streams meet he will revive," whereupon they crossed their clubs between the streams and held them there until the blood hardened. The blood coagulated at that time turned dark and now forms the various lava dikes of the Navajo country.

Many monsters were rendered inert, others changed their character and became useful to man. The children of the Eye-Killers were transformed into two kinds of cactus, the tips of the ears, nose, fingers and toes of the elders became antelope. Tips of body parts of another pair of monsters became deer. Finally no large evils remained, and the earth was habitable.

However, Enemy-Slayer went about the earth to see what it was like, at the same time looking for something to do. At last he came to the house of Gray-Haired-Cactus. The dwelling was unattractive, and the people in it were disgusting. They looked like skeletons, they had sore eyes, matter stuck to their eyelashes, mucus ran from their noses. He determined to slay these too.

"I'll kill you," he vowed, as they, awe-stricken, stared at his armor. "What use are you to mankind? Many of the others I killed were not as bad as you, but they had to be destroyed."

These were Hunger, Craving-for-Meat, Poverty, Sleep, Desire, and Want. Sleep sat nearest to the visitor. Just as he was thinking of killing them, Sleep brought his finger gently down over the nose of Enemy-Slayer, mentioning his name. Whereupon he fell over and was sound asleep. He snored and slept on even though the people spat on him and smeared him with their filth, thus making sport of him. When he awoke and found he looked more wretched than they, his anger knew no bounds. He had grasped his powerful club and was just about to bring it down when Sleep again made him impotent.

After this had all happened four times, Sleep said to him, "This which you had intended to do, to kill us, you won't do." And this in spite of the fact that Enemy-Slayer had merely thought of killing the gray evils, had never said so. Sleep continued: "Your mother knows Sleep. Has she never told you about it? You have killed the strong harmful things, but you will not kill us. Ask your mother about it."

Enemy-Slayer was not much pacified, but went home to his mother, who said to him: "What are you looking for? Where have you been? You have now finished all your work."

He answered her indignantly: "Nothing to do? Why,

yonder I came upon some ugly things whose names I do not know. They insulted me terribly, but when I tried to kill them they said you knew all about it. Even now I could go back and do away with them."

"No, my baby, these you surely must not kill. Those others were great, you killed them because your father helped you. But these things you should not kill because they meet midway. They are not altogether good or entirely bad. Poverty and hunger meet somewhere between that which causes satisfaction and that which causes pain. That is why they should be left."

And the Holy Boys left them as their mother decreed.

Although the world had been remade and was useful to man, the Twins continued their adventures, getting acquainted with all parts of the universe and bringing back with them from each visit some essential gift for the Shooting Chant.

XXIII

SUN'S HOUSE

THE first day of Marie's sing is a concentrated sample of the four days we put in cleansing ourselves and preparing sacrifices for the various gods. The next three days are similar except for minor variations and intensity. The early morning paintings change a little. Horned snakes are painted on the first morning; on the second there are straight and zigzag arrows; on the next, sidewinders, and on the fourth, arrows again. The cloud of the first day is black with Sky People, of the second, blue with Water People, of the third, yellow with Sun People, and of the last, pink with Summer People. The only apparent change is in the color; the design is exactly the same for the four days. The second day the fire is not as hot as on the first, the emesis not so violent, or nearly so long drawn out. These events of the third day are again conscientiously done, but even then not as strenuous as on the first.

On the second night the kitty quietly followed the guests into the hogan. Curley's-Son saw it, went to the water bucket, filled a pan with water and unobtrusively enticed it out past the door curtain. Dan and Ben did not even see him do it. When he returned, the cat remained outside.

By the end of the fourth day invitations have been offered to Wind, Water-Monster, Water-Horse, Summer, Black Sky,

Earth, Sun, Moon, Pollen Boy, and Cornfly Girl, besides to the Horned-Rattlers; all beings who assisted the first legendary heroes, the Holy Twins, to whose sufferings we owe the Shooting Chant, and who for that reason will assist us. When I came this year, I brought Red-Point a flask of water from "the eastern ocean." He uses it for painting the prayersticks of the second day. It has not been secured with the proper ceremony, but perhaps it "will bring rain. We are trying it."

During the intervals between the ceremonial acts of each day the men are working. To Marie and Ninaba they seem brief indeed, for they seize upon these moments for naps. To me, though I am not weaving, the hours seem like minutes. I am mulling over the myth of the Shooting Chant, finding, in the narrative of the adventures of the two sons of the Sun, explanations and understanding as well as the unity of all the ostensibly unconnected small acts of each performance. But to the men who are working, time has ceased to exist. They have a great deal to do, and only a short time in which to do it.

Red-Point has determined to make this sing as complete as he possibly can. So he has chosen an elaborate form of it called the Chant-of-the-Sun's-House. He has sent out announcements of the event, and each day a few of his friends have come; but the hands are few compared with the work to be done. During the time he worked as a missionary John did not participate actively in sings. If he went to one he did so because "he had to see someone on business." But he comes to ours on the second day, and because Red-Point is short-handed, but more because his hands itch, as do mine, to work with the attractive sticks and paints, he begs to be allowed to help. The Chanter is pleased to let him try.

All the men including John work tirelessly, although, as is the Navajo custom, without haste. There are endless details to be attended to. A chant of this sort requires an unlimited supply of water and wood, to mention only two mundane needs. The largest task on hand is the repainting of the Sun's-House which is the symbol of supernatural power for the Chant. It is a booth not more than eighteen inches deep over the front of which hangs a curtain of sticks like a portière. This is about five feet wide by three high. Red-Point has not sung the Chant-of-the-Sun's-House for eight years, and the curtain must be painted anew. The pattern is exactly the same as the central part of the Sun's-House sand-painting which Atlnaba so carefully wove into a tapestry last year. Wide stripes of white, black, green, and yellow occupy most of the space. With the yellow stripe as background four deities, Sun, Moon, Black Wind, and Yellow Wind, form houses for the four different kinds of snakes. Around each is a rainbow, blue (Red-Point uses green) outside, red inside. Encircling three sides of the whole is another rainbow of the same sort, no detail of which is omitted.

Now if I were painting this curtain from Atlnaba's rug or Red-Point's copy in water colors, it would not be so much work. I should paint a stick all white and lay it horizontally for the top, two or three green and lay them parallel with the first and so on. The last few which compose the snakes' houses would be the only tedious ones. But the Chanter and his assistants cannot do it this way. The sticks must hang vertically. This means that every piece less than half an inch in diameter must represent a cross-section of the whole. The designs must be applied in mosaic fashion. As a weaver must carry in her mind her entire pattern and at the same time divide it into an infinite number of single-strand stripes, so must the painters of the Sun's-House. Each "strand" of their painting is one stick wide.

After two days of intermittent work at this John comes to my house just before sundown to prefer a request. "You look tired," I say as I offer him a smoke. "I am," he replies smiling. "It's lots of work."

"I never realized how much work a sing is," I say. "I simply cannot understand how Red-Point does it. He superintends everything by day; he never loses sight of a thing, and everything necessary is ready at the proper moment. He hardly sleeps at night. Last night it was eleven before the sing was over and this morning I heard him singing at four-thirty."

"Yes," continues John. "I just came up for a little visit yesterday morning. I did not intend to stay this long. But they need help, and I offered to try my hand at the painting."

"Did you ever help before?"

"Never."

"It looks like a nice thing to do."

"It is," John replies. "The old man said I did better than some of the others who had done it before."

A pause ensues, broken finally by John. "One of the boys has been hunting his horse all day and has not found it. They need some medicine for tomorrow night and now there is hardly time for him to get it even if he could catch his horse."

"Where does he have to go for it?" I inquire.

"The nearest is Crystal."

"Why, that is sixty miles!" I exclaim.

"Yes. The old man is pretty disappointed because he

wanted this done so complete. I suggested that maybe you would be willing to go for it. I said I would be glad to do it, but I do not know how to cut the medicine properly nor do I know the prayers."

"I told him at the beginning that I should be glad to do anything of that sort I could," I protest. "I knew he needed this distant medicine fresh, but I didn't know when."

"The roads are dry and hard now. I think if we start about sunrise tomorrow we could get it in time. He said one of the boys would go with us. I said maybe you wouldn't mind getting up so early."

"All right," I agree, "but I think I better get gas tonight. I haven't enough, and no trader will be up that early."

"I will take my horse home and come back with you. I am kind of worried about my horses. I left them in the corral without any hay. And nobody is home. I will let them out and look around the place."

I drive to Ganado, get gas and supplies, and visit my friends for several hours. I am sorry to miss a part of the ceremony but am glad the part I have to miss is not new, merely a repetition of what has gone before. About nine I pick up John and we arrive at Red-Point's hogan as the men are eating, preparatory to the evening sing. A discussion is under way as Tom sits hatted and kerchiefed as if he were going somewhere. Just before we arrived the man I call the "Man-with-the-Voice-Wrapped-Up-in-Cotton-Batting" had inquired where he was going. He answered, "To the southeast to get Douglas fir."

As we come in, someone suggests: "But it is just as far that way as to Crystal. Both kinds grow at Crystal. Why don't you get it all on one trip?"

John now takes command. "When do you have to have it?"

"At noon tomorrow."

John quietly and persuasively addresses himself to me. "Gladys, would you mind starting tonight? We could throw your bed in the car and go as far as we get, then camp, and in the morning cut our medicines. If we have good luck we could be back by noon, when they need this Douglas fir. The roads are good now, and there is no sign of rain."

"Sure, I can be ready in five minutes. I'll be down to eat before we start. I will pick you up, and you can load the car on the way out."

So agreeing, I repair to my house to assemble my camp kit and strap my blanket roll. I join John and Tom at the cooking shade in a few minutes, and after a hearty meal we are off. Never has the road been better, and I almost pray Jonathan will not do anything to delay us. He runs like a charm, and we find ourselves near our destination a little after midnight. In the darkness John and Tom have missed the dim tracks which lead to the Pass where the trees we seek grow, and John suggests we camp here until daylight. We do so, to find ourselves eaten up by mosquitoes. John and Tom are so weary that even the millions of these pests do not seriously annoy their slumbers. For once in my life I anticipate the dawn; more eagerly than Red-Point I discern its first pale gleam. Out of pity for the guides I linger a bit over my abbreviated ablutions and fixing my bed for travelling. But these beasts are unendurable; besides we have work to do, so I call the boys. I persist loudly before they remember where they are and why. The mosquitoes soon bring back consciousness.

In the cool of early dawn we drive a few miles to a road

I had travelled once before. It winds through green pastures watered by a clear, fresh-running brook. As we ascend the steep slope of the mountain, the meadows narrow, and the road is bordered on both sides by dense rows of tall firs and spruces. There is no undergrowth, and the long luscious grass is dotted here with a blue flower, there with a yellow, and farther on with a bright dash of scarlet. We cross the stream and arrive at our destination, a flat on the edge of a ravine. Gigantic pines grow on the flat; we stop to camp near a Douglas fir which is at least eighty feet high. As John lights a fire and collects with little effort the fuel to enlarge it, I remember that upon the occasion of my previous visit during which it had rained continuously, I had registered this as one of my patterns for paradise.

The men are off to cut the branches of the Douglas fir and Colorado blue spruce, both of which grow across the ravine. As I am making the coffee, I decide to be decent enough to wait politely until the boys come back. Within the short time it takes it to boil my decency evaporates. I do not know how long they will be gone, I argue to myself. I take a cup of coffee and a cinnamon roll, another cup and another roll. I am very sleepy. There are no mosquitoes here, the morning is even too young for flies. I have slept soundly for an hour and a half when the boys return and we have a regular breakfast.

We start back with a large gunny sack of the fir branches. Tom had cut several pieces of blue spruce very carefully so that each formed a cross with two arms; to the butt end he had tied a knot of the blue cloth in which he carries them. During the trip home he takes care always that the spruce branches never leave the cloth; when we are moving the bundle lies lightly on his lap, when we stop he lays it tenderly on the seat.

"How did you cut the medicine?" I ask John as we drive along.

"Red-Point gave Tom a flint knife from his bundle and a little sack of pollen. He told him the prayer to say as he cut a branch and sprinkled it with pollen. You know Tom has been learning from Red-Point."

A few miles west of Fort Defiance we stop once more for some sticks of wild rose, which complete the list of medicines for which we were sent. Jonathan buzzes along in a determined and businesslike manner, and at 11:35 we enter the ceremonial hogan to the congratulations of the men making the prayersticks there.

On the night which begins the fifth day the performance differs only slightly from the previous four. The Sun's-House is finished and stands at the back of the hogan, a protection and a blessing to it. The top and sides of the booth are covered thickly with the green fir branches, through the holes of the Sun, Moon and Wind houses wooden snakes move back and forth. Above the curtain four carvings of clouds stick up. In Atlnaba's weaving birds stood on these clouds. Here by invisible means a bluebird, a bluejay, a blackbird, a wild canary, and a yellow warbler, very realistic, fly about above the booth as they sing clearly and sweetly. From now on this pantomime accompanies each performance. Often Curley's-Son is strangely absent.

Old-Mexican's-Son sleeps in the hogan this night. The next morning as I drive him home he reports, "You know there is something to that Sun's-House. About three-thirty I got awake and felt something like a presence. I told Red-Point, and he said, 'That's right, no one can sleep with the Sun's-House present.' Very early he woke up Marie and Ninaba and placed them in front of it. As the pollen carried a prayer, the birds sang, and they sounded just like bluebirds, too. Then Red-Point made them go outside and facing the rising sun; they set up the things from his bundle which will guard the house from evil while they are making the sand-painting of the day. As he stuck each object in the sandpile, he chanted a long prayer. You know there is something in these Navajo prayers that gets me. That's why I like to go to sings."

"It was the prayer which woke me," I agree. "I couldn't hear the words but it is the setting which is holy. The night the sheep were struck by lightning I woke about midnight and heard Red-Point praying down near the sheep corral. The parts of the sing the white people never see are the most impressive. The lighting of the prayersticks and these prayers in solitude carry the answer to the power of the chant. Even I who do not believe can understand how these acts can really cure these people because they believe so implicitly."

As we ride on in silence I muse, "It could not be otherwise when from babyhood a Navajo has heard:

"*The curtain of daybreak is hanging.*
Daylight Boy, it is hanging.
From the land of day it is hanging.
Before him as it dawns, it is hanging.
Behind him as it dawns, it is hanging.
Before him in beauty, it is hanging.
Behind him in beauty, it is hanging.
From his voice in beauty, it is hanging.

[188]

"In solitude:

"*Holy-Young-Man sought the gods and found them.*
On the high mountain peaks he sought the gods and
    found them.
Truly with my sacrifice he sought the gods and found
    them.
Somebody doubts it, so I have heard.

"*I do not doubt it.*"

XXIV

THE GODS ACCEPT

I KNOW that today the first sand-painting is to be made, so I stay at Ganado only long enough to eat breakfast. Because Red-Point had said that he was going to let me "see everything," and that he was going to "tell me about everything," I suppose I am to be allowed in the hogan while the men are laying the sand-painting. I want especially to see it while it is being made. I know the technique but never tire of watching those who strew the sand. Furthermore, the complete beauty of a sand-painting is obscured by the last touches put upon it, for after all the smallest symbolic and artistic details have been attended to, one of the helpers fills in all the background space with wavy black lines of sand. The first act required of the patients when they come in with the "other women" who are part of the audience is to sprinkle white cornmeal over each figure of the painting and around according to the Chanter's instructions. No patient is skilful about this, nor need he be, and the audience, in the brief time at its disposal, sees the painting covered with black and white smudges unevenly applied. For this reason I hope to see the paintings made, so as to get a clearer idea of their patterns.

Before the men start on it, however, Tom informs me that I may not come. "You see, women never see the painting," he explains. "That is the reason."

Marie and I both have plenty of leisure this day. The sun was scarce up when the dawn prayer was over, and she and Ninaba have nothing to do but wait until they are called for the painting. The paintings of all four days are to be large ones; so the men begin about nine o'clock, and they will not be finished until nearly sunset.

Red-Point starts the men to work, and about ten-thirty he and Marie come to see me. "Tell her I promised to let her see everything," he instructs Marie, "but we never have even our own women in the hogan when the painting is being laid."

"Why is that?" I ask, thinking that it is to protect the "powers" from the contamination of the female sex.

"We have always been taught that way. It is in the story. So you must not feel sorry because you cannot come in."

"Some of these men who are here to help said he oughtn't to allow a white woman in our sing," Marie explains. "But my father says you are his child and he would not refuse to have his own child. Besides, he says his teacher told him if outsiders want to be sung over, he should do it. Once there was a Hopi who asked him to sing, and he did; then there was a white man at Chinlee; and of course he always sings for Old-Mexican's-Son when he wants him."

I assure them I am not offended, and as he finishes off his cigarette Red-Point declares, "And I will sing over you some-time too, let the Navajo say what they will!" So saying, he jumps up. "Well, I must go back and watch those boys!" And he leaps up the two high steps of my house.

I answer his challenge as Marie stays, "Well, I should not mind if no whites would come."

"Just like Ninaba," smiles Marie. "She says she don't like

to have white people there, just Weaving-Woman is all right. But that's all."

I return to the subject of women witnessing the sand-painting, and Marie explains more fully, "Women never see the men working at it. Only if they have had a sand-painting made for them like my mother, Atlnaba, and Ben Wilson's Wife, then they can go in any time. After this Ninaba and I can go in when they are making the ones we have had. You see they will always be ours after that."

"If your father would sing over me, would the four paintings be mine?" I ask.

"Yes," responds Marie, as she sees I understand.

"Do you know which painting they are making?"

"No, the patient is not supposed to know it until she goes in when it is finished."

"How does your father know which one to use?"

"You know he has forty-seven. Some are large and others are small. If the people pay the singer lots they can have the big ones. They can choose which they want. My father is making the largest for this sing. He asked me which I wanted. But I told him to make any ones he and Tom and Tom's brother want."

"Did you ever see the double painting?" I ask. "I wish they would make that one."

"No, never in sand. But they said they were going to use that one because the house is big enough. But I don't know if it will be today."

"We had an awful nice trip the other night," I say, changing the subject. "I wish your father would go on a trip with me for medicine sometime."

"He would like to," she says. "He said he wished he could

have gone along that time. You know all of the medicine must be collected in a special way. If it isn't done that way, it is not so good. Now that water you brought from the Hudson. It would be better, if my father had got it. But he said we'll try it anyway."

"I know," I reply. "That is why I'd like to have him along. Besides, he knows where everything grows and what it is good for."

"I guess I'll go and try to sleep a little." And Marie departs.

The day is a quiet one. I engage in my ordinary pursuits always with an eye to the ceremonial hogan. Shortly after noon there is a bustle of excitement before the door. In their customary inquisitive manner the goats have come over to nose into the sacred objects, twenty-two of them from Red-Point's bundle, which were painstakingly arranged in and on a pile of clean sand before the house. This makes an altar and, as Old-Mexican's-Son explained, protects the house and all in it during the time the sacred sand is being used. When the painting is finished, the objects will be taken in and placed in order on and near it. When I see the men take them in, I know we shall soon be called.

The goats do little harm before they are discovered by the ever-vigilant Red-Point. "Chase them off," he calls to Ruby. Tom and Curley's-Son leap from their work, and as Ruby drives off the herd, they bring a large crate from which they remove the bottom. This they place over the altar, taking care not to allow even a down feather of a prayerstick to touch the wood. From this time on the crate will protect the altar which guards the house from invisible dangers.

The July days are long and it is not until after six that we are called. I enter the hogan just after the patients have sprinkled the cornmeal over the painting, which happens to be the double one. By that is meant that there are really two paintings in one.

"In the story," at a distant period when the Holy Twins were going about the earth making things livable for man, the Thunders laid down this painting on the top of Black Mountain in order to sanctify themselves. Then they bethought themselves and said: "Earth People ought to know this. Let someone go down and get one of them."

So Mountain-Sheep was stationed at a certain point and on the opposite side at a place called Hot-Springs a cornstalk with twelve ears was set up. Just then First-born, the more powerful of the twins, came up. He had been forbidden to come to the place where the Mountain-Sheep stood and his brother, Child-of-the-Water, had been warned against the Place-of-the-Large-Cornstalk. As he came up to the Mountain-Sheep, First-born thought, "Ha! This is the reason they didn't want me to come here." So he killed the animal. Just as he drew it aside to the base of a Douglas fir thinking to skin it, lightning struck and he was picked up by it.

Shortly after a bear came along. When he saw what had happened, he said, "Although it may look bad, nevertheless, my daughter's son will return without harm." Then while singing songs, he rubbed his back against the aspen, red willow, fir, and chokecherry trees successively. All these medicines are used for the circle prayersticks on the various days when the emetic is administered. Because of this and because Big-Fly and Otter were with him, First-born was saved.

At the same time all this was happening to First-born his

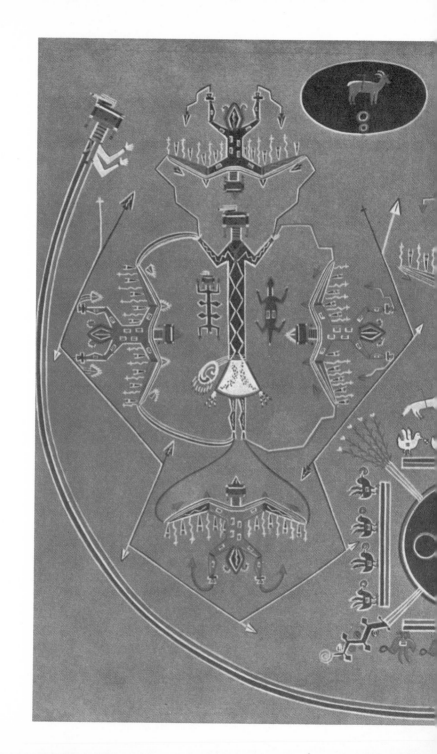

NORTH

Frank Johnson Newcomb, 1934

brother was on his way to Hot-Springs where he saw the great cornstalk. He broke off the fifth ear but as he did so, he was swallowed by a monster fish. However, he always carried an arrow-point in his right hand and with this was able to cut the fish open. Five arrow-points about his neck helped to save him. With the five medicines he always held in his left hand he healed the side of the fish, after he had cut it open.

The painting called "Opposite-each-other" commemorates this expedition of the Holy Boys. The black mountain at the west of the picture represents Butte-Reaching-to-the-Sky. It stands about fifteen inches high, made like pottery of kneaded clay.

"After it has been made, the place where it is to stand is levelled off. A cross is made of pollen, and some is sprinkled over it. Then a small portion of charcoal made from burnt herbs is sprinkled on it to represent darkness. White sand sprinkled over this represents the dawn; blue sand, blue sky; and yellow sand, yellow evening light. On the flat top part it is all yellow to represent pollen, and beside this yellow is a small black circle, and across this a red cross. This represents the fire inside.

"All around the base is black, and four encircling lines are made around it, white, yellow, blue, and red, making four lines around a black center. Around this standing butte four small bowls of water are set, all being within the black circle. Around the rim of the bowls are four lines, the white representing water foam; the yellow, pollen; blue with red, the rainbow. In the bowls on the water there are four rainbows in the four directions, the inner red, the outer, blue. Then moss which is found under sagebrush is put around the edge of these water bowls. They are shown as being on the mountain in the painting.

"Around the black center of the base of the butte there are four rainbows in each direction, inner blue, outer red.[1] Four open spaces are left at the ends of these rainbows. On top of the rainbow in the east four white ducks are made with their heads turned as if they were moving south. On the sun raft to the west are four yellow ones with heads pointing north. In the south they are blue with heads west; in the north, black with heads east. So all the heads face the same way, that is, sunwise. Above the head of the eastern duck as guardian toward the north a wolf lies in white, and toward the south a black bear is made; the noses of these animals face each other with a space of five fingers between, their fronts to the west.

"In the space between, in line with the head and facing west, yellow thunder lies. This finishes all in the west part of the room.

"In the north the figure of First-born is laid first as the center figure. East of him lies black thunder with its head toward him. From the tip of its wing a line runs into his hands. At the south of First-born lies the otter. On the other side the horsefly lies on his back. Facing him at the west the blue thunderbird lies, at the south a yellow one, at the north a pink one; all these lie with heads toward First-born.

"From the tip of the blue thunderbird at the west a line of straight lightning runs to the sole of each foot. From the west wing of the yellow thunderbird of the south a sun-ray line runs into the sole of his foot. From its east wing one runs into the tip of his hand. From the west wing-tip of the pink bird at the north a stretched rainbow runs to the sole of his foot, from its east wing-tip one leads to his hand.

"From the space between the rainbows around the butte at the west plants run out, bean toward the south, squash toward the west, tobacco toward the north. In the space toward the east corn roots are sprinkled and make a turn to where Second-born will be placed, exactly in a line with him. The cornstalk is made with an ear on each side.

"After the corn is finished Second-born is laid down, his head in line with that of First-born, their feet stepping in line with each

[1] The difference between the picture here portrayed and the one made for Marie is explained on p. 155.

other. In his right hand he holds a black flint with a shaft of zigzag lightning. Around his neck five points on a sun-ray shaft are wound, the lowest one next his body is black flint, the next is white, then blue, yellow, and finally pink, all white-bordered.

"In his left he holds five medicines, the one nearest him being black, then white, blue, yellow, and finally pink being east. Above his head facing him lies the black fish,[1] below his feet the yellow one, at the south, the blue one, at the north, the white one. All have their heads toward him. From the mouth of the black one in the east runs a zigzag lightning. The lines forming it separate and run under the armpits of the figure. This is the one that swallowed him.

"The one at the west has a straight lightning curving out from the mouth, and returning to it. In the south a sun-ray is arranged the same way and in the north a rainbow. A mountain entirely black with a white line around its base is placed even with the door toward the north. Not far from the center toward the west is a cup of water, and on top of the range is another cup. On the top of the mountain on the north side of the cup lies a blue mountain sheep, with head toward east and facing south. A piece of Douglas fir and one of blue spruce cut neatly for the purpose are placed on top of the mountain range at the south. Then that is finished.

"On the south side in line with the tip of the cornstalk Mt. Taylor is placed. It is about the shape and size of an anthill. On the west side of it a cup of water is placed. From the east a black quarter; from west, yellow; from the south, blue; from the north, white; so four lines coming from the four directions meet at the top. All the cups of water are made alike.

"Now around First-born and the Thunder People alone a zigzag lightning is used for an encircling line, but the rainbow is the encircling border of the whole sand-painting, its skirt is south, head north. That finishes it."[2]

Because the sand-painting is double, there are two choruses today, one on the north, one on the south side of the hogan.

[1] In Red-Point's picture the black and white fish were interchanged.
[2] Literal translation from the myth of the Shooting Chant.

They sing alternately and in unison, Red-Point giving them the cue for the order of songs. The leader of one knows the Shooting Chant too, but occasionally he starts the wrong set of songs and Red-Point corrects him. While Marie and Ninaba remove their moccasins and shirts, Red-Point sprinkles liquid over the painting with a medicine sprinkler.

He bids Marie sit on the body of First-born and Ninaba on that of Child-of-the-Water, with their feet extended to the east. As the songs proceed, and suiting each act to a particular word in the song, Red-Point wets his hands with water from one of the medicine cups, applies them damp to the feet of certain gods in the painting, that means not only First-born, Child-of-the-Water and the Thunders, but also Big-Fly and Otter, the fish, the cornstalk, the lightnings, the Rainbow encircling border, and all other figures, for these are all deities who have accepted the invitations. After touching these points of the painting, Red-Point presses his hands to the feet of the patients.

On another round of the same sort he communicates the power of the hands of the deities to those of the patients, then that of the heart and head. There is an unusually large number of songs for this painting, and the patients sit for some minutes during which nothing but the singing occurs. Altogether the performance takes not more than half an hour. The final incense is burned, and Red-Point orders the patients out. We women follow, Atlnaba carrying the clothes of the patients. As we hold their things while they dress, the helpers run out to the four directions, where they hastily deposit the sand which had composed the painting.

The elements of the Chant, purification, offerings for invitation, the drawing-in of supernatural powers, the application of them being present, and their careful disposal, all of these have appeared again and again. On the eighth morning the patients undergo another type of purification, the shampoo and bath. A basket stands in the west part of the house on a nicely shaped mound of coarse sand. Between it and the sand are fresh sprigs of five medicines. In the basket lies a cylindrically cut piece of soapweed root soaking in a small amount of water. Singing the while, Red-Point prepares the sacred bath. He rolls the soaproot between his hands for some time. The water becomes ever more foamy as he sings and rubs. He adds more water from the bucket, until the foam rises comfortably above the rim of the basket like a fluffy meringue on a pie.

He now makes the ceremonial crosses of the four pollens, black, white, blue, yellow, one on top of another, on the foam and sprinkles each around it. When he reaches the proper song, Marie and Ninaba, having left their clothes on a blanket, kneel before the basket and with Red-Point's help wash their hair. He pours the rinsing water over and bids them wash carefully their beads, bracelets and hair strings. The herdboy fetches and carries today, for Maria Antonia has charge of the bath. Red-Point retires to his sheepskin, as four old women and Atlnaba, led by Maria Antonia, stand holding blankets in outstretched arms to form a semicircular screen around the patients while they vigorously apply the sudsy water to their entire bodies. They stand on the sand, feet on particular medicines, as they do this. The old women bid them hurry, and as soon as every drop from the basket has been applied, rinse them with dippers of fresh water from the bucket. The patients catch it in cupped hands and wash their faces. Hastily

Maria Antonia hands each a skirt to be slipped over the original one, which is precipitately unfastened, let down, and removed.

The women take down the screen and the bedraggled patients stand for a moment while the wet sand and medicines are swept from sight and replaced by a dry blanket. Maria Antonia now applies cornmeal to their backs while they rub arms, legs, and chest with it. Red-Point draws a generous amount under their chins, on their cheeks, and over the top of their heads. They then use all the rest in the basket to strew over shirts, moccasins, and especially jewelry before they dress. The bath is over. The cornmeal is the substitute for a Turkish towel; it stays with the bather somewhat longer.

There is a rumor that the picture of the last day is to be the Earth-Sky one. I am disappointed because I like it least of any I have ever seen reproduced. At three o'clock when it is finished, I am surprised at its beauty as it lies "strung out" in the most graceful proportions on the floor of the hogan, which affords it ample space. I have seen the pattern woven into blankets—hideous, I consider them. I always thought it was because bad colors were used and because there was such a large space of solid color, blue for the earth, black for the sky. I find now I was right about the color but not about its extent. The copies are bad primarily because of the crude proportions, short and awkwardly wide. Here are elongated figures, so graceful as to have little in common with the perversions I have seen. The large expanse of color adds to the effect, for it consists of black and the inimitable shade of blue, a natural color which is the despair of all copyists, and which the dim shaded light of the hogan brings out to perfection.

It is well the picture is done early today, for the rite includes not only most of the acts which were performed previously but several new ones, and these are tedious. One is the body painting. As we watch, and as the chorus sings, Red-Point carefully paints Ninaba, and one of his friends paints Marie. A blue spot at the middle of the chest is the sun, a white at the center of the back, the moon. Black, white, blue, and yellow stripes running over the shoulders and under the arms connect the two. The black represent zigzag lightning; the white, straight lightning; the blue, sun-ray; and the yellow, the rainbow. There is a cloud figure on each fore- and each upper-arm; the two are connected by stripes of the same colors as those on the shoulders.

Similarly the painter places four stripes on each shin. I see a fly on Ninaba's left shoulder as her grandfather traces a line on her right arm. I know it tickles her, but she does not move—it would spoil his line. Finally he reaches the foot. On her right instep he traces a white-horned rattler and on her left a yellow one. I shudder as he carries the head of each under the first joint of the great toe. Neither Marie nor Ninaba bats an eye at this.

All the details have been brushed in. Red-Point now paints Ninaba's face as his friend paints Marie's. Not a millimeter of skin is left in its natural color. Four wide stripes cover all, white over the forehead, black across the eyes, blue over the nose and cheeks, and yellow across mouth and chin. I cannot believe this is my shy little daughter as her eyes roll in an unnatural expanse of whiteness and her teeth glisten fiercely from the surrounding yellow. Marie's sweet, jolly face is also disguised out of all semblance of its usual expression.

Red-Point and his assistant finally finish the painting to his satisfaction. The patients put on their jewelry. Red-Point mixes a little sand from the feet of the gods of the sand-painting and puts it in their moccasins. He then leads them on to the painting. They go through the course of treatment which combines all they have had before on the three paintings of the previous days and on the preceding seven nights, and to them several others are added. Red-Point has braided a necklace and wristbands for each from strips of yucca leaf and intertwined at intervals sprigs of Douglas fir and four turkey feathers. He puts these on the patients ceremonially at a word in a special song.

A feather medicine bundle lies on the painting. This he ties to the locks of hair which he has smeared with white during the painting. To a small lock of each girl he ties a string on which a tiny cowry shell and a small, very blue bead of turquoise have been fastened. A ball about as big as a walnut is administered. It is rough and dry, being a compound of many things like fish's blood, and pollen. It is like a huge, sandy, woolly, sweetish, bitter pill. The patients chew it up and swallow it with water Red-Point gives them in four mouthfuls.

The pollen ball represents the agate man which the Sun put into Enemy-Slayer or the turquoise one which stands in the body of his brother. The sun board of the bundle is pressed hard against the stomach, the moon board against the back. This is done to put the turquoise in place. Finally, after breathing the sun outside the hogan and dressing, the patients return and eat unseasoned cornmush to keep the ball in position. This part of the rite is over and they may sleep until they are called for the vigil of the last night. They must under no conditions remove the collar and bracelets of yucca, nor must they take off their moccasins or lose any of the sand out of them. Since they must keep awake this entire night, the few hours between the painting and ten o'clock will be their last chance to sleep for twenty-four hours.

At sunset, which begins the ninth day of the Chant, I am sitting in the car reading dreamily and uncomprehendingly. The glow on the earth is of a quiet healing sort. Every day since Red-Point used the Hudson River water there have been light showers and White-Sands has become green. I am sitting in the car because a sweet female rain dampens the ground. When there is not a double rainbow through the glistening curtain, small ends of the rainbow brighten the horizon. I am thinking about the Shooting Chant. When Marie told me it would continue nine days, it had seemed to me impossible that such a long time could ever pass by in this ceremonial manner. And now, almost before I know it, eight of them are gone. There were the four days of cleansing and preparation of sacrifices. They sped by. Then four more when the Corn-stalk-with-Twelve-Ears, the Double-Painting, the Buffalo-Painting and the Earth-and-Sky were laid, applied, and deposited. They flew by.

And now a sense of complacency lies over White-Sands, as gentle and as gratifying as the curtain of raindrops which hangs over it. The satisfaction lies, I think, as I half recline, in having carried out a complicated, fatiguing, nerve-trying ritual to its prescribed end. A sense of restoration pervades the place as Red-Point stalks up. He climbs up beside me in the car. As he lights the proffered cigarette, he looks through the smoke and says, "White-Sands is beautiful."

Before either of us realizes it, we are intoning a litany: "The fields are beautiful," I respond.

"The vegetation is beautiful," he encourages.

"The trees are beautiful."

"The houses are beautiful."

"The women are beautiful."

"The men are beautiful."

And together we say, "The children are beautiful."

Then I, "The Chant is beautiful."

"The offerings are beautiful."

"The prayers are beautiful."

"The paintings are beautiful. All has been restored in beauty," concludes the old Chanter, as he once again strides off to attend to the details of the final night.

XXV

EFFECTS

THE songs are over. The singing and drumming continue with only a few short intermissions all night. The Chanter, chorus, and patients may not even doze off, but the rest of us take a cat nap now and then. And now after breakfast, when all is still and peaceful, Marie and Ninaba come to see me. They rub their sleepy eyes, as Marie tells me: "We may not sleep as long as the sun is up. For the next four days we must get up at sunrise, and we must not sleep again until after sunset. That is because we had the Sun's-House. So when I was nearly falling off, my father said, 'Go up and see Weaving-Woman, and tell her to keep you awake.' "

"I'll do that all right," I laugh. "I shall take no pity on you when you are getting tired of my questions, but I'll just keep on"—referring to our work in language. Marie may not work; but teaching me Navajo is not work, and I shall nag at her with my eternal curiosity.

If the patients sleep in the daytime they may have bad dreams, and that would keep the pollen ball from remaining in place.

They still wear the large bunch of feathers and the small beads on their hair. They have rubbed, perhaps not purposely, a great deal of the paint off their faces. But they may not wash or comb their hair for four days, nor may they remove

clothes or moccasins. The necklaces and wristbands of yucca
and fir are still pricking into their flesh, a minor torture.
They do not stay long this time, for Red-Point once more
calls them. He unties the feather bundle from each head and
from it takes a down feather which he bids them carry. Then
all three walk about a quarter of a mile to the west, where
Red-Point selects a small piñon tree before which they stand.
He ties the down feathers to the tip of the tree, after sprinkling pollen at the four quarters, around, up and down. Then
he removes the yucca necklaces and secures them over the
upper central branches of the tree. The wristbands he places
on branches at each side. As they stand there side by side,
he speaks the prayer of the young pine four times, and his
daughters repeat it after him:

> *Dark young pine, at the center of the earth originating,*
> *I have made your sacrifice.*
> *Whiteshell, turquoise, abalone beautiful,*
> *Jet beautiful, fool's gold beautiful, blue pollen beautiful,*
>   *reed pollen, pollen beautiful, your sacrifice I have*
>   *made.*
> *This day your child I have become, I say.*
>
> *Watch over me.*
> *Hold your hand before me in protection.*
> *Stand guard for me, speak in defense of me.*
> *As I speak for you, so do ye.*
> *As you speak for me, thus shall I do.*
>   *May it be beautiful before me,*
>   *May it be beautiful behind me,*
>   *May it be beautiful below me,*

May it be beautiful above me,
May it be beautiful all around me.

I am restored in beauty,
I am restored in beauty,
I am restored in beauty,
I am restored in beauty.

After all sprinkle pollen once more they return home.

On subsequent visits of Marie, I learn that the kind of work they may not do has to do with fire and water. They must not go near fire or use water, although they may drink some. They have had the sacred patterns put on their bodies with care and song, and for that reason will be benefited. But they must not touch anyone who has never had the sing, nor should such ones touch their things. Only those who have had the sing may eat with them and wash the dishes they use, for the blessings of the chant are permanent. What is done now is done for all time. For four days they will observe these restrictions; for four nights more they will sleep in the hogan under Red-Point's eye. To those who have not had the sing, they might communicate power in an irregular and disorderly manner, that would bring special harm to the person encountered.

"Harriet said when her mother had the sing, she washed after two days," I tell Marie, speaking of a girl who had visited us.

Marie's scorn knows no bounds. "Yes, and she was bitten by a snake that very summer. That's what is the matter with Totlani's-Wife, too. She had this sing over at Water-in-the-

Earth, and she started to cook the very day after the all-night sing. My father says that is the reason she is so sick."

Totlani's-Wife is dying of cancer. Some say it is because she wove too many sand-painting blankets, since before her illness she was industrious and enterprising. Red-Point is sure he could cure her, for although she has already had the Shooting Chant sung for her, he is sure it was not done properly.

"She is worse, did you know?" I tell Marie. "She got a cold much like you had, only worse, and she was spitting blood. They had a man to tell what sing she ought to have when I was there day before yesterday. He said she ought to have the Female Shooting Chant and after that the War Dance."

"It's too bad," says Marie. "You know after the first day when I had that awful headache, my father said my hands were cooler. It was the sing that made it. After that I didn't have headache any more either."

"It seems as though your father never makes a mistake. I know, of course, that he has to say the prayers just exactly right. You said them all right, too, but what does he do when someone can't keep up? If I had a sing, I am sure I'd make mistakes. Would he be able to sing so that it would not matter?"

"Yes, that's the way they do. Ninaba got off the track, too, but he can make that all right with a prayer. We don't know what to do either. They have to tell us."

Dan rides up as we talk. The men are going to brand cattle. Do we want to watch them? In no time we have a full auto. Yikadezba and Djiba as usual implore us to take them. "They can come this time," I say. "Ninaba can hold Djiba."

"No, we are not allowed to touch the children. They have

never had the sing." The women negotiate. They agree that the children will walk to the branding with Atlnaba.

On the way Marie communicates another bit of gossip. "Mary said she was going to come up to the sing, but she couldn't get anyone to bring her. She was coming to make fun. She said she wouldn't have a sing with those dirty old medicine-men."

"I think a person doesn't have to believe it," I reply, "but I don't think she needs to make fun of it."

"She's a Christian!" bursts forth Marie indignantly. "That's the reason she has such funny babies!"

Mary has had one child born without eyes and another without a skull. Both lived for some time, a horror to Indians and whites alike. The doctor says she has chronic malconception; the Navajo say it is irreverence.

The branding is a pleasant diversion.

Another full day goes by when a party of the family, Marie and Ninaba included, go by wagon to a cañon toward the east where they carefully deposit Butte-Reaching-to-the-Sky. This is a sculptured part of the double painting made of pottery clay. Red-Point goes with them and the disposal is made ritualistically.

Before we know it, the four days are gone. At sunrise after the thirteenth night from the beginning of the chant, Marie and Ninaba untie the beads from their hair, shampoo it and wash their entire bodies in yucca suds. Each ties her bead to her hair string and from this time on will wear it always. If ever there is a storm, an epidemic, or she "gets into a tight place," she may shake the bead at the offender as she utters a prayer, and all danger will disappear.

XXVI

THE KINNI'S-SONS

THE four days during which Marie and Ninaba imbibed the strength of their paintings have been days of quiet mental work and relaxation. I leave White-Sands to get the saddle-blanket patterns from Mr. Short-Pants and Mr. Little-Man-with-the-Spectacles. They live at Thoreau, a place on the railroad a few miles east of the Continental Divide. Many of the Navajo women know how to make the more modest, dull blankets, but since the American buying public wants something more striking for "Papa's study," they do not generally receive much encouragement to bring them in. In fact, few of the traders know they are different, almost none know what the differences are. The blankets require great care in counting, not only when the warp is strung up but even during the entire time they are being woven. The Navajo make them for their men-folk, by whom they are duly appreciated and used.

The traders at Thoreau have for two years been collecting looms with unfinished webs. The very day I announce myself sees me established in their blanket room surrounded by blankets of all kinds and the many looms. I can draw plans for stringing and weaving in my notebook without actually setting up and weaving each pattern. At Red-Point's I progressed from one step to another by having the women show

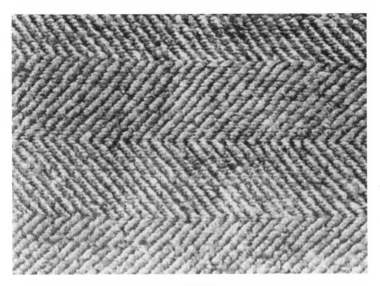

BRAIDED

Courtesy of Lloyd Ambrose

DIAMOND

COOK SHADE FOR WAR DANCE

FIREWOOD

me. Often I did not know what my goal was. My learning was always particular. And so it would be here too, had not these gentlemen taken the trouble for several years to secure information on the different rugs as they came in, ever finding new surprises, even in a business long followed.

The difference between these weaves and the ordinary kind I have learned is that the design in these depends upon elaborate stringing of the warp. We have used so far only two healds making two sheds, and we have secured all the variation in our designs by manipulation of the weft. Because of that manipulation, we have, too, always achieved the same design on both sides of our rugs. I see that these weaves, new to me, depend upon the way the warps are strung, all of them carefully counted in varying series and looped on two, three, or four healds. The weft is usually a three-color combination, although it need not be. Each of the three weft strands is carried across the entire width of the blanket as the healds are thrown. It is necessary, then, for me to mark in my diagrams the number and order of the threads on each of the healds, and to note the alternation of the weft strands.

The design resulting from the combination of different sheds and variation of weft color in the most complicated is a diagonal. It may be varied by different shifts almost indefinitely, but it remains the basic design. Another division of the sheds thrown in the proper order for a given distance, then reversed, results in a diamond, large or small depending entirely upon the number of warps in the set-up. It is not difficult from these loom models to grasp the essentials of the shedding quickly. It is necessary in addition to dissect the weft throwing. Since the loom models are loose, it is easy enough to push up the wefts row by row and coördinate them with the healds. But I find I must do this for a goodly number of rows, depending of course upon the size of the diamond. For, after half the shape of the diamond is secured, the order of throwing the sheds is reversed to form the second half.

I work on these patterns, advancing from the simpler to the more complex. I am occasionally puzzled by the fact that the warps as strung do not correspond to them as woven. In such case, Mr. Short-Pants finds me a second model. He has no duplicates for one or two, and I decide to leave them until I know more.

I am now ready for practical work. Mr. Short-Pants takes me to see Mrs. Kinni's-Son. She lives only two miles north of Thoreau. We find her weaving at a loom set up under a tree. The family is a dull one, but the setting is even more color-ful than White-Sands. There is a piñon-dotted plain extend-ing from steep redstone cliffs which stand like a bulwark about a mile behind the settlement. The place is well watered, the grass grows bright green and thick over the red sand ground. The view is brilliant, far, and clean.

The tree under which the large loom stands is in front of a rude structure of planks, a house unlike that of whites or Navajo. In this house the cooking is done. A few paces south is another building somewhat like it, the boards of its sides and roof so placed as to leave large cracks through which the sun filters temperamentally. There is a stove in the center of the building, and a loomframe at the north side.

Mrs. Kinni's-Son is weaving a blanket such as we have come to talk about. Her daughter, a handsome half-grown girl, sits near her, carding and observing us smilingly. Mr. Short-Pants explains that I want Mrs. Kinni's-Son to set me up a loom for which I will pay the same price he pays her at the post. Besides I will pay her five dollars a week for teaching. After the blanket is strung up, she will not have to work at it, but can card or spin while I am weaving. We emphasize the fact that this way she will be able to earn more than twice what she would with her own weaving. She agrees, although her expression shows she does not quite comprehend.

As we sit longer and watch her weaving, her husband comes up. He is not cordial like Red-Point, but has rather an attitude of "What are *you* doing here?" He is of medium stature and stocky, good-looking, but lacks the friendly appeal I have come to admire in the Navajo. We explain our plan to him, talk a little on other things, explain it again. He has a son who speaks English; so if we come to a discussion too involved for my Navajo talents, he will interpret. We agree, after more and longer argument about money, that I may start work tomorrow. I have the feeling I shall not become attached to this family in any way. I shall learn my lessons, pay my money, and be done.

I arrive next day to find the women busy preparing yarn. Kinni's-Son is not home. Mrs. Kinni's-Son has warp, and at once sets up a blanket. It is a little less than three hands wide by less than four long. It does not take her long to string it or to twine the end finish. She deftly fastens the movable loom to the loomframe in the house. Then she seats herself before it and starts to count out the threads for the heald loops.

Although she has set up dozens of these blankets, her procedure is one of experimentation. Carefully counting, she takes up threads on her batten. When she has cast it through the entire width she inserts a reed and withdraws the batten. She makes the first two sheds rather fast. But she finds the count for the third wrong and tries again.

I watch her intently. I have my notebook open at my diagram for this pattern, and I know which warps she should take up. But she has made many of these blankets, and I want to see how she does it. She tries and fails a number of times and at last, discouraged, has her daughter at it. The daughter has been watching for a time and giving oral suggestions. She now trades places with her mother, flips the threads and separates them surely and expertly, each group for its rod. It does not take her more than about twenty minutes to get them in order. Her mother then fastens the proper paired or single threads into the loops over the heald rods. At last the sheds may be thrown. It has taken her at least an hour and a half to do this part of the work.

She weaves a few rows to illustrate for me the order of inserting the woof threads, and of throwing the sheds, then hands the comb to me. I note particularly that she pounds down the yarn with her batten, a proceeding Marie forbade when I first started to weave. In every case we shall throw the weft clear across the width of the warp so that we have each color wound on a reed, and our work proceeds rapidly. I must keep in mind the order of the sheds to be thrown and coordinate that series with the proper sequence of weft colors. If I make no mistakes for this blanket I will get a cleancut row of diagonal lines, white, black, gray, white, black, gray.

Mrs. Kinni's-Son is not nearly as intelligent as Red-Point's women, but in some respects she is a better teacher for she throws me on my own responsibility. I weave along, making occasional mistakes which I take out, but withal my progress is apparent. It is surprising how one has to concentrate on the order of this type of weaving. I think it is because I am new at it, but Mr. Short-Pants tells me that all the women he knows become impatient, even angry, if someone talks to them while they are making these weaves. This fact alone, in the face of the Navajo liking for visiting and conversation, may account, I think, for the scarcity of these blankets in trade.

Mrs. Kinni's-Son does not feel it necessary to watch my every move and leaves me to my own devices. About eleven o'clock there is a stir in the other house, and soon the delicious smoke of burning cedar assails my nostrils. The girls have started the midday meal. When I get hungry I move my car with its contents toward the red cliffs and have my brief lunch. I return to my work to find the women all busy preparing yarn. I arrived at a time when they had none ready. I hear the rhythmic *scratch scratch* of the towcards in the strong hands of one of the girls, and the busy comfortable whir of Mrs. Kinni's-Son's spindle as it rapidly twirls on the hard ground. I add to the chorus the regular thud of my comb at the weaving.

I had intended to have Mrs. Kinni's-Son set me up a loom for each type of stringing. But I have made a two-inch stripe of diagonals leaning from right to left; I have reversed the healds and achieved the same kind of a stripe which leans from left to right. Another band of diagonals leaning in the opposite direction convinces me I have mastered this lesson. There are imperfections, of course, but I want to understand principles. I shall doubtless never weave enough to become wholly expert. I shall be contented with understanding. Not of course because I do not have dozens of patterns in my head, but because I have too many things to do.

I am thinking these things with a sigh of resignation when Kinni's-Son comes in with his son. He starts in on a long argument which is to have almost daily repetition, and the burden of which is: "This kind of weaving is hard. Not many women know how to do it. You ought, therefore, to pay my wife a large sum for having her teach you."

I point out that, while she is teaching me, she is getting more than any of the educated girls who are working, and at the same time she can be working for herself. I try to be patient as I explain these things. These people live near the railroad. They have been exploited for years by white people. They are on the defensive against exploitation but they really have no defense. "You will learn to weave, and you will teach the white women to weave so that the Navajo women won't be able to earn money any more."

I should not be able to suppress a smile if another white person or even Marie were with me, but alone as I am, it seems too pathetic to be funny. I tell him how my family would starve if they depended on my weaving for a living. I tell him how bad and how slow I am at spinning. After a time he is silenced but not convinced. Again we go over, detail by detail, the amount I am going to pay his wife. He is very insistent, and I continue to elucidate. I tell him I make a point never to pay before a job is done. As soon as this blanket comes down, I will pay his wife for it, just as the trader would if she brought it to the post. If, before the time comes, a week goes by, I will pay her five dollars for teaching me.

Luckily for me, Kinni's-Son is not home every day. But every day he is there we go through exactly the same performance. His wife seems to like to have me there. She "shows" me all about the weaving, she cheerfully corrects my Navajo, she sits behind me and spins sociably as I work. When I pay her the first time, her son tells me "she is glad." My surmise, corroborated by white observers and other Navajo, is that Kinni's-Son is supported largely by the industry of his women, and he wants to be supported as well as possible.

I decide that, since I understand the principle of this first diagonal method there is no use in having a number of looms. I have the counts in my notebook, the coördination in my head. I will take the heald loops out of this one, restring them for another pattern, and have two or three designs on the same loom. I tell this to Mrs. Kinni's-Son and tell her I wish to arrange my own sheds. I follow her lead in picking up the threads on the batten, but I read the proper threads from my notebook. It takes me twenty minutes. As I do it she remarks to her daughter, "Her paper tells her."

After I have it finished I ask for her approval. She seats herself once more before the loom to try it out, and as she does so she says it is wrong. I argue with her and ask her where. She tests the pattern by weaving and sees the threads have the correct relationship warp to warp, weft to weft, warp to weft. She says no more, but she is bothered, I know, by the fact that I omitted a preliminary separation of the warp threads for which I can see no purpose.

The new pattern is a continuous succession of small concentric diamonds. One vertical row has a gray center diamond succeeded by a black and a red. The next vertical row which dovetails into it has a red center, and is surrounded by a red and a black diamond. On the opposite side the order is reversed as it is in all cloth where the weft is thrown through the entire width of the shed. I weave nearly a hand in this pattern. I understand it well, but a single mistake ruins the effect and I have made more than one. I want to get several rows of perfect diamonds at least.

I have told the Kinni's-Sons I am going to stay three or four weeks. I had no idea how long it would take me to learn the weaves, and besides, I have a great many other things to do. On the third day I ask Mrs. Kinni's-Son to loop the healds for a third pattern on this set of warp. I can do it myself, I am confident, but I want to see if she always uses the method of trial and error or if she just got flustered the first day. I find that again she uses the same system, although it does not take her so long to get it right this time. Once more her daughter tells her where she is wrong after repeated trials.

There can be no doubt that she knows how the threads appear, and it is evident that she has not systematically memorized the counts. Each time she sets one up she must start from the very beginning.

When Kinni's-Son sees my progress, he is amazed and baffled. He starts on his long speech of fear about white competition. He has been driven by my speed in learning to the following peroration: "This is hard to learn. Not many persons know how to do this kind of weaving. It took my wife a long time to learn it. You have learned it so quick you ought to pay her five dollars a day instead of five dollars a week for teaching you."

XXVII

STANDARDS

AT THE post there is one of the most beautiful modern rugs I have ever seen. It is of medium size, and the combination of colors is a stroke of genius. Besides, it is woven with a different technique. Although it has a pattern apparently secured by our ordinary weft weave, there is a twilled effect in the way the stitches lie. I consider this rug for a while, and after a time I think I know how to do it. It is a combination of the more complicated warp stringing and the weft weave. The set-up is as for the diamond, but this time the diamond is really large; there are only two complete diamonds to the width of the entire rug, about three feet.

I will try it myself, but I must—once more because of lack of time—make mine small. I pattern mine from the handsome one, designing only a quarter of it and in much simpler colors.

The process is one of the most complicated to which the Navajo attain because of the combination of principles. But it is not particularly difficult in actual execution. Mrs. Kinni's-Son agrees with my analysis and lets me set it up. I smile to myself, remembering how my white friends at Ganado tease me about my liking for stripes, as I weave a foundation of four stripes, each outlined by a contrasting color.

I have woven half of my third, a gray stripe, when I run out of gray yarn. I expect Mrs. Kinni's-Son will have some more. She has, but it does not match what I have been using. There are many shades of gray. One kind is made by mixing white and black in carding. Many workers match up their carded pads as they work and secure uniformity. Atlnaba is always very careful about this. There will of course be many shades, lighter or darker, according to the amount of white or black that is used. This type we call "carded gray." But there is another kind, "natural gray." It is yarn spun from the wool of a grayish sheep. It should more properly be called tan.

This color is all right in its place; my idea of its place is with the tans and combinations of colors suited to them. The gray I had started with is soft and dark, exactly like that I had used at Red-Point's. The new ball Mrs. Kinni's-Son offers me is "sheep-gray." She sees no reason why the two should not be used together. She knows they are different, but her standards are not up to Atlnaba's.

I use the yarn but only with inward mutterings and grumblings: "That is the reason they get such effects as several at the post. Whole blankets woven and ruined by mismatching." If I were making a point of standards I should not be satisfied until we had spun the proper shade. But I am interested in getting on with my sample, which I am not going to finish anyway.

I see I shall soon need white. Mrs. Kinni's-Son sends the girl for a white skein. White is a euphemism for what she brings. It is a skein of nice yarn but the color of sheep during the rainy season. I gasp to think they would even consider using that, but the girl sits down and unwinds the skein preparatory to winding it in a ball. When she gives it to me, I say it is too dirty to use. I know the dirt could never be taken out of a rug once it had been woven into it. I do not believe either mother or daughter would use it in her own weaving. I think: "Atlnaba would send Ninaba to wash that for me. More likely she would have washed it herself ere this. It certainly is a contrast the way 'my family' has so many supplies on hand. Here they are never even a skein ahead of the rug they are making—lucky if they have enough to finish even that."

I decide I will not compromise by using this soiled stuff. I will wash it myself first. I have in my kit a small quantity of white I have spun myself. It is very lumpy and uneven but white and fleecy. I will use this as a makeshift for the afternoon. I take the ball of white with me and wash it, whereupon it becomes as good as any yarn.

I come to the triangle and weave a few inches before the day is done. The next time I come Mrs. Kinni's-Son tells me complaisantly that the sheds were wrong and she took them out and put them in again correctly. She cannot understand my unexpressed annoyance at the fact that I did not see her do it. Luckily I have my diagram and I can see wherein she changed it, but I should have liked a chance to ask why. I could see nothing wrong with the weaving, although I understand perfectly it would be too late to correct it when we come to the point of the theoretical diamond, that is, at the half of the weaving.

I dawdle considerably about weaving this rug. I want to keep my promise to the Kinni's-Sons about staying, but I do not want to finish this rug, nor do I want to set up another one here. So I work at other things. But I finally reach the center of the blanket and reverse the order of my healds. I decide to do "just one more row" then "one more series of healds" before I stop. Clouds have come up in the northeast, wind blows violently. I work until big cutting drops come through the cracks of the roof, then hastily cover the blanket and wool with a sheepskin, throw over my shoulders the army blanket on which I have been sitting, and emerge into a perfect torrent. The inhabitants of the place scuttle for cover in the hogan. The boy has already started a fire of cedar and the raindrops hiss as they strike the metal pipe which carries away the smoke.

Everybody laughs as he moves his seat constantly from one dry place to another when the hard rain finds the weak points of the roof. This is the permanent building of the Kinni's-Son family. It, like the wooden houses, and in contrast to the hogans at Red-Point's, is bare. These people do not have extra supplies. There is hardly a thing one can mention, certainly nothing one needs, that Maria Antonia or Atlnaba cannot produce. Even this brief acquaintance with another family brings out the contrast and exaggerates the superiority of "my family."

Within fifteen minutes the settlement is a lake. Kinni's-Son, his son, and a boy who is visiting now go out although it is still pouring, to divert the wash which threatens to flood the corn behind the shed where my blanket stands on the loom. It is raining more gently when a cry comes from the younger girl that the puppy is drowning.

Three of the young people, shoeless by this time, wade about three-quarters of a mile to rescue it, and after a time they bring it in to the fire wet, shivering, and frightened, a drenched ball of fur, but showing even at this early age the peculiar lines which can best be described as "Navajo."

The rain has nearly stopped, and I wade gingerly, for rubber soles slip, from island to island of this newly made pond extending from hogan to weaving shed. On the way I pass the cookhouse. It was dug out about a foot when constructed and in it the water naturally seeks its level. Coffee pot and wash basin, empty water bucket and frying pan float madly about as the water swirls through.

Where the loom is, the floor is patterned accurately with ridges regularly pecked out by the drops beating vigorously through the cracks of the roof. This floor is very damp but no water stands on it. I am disappointed not to be able to continue weaving and Mrs. Kinni's-Son with a shovel pats dry sand before the loom where we sit. We have our sheepskin and blanket spread once more and she is starting a fire in the stove when another shower drives us out. I wait for this one to sink in a bit, then decide to come another day to take down the blanket.

After two days of hard showers we get the clean brightness which only the Southwest knows, and I finish my work with the Kinni's-Sons.

During the intermissions of my weaving I have been working out the other weaves my friends have demonstrated on their small looms. All save one of the others are simple, and I do not need practice in learning them. The exception is the double-faced blanket, which is always viewed with a kind of awe by the uninitiated. It is a rare type, and when woven seems to be regarded as play with a technique. There are two looms strung with it at the post, but neither of them "comes out" when I try to reconstruct the process. Mrs. Kinni's-Son does not make this kind. Juan's-Wife comes into the store. She is a neat, efficient-looking woman with features somewhat severely chiselled. Her rare smile is quiet like the sun shining from under a deep long cloud. We ask her if she made this one.

She answers scornfully as she stretches the loom and carefully scans it, "Do you think I would weave anything as bad as that?"

I had come to the conclusion that someone had changed the sheds after the weaving had been done. Perhaps someone at the store, I thought. But I could not account for the fact that neither of the two looms worked. Juan's-Wife says she is going to Gallup for two days; but after that she will set one up at her hogan, and I shall come up and see it. She will show me how to weave it. After the agreed interval of time I go. It is at the end of my stay at Thoreau.

Juan's-Wife's father, who is the patriarch of the neat, cordial, prosperous group of houses, welcomes me, says I shall come here to live. He says he will build me a hogan if I do. Whereupon I conclude: "It isn't the railroad, for these people are as near as the Kinni's-Sons. It is the difference in families which accounts for the great difference in attitudes."

Juan's-Wife has made three-quarters of a rug with a bright orange, red, and black swastika design on one side, on the opposite side a speckled brown and white. She weaves a few rows as I watch; I think I understand the manipulation, and she offers me the comb. I weave, she watches me, lets me work by myself except when she sees I am drawing in a weft, whereupon she corrects it.

This web which seems so miraculous is actually one of the easiest of all the weaves. Each heald is looped with combinations of one and three warps. Two of the healds regulate the warps for the design of the face of the cloth, the other two those for the reverse side. The web is heavy but one of the most interesting, although I have never seen one I considered really beautiful. I have brought the two looms with me from the post, for I wish to see wherein they are wrong. When I ask Juan's-Wife she says laughingly: "The woman who made that did not want anyone else to learn how she did it. So when she stopped weaving she took out the loops and restrung them wrong."

XXVIII

WHITE-SANDS DESOLATED

EARLY in a fourth summer I appear once more at White-Sands. I am alone and of course expect my usual joyous welcome. I drive up early in the morning. Daily activities should be started, but even so I expect some of the family to be at home. Not a single dog protests my arrival. Maria Antonia's shade is crazier than ever, but not picturesquely so; it looks forlorn. Closer approach shows a lock in the hasp of the large hogan, bars across the shade entrance. A premonition comes over me. It may be Maria Antonia is at the garden, but this looks like a more permanent absence. For there are no chickens and the ground around the house is not hard. Strong frequent winds have blown sand about it, sand long unmarked by little tracks of children and goats. Atlnaba's house and Marie's confirm my suspicions—not a sign of life.

Deeply disappointed, I go up to my own house. On the way I find a strange vacancy: the house of Yikadezba's-Mother is gone; only a ring of black ashes indicates it had ever been. The storage hole which for three years I have considered one of my homes, that simple place where I have had a complete sense of well-being is utterly desolate. It looks like a sand dune. Great heaps of sand, borne by never-ceasing dry winds, fill in the vacant spaces which set off the storage pit from the rest of the landscape. In fact, Jonathan pursuing his usual track, almost gets stuck.

In the former three years of my sojourn Tom had cleaned out the place before my arrival. Today it smells of sheep, there is a lot of loose dirt on the floor, the extra eagle feathers which Red-Point has kept there for two years are pulled all over the place as if by an animal. The poker resting on the ridgepole alone seems like home. There is no temptation to stay. Outside I find large posts standing close to the storehouse, so near as to spoil the freedom of my sleeping-place. But the posts, so carefully cut and partially set up, look as if the builder had been suddenly interrupted in the midst of his exacting labor.

My experience has taught me not to give up in the quest for my family. The bleakness of White-Sands is due to more than temporary absence, but I will try the garden. A short drive to a fenced-in sand dune, and the same desolation. Last year I had walked through it to Maria Antonia at the opposite end, wondering when they were going to plant it. She had later pointed with the greatest pride to tiny green blades pushing with all their force through the deep sand. I had marvelled at the stalwart fight these seeds had made in the face of the odds against them. Like the hardy junipers, aged but small piñons, intrepid and valiant like the Navajo themselves. But this day I find no stooping black speck at the end of the "garden." There are green shoots, but it is as deserted as White-Sands.

My next try is the sheep camp over the hill from the garden. Last year we had frequently visited Atlnaba there, where neat clean corrals were built and used for the lambing. It should be over now, but it had strung along before, it might now. I approach from the wrong side and come to the wash, which like house and garden has been the butt of the wind for months. I see a moving red speck on the opposite hillside, the dogs have started at the sound of the motor and run toward me barking as ominously as ever.

I decide I'd rather walk through that sand more surely than shovel Jonathan out more doubtfully for the greater part of the day. As I walk toward the piñon-dotted hill I see lively wads of white farther on. Suddenly the moving red spot comes from behind a tree. "Hello, Tom! Where is everybody?"

"We're living here now. I came down because I thought someone was stuck in the sand."

"No, I left the car on the other side. It looked too deep and steep for me, so I thought it less work to walk."

And now Marie advances, lays her head on my breast, as I put my arm around her waist. The tears well from her eyes. I repeat: "Are you all staying here now? I went to White-Sands, and no one was there. Where is your sister's hogan? It looked as if it was burned?"

"That little 'Kadezba died," says Marie with a sob in her voice. I grasp her tighter as for minutes we remain silent.

She then goes on to explain. "It was May the sixteenth. My sister wasn't here when she got sick, and she didn't know what to do. She just seemed a little sick for two days; then she brought her here, but it was too late for my father to sing or to call the doctor or anything. I think she must 'a' had pneumonia. So we are staying here now."

She leads me to a shade, roofless but well made of posts slanting inward and covered thickly with green boughs of juniper and piñon. Here Red-Point, Maria Antonia, and

Atlnaba greet me tearfully. As we smoke, I get a little of the news. "It has been terrible dry. It didn't rain since you went away."

"It hadn't rained much up to that time either. Did you have any snow?"

"Yes, lots. The grass was good at first, but somehow the snow melted so it didn't go into the ground."

There has been much sickness and death, especially among the people we know well and think much of. "My father was to sing that same sing I had over Totlani's-Wife, but she died early in the spring," communicates Marie, and there is a silence at this announcement.

"Poor thing! I never thought she'd get over that illness she had last summer," I condone at last.

"Yes, she got so she could walk around the house again and she was well. But she got another cold and she didn't die from the cancer but from pneumonia."

"I hear John is Judge at Fort Defiance!"

"Yes," answers Marie with the old light in her eye, "and his wife has a baby."

"Is there any place I can stay?" I ask Tom.

"Yes, I have picked one for you. I'll show you."

We walk over a sage-covered slope to a protecting pine which Tom indicates as a possible residence, far enough from their settlement of shades not to be intrusive, near enough to be a part of it. "I'll bring my things tomorrow when you can fix it up for me."

"Tomorrow" I arrive bag and baggage. In no time at all Tom has dug out a place under the piñon so that it is hard and clean. Using such supports as are convenient near the tree, he adds others so as to make part of a shade. I do not intend to stay long this time, so it will do. I want to collect plants and experiment with vegetal dyes, something my family does not make. I am hoping Red-Point will go with us, but he cannot do so until the end of July at the very earliest. There is to be a War Dance soon at Water-in-the-Ground, and the family have decided to participate. This is a tremendous undertaking, and the combined resources of all the members of the family will be none too much. I resolve to see this through.

Marie tells me Big-Man is here. He is going to have a prayer for Djiba's-Mother. Yikadezba's-Mother, at the death of her oldest child, has become Djiba's-Mother, named for her oldest living child. She is not exactly sick, but does not feel real well. She is tired, and her mind is somehow not in order. She gets dizzy and feels all mixed up. Her husband has consulted a diviner who finds that Ben has his mountain camp on an old deer trail. In the old days the Navajo chased the deer over it to impound them. Then the deer would turn back and get "all mixed up" when they saw the men who were hunting them. The mind of Djiba's-Mother is like that now. They will have the prayer today.

A little later Marie calls me to her father's shade. The family is there, and as I look around, the faces of the women are drawn with sorrow. Djiba's-Mother, who is nursing her first son, about five months old, looks thin and ill to me. She is worried and sad; perhaps that is why her mind is not in order. Big-Man has made a "prayer painting" in sand. He treats Djiba's-Mother much as Marie and Ninaba were treated from the big paintings of the Shooting Chant. She holds her baby and nothing which is done for her is omitted for him.

He undergoes the blowing, anointing, pressing, and the rest without a protest.

The evening part of the prayer includes the "blackening." Red-Point calls me about an hour before Big-Man begins to sing. He has several flat stones and some sticks which he uses as tongs, and larger or smaller amounts of plants assembled before him as he sits near the glowing cedar fire. With consummate skill he burns the weeds. Some are dry like straw. Holding them with his improvised tongs, he ignites a bunch at the flame and hastily lays them on one of the flat stones to burn up. Others are hard, thick, but dry roots. These he puts into a small bed of hot coals and leaves to burn into charcoal. There is a large amount of a greener sort. This he ignites but coaxes to burn on one of the stones for quite some time. The root charcoal is hard even when burned, so he grinds it fine. The finished product is a mass of fine soot which he lays aside for Big-Man to use later.

About nine-thirty the medicine-man begins singing. For an hour ceremonial acts familiar to me continue. Every time a medicine is applied to, or drunk by, the patient it is passed about to the rest of us. The women take great care to include all the children who are present in all of these matters. They are treated while asleep or even wakened for some of the acts. The blackening is next in order. Djiba's-Mother is thoroughly blackened by rubbing the specially burned charcoal over all her body except her head and face. Then her baby who is sleeping, is aroused, undressed, and held standing with his tiny feet in the charcoal, while his mother and grandfather see to it that he is thoroughly covered with it. He does not even whimper.

His mother will leave the paint on for two days, but she has no other taboos.

The next morning Red-Point leaves to sing at Black Mountain.

XXIX

WAR DANCE

Maria Antonia, who is never really well, is feeling even worse than usual. Her cough is bad; she feels weak and has little energy. She is sixty-three but sees no reason why at that age she should be able to do less than she did at thirty-five. Occasionally she has a little stabbing pain in her left side. Red-Point has heard that some people who live near Water-in-the-Ground are going to have a War Dance. After consultation the family agree that it would be well for Maria Antonia to join the patients. The whole family will contribute not only labor but also all their financial means.

The War Dance is held more frequently than any of the Navajo sings. It has been witnessed by more whites than any other. Whites understand none of the rites completely, but this one, because the social and secular side of it is more apparent, is even more thoroughly misunderstood and misrepresented. Man gets out of sympathy with nature, with the elements, or with the universe, and disease comes upon him. A diviner has the power to tell what the cause of the disorder is; once the cause is determined, steps in the form of one chant or another can be taken.

Causes are not, however, restricted to a man's own span of life. It may be that one of his parents has come into contact with danger in a disorderly manner during the time his mother

was carrying him. The particular dangers consist in dealing
with enemies or foreigners. If a warrior has killed or injured
his enemy by hitting him in the head or chest, that same
fighter unless he has the War Dance held for him, may become ill with an affliction of the head or chest. His unborn
child may also be later so afflicted. The Ancient People, prehistoric inhabitants of the many ruins of the Navajo country,
were traditional enemies. Their power for harm has not ceased
because they are dead; if anything, death enhances their
danger. The sight of a bone of one of these people may have
the same effects on a person or his offspring as actual contact
with an enemy. Even if he has not consciously beheld such a
disintegrated but still sentient relic it may be that he has
passed one, perhaps even stepped on it, unknowingly. If indefinite dangers like this beset a man himself, who can account
for the experiences of his parents?

Maria Antonia was born the year the Navajo were released
from their captivity at Fort Sumner. Contacts there and later
were almost entirely with soldiers. Since the benefit of other
sings has been only temporary this one may have more permanent results. So, like Totlani's-Wife and many other of her
friends and acquaintances, Maria Antonia will try this.

The War Dance will begin Thursday. On Wednesday all
the cooking utensils, bedding, and odds and ends necessary
for a short sojourn, as well as much goods by the yard and
ceremonial paraphernalia, are loaded into the wagons and
taken to Water-in-the-Ground. Ninaba and Angela, Ruby's
sister, who is visiting, have been instructed to drive the sheep
in the same direction today. After all are well started I take
Maria Antonia and Djiba. We drive nine miles to the scene
of our part of the ceremony. Here is a tremendous shade

perhaps thirty-five by twenty feet in dimensions. It is new, the posts are closely set, the roofing boughs are fresh and green.

There are few people here this early, but the chief cooks of the other family participating have established themselves with their families and pets in the northern half of the shade. Our women will use the southern half, and this will be our home for several days. Here hundreds of visitors will be fed at all hours, here all supplies are kept. Three wagons with barrels of water stand outside. In front of the shade there is a huge pile of wood; not far to the right are three large clean Spanish ovens made of adobe. This is the center of the entertainment. A War Dance consists largely of entertainment.

There are three patients besides Maria Antonia, an old woman with white hair and no teeth, but very spry; her fourteen-year-old son; and a man who is no relation to any of them. Marie knows his name but does not know the old woman. Her eyes are quick and bright and humorous. The patients remain for most of the five days of the performance in a summer hogan five hundred or six hundred yards away from the cooking shade. This hogan and the small shade in front of it are the stage for the sacred part of the sing.

The most important property of the Dance is a trophy which represents the ghost of the enemy. In the old days it was an enemy scalp or bone of the Ancient People. Today a lock of hair, or a piece of skin of some person not a Navajo may be used. It need not be taken in war but must belong to an alien. Scalps from the medicine bundle of a chanter are not unknown. It takes several hours to make the trophy stick, which is marked and tied with many things.

"Changing-Woman, who is the Earth Mother, bore two sons, First-born and Child-of-the-Water, who derived such power from their father, the Sun, that they were able to overcome the dreadful monsters which encumbered the earth and prevented people from populating it. When they were four days old—that is, old enough to think—they asked their mother, 'Where does Big-Monster live?' 'Sh!' she warned. 'Don't mention his name.' But they insisted, so she told them. They went off and not only attacked but killed the monster for all time. First-born brought home a part of the body of Big-Monster which he hung in a tree in front of his mother's house to prove his prowess. This he and his brother continued to do, until all the monsters were killed and the earth was a decent place to live in.

"Changing-Woman herself had a great deal of power, but each time she looked at one of the trophies she purified herself with pollen and a prayer."

About three o'clock on Thursday, the first counted day of the sing, the trophy stick is ready. "Our" party is ready to take it to Sunrise, about fourteen miles west, where the opposing party awaits it. By this time several hundred people have gathered. All of them want to go to Sunrise with me! I tell Marie I cannot take all who want to go, she must choose which they will be. We start with seven. Marie chooses to take her mother's co-patient and another stranger, then there are Tom, Atlnaba, and of course Dan. The man patient is in the party of horsemen, and the fourteen-year-old boy on horseback carries the trophy. Maria Antonia is the only patient who remains.

White-Haired-Woman guides us over a short cut—shorter in miles than in hours—which leads past her winter hogan to Sunrise. For miles we climb up and dip into thick-grassed slopes, and for as many miles see scarcely a sheep or a trace of one. The reason, White-Haired-Woman tells us, "No water to drink." We get stuck in deep sand once. The car disgorges its load; all push, and we are out. Tom knows a detour. The crowd is assembled at Sunrise, where not a blade of green is visible on any side. Against jagged cliffs stands a cooking shade about half as large as ours. In it particular guests, which include our party, are fed. People walk over one another, there is scarce room to set a coffee cup. Order and organization, which are so noticeable at all affairs at Red-Point's, are conspicuously absent. Set on the sand some distance before the house are tubs of boiled mutton, wash-boilers full of coffee, and gunny sacks full of bread. The food is devoured by the hordes of guests.

The people of the opposing party offer us all possible hospitality. Marie does not even know who they are. After the feast we wait for the Girls' Dance (usually called Squaw Dance) to begin. The trophy stick stands in a basket in a hogan where for hours it is the sole occupant. Not until eleven o'clock does the trophy-bearer march out with it and thereby start the dance. She must be a virgin and must never let the trophy touch the ground from the time she first carries it until the whole dance is over. The Sunrise party have made the choice. The child is very young, does not look more than seven to me. I learn later from Marie that she is so young that there are two who take turns because one gets tired.

Her mother accompanies her as she comes from the hogan carrying the trophy and seeks a young man to dance with her. The mother tells her to grab a young man by the coat and draw him out into the center of the dancing place. A large chorus stands on one side and sings vigorously, pausing for only short intervals until sunrise.

This is the dance of which white people make all manner of fun. The girls force the young men to dance. They will not let one go until he has paid for his dance. A Navajo man can get away by paying a dime, a white man is expected to pay at least a quarter. But even if he gets off by paying his coin, any presentable young buck will be invited again and again. He may therefore save money by dancing for a long time with the same girl. He may enjoy this, may even pay a girl to dance with him and no one else the whole evening. On the other hand, his lack of a coin may make him a girl's prisoner for hours.

The step of this dance is monotonous, a kind of disinterested shuffling of one partner around the other. Often the man appears to be dragged by the girl, who holds him by the coat if she follows old ways. More intimate positions may be assumed, and those who dance together for a long time take on a look as fatuous as that I have seen on our dance floors. Many girls dance it. A girl who is not respectable is referred to as one "who had to dance for her mother," meaning that her mother forced her to dance and exacted from her the proceeds. This is what John meant when he said his relatives must pick him a woman who does not dance. It is what Marie means when she says, "My sister will never let Ninaba dance."

Each of three nights of the War Dance are passed in this manner, one here at Sunrise, the two following at Water-in-the-Ground. By dawn the next morning most of the audience is strewn here and there on the ground fast asleep. Shortly after sunrise people begin to gather before the hogan, and one by one they take gifts into it, yards of calico, boxes and boxes of crackerjack, uncounted bottles of soda pop, sacks of candy, oranges, silk handkerchiefs, a fine Pendleton blanket.

After a goodly amount has been accumulated and the crowd is as close as it can get to the house, small objects suddenly begin to fly out of the smokehole and door. Women from our party form a semicircle in front of the door; men and boys stand behind them. Women from the Sunrise side come out and place calico around the necks of our party. They give them as much of the other things as they can carry. Some of the recipients have fifteen or more boxes of crackerjack and bottles of pop, others have scarcely any. Complaints are most emphatic from those who receive the most.

Everyone who came with me "got lots." Tom tells me a man gave him a steer. We now have the bulky encumbrances of each passenger and besides another hitcher begging me to take her. Nothing is so hard as for a Navajo to say "No." One other thing that grieves him sorely is not to be able to pack all his belongings. Both contingencies now arise. I absolutely refuse to take on this woman. Lack of space is a good excuse, but Marie finds it hard to make; the woman finds it impossible to understand such an excuse. Meanwhile Tom is planning the load. He ties here and straps there, feet must cease to exist. At that he is obliged to send one large bundle on a wagon going back to Water-in-the-Ground. He could get everything in Jonathan if our receipts were expressed in almost any terms but pop bottles. They stubbornly refuse tighter cinching and end up by riding in the laps of their owners. I don't dare inquire about the steer, we might somehow have to take that too. I drive back the longer but smoother and less sandy way; we arrive at Water-in-the-Ground with every bottle intact.

XXX

KILLING THE GHOST

THE crowd, including the participants from Sunrise and the little girls who carry the trophy, is large enough the second night to make the Dance a complete success. But at daybreak the next day the place takes on the appearance of a fair. Covered wagons stand about, more drive up in a spirited fashion. There is no counting of the horsemen in their wide sombreros, cerise neckerchiefs and Irish green shirts. Horses stand in quiet groups, reins slung over a twig of sagebrush, as their riders file in one door of the shade, eat what seems to be their fill, and file out again, only to appear at the table at the other end where their appetites seem equally good.

After a time the interest in the ceremonial shade dominates the attention. The men mount their horses and stand ready. The people on foot gather in a wide space not far from the shade where the patients are. Even the cooks pull the meat to the side of the fires, cover surplus food against marauding dogs, and stand modestly outside the shade, hands protecting eyes, as they watch. Plenty of time has been given for warning, but suddenly one large band of horsemen rides fiercely up and attacks another. In the second band is the boy holding the trophy stick. There are shots from blank cartridges and warwhoops; dust rises in dense clouds from the charging hoofs. Very exciting is the attack made by the Sunrise party upon ours with the trophy—as brief and meaningful as it is amusing.

The horsemen collect themselves leisurely and remain mounted in a throng near the ceremonial shade. The guests congregate now for another distribution of gifts. It is our turn to honor the Sunrise party. I thought they had a large crowd yesterday morning, but I find I had no idea what a crowd is. The space before the hut is so full that the donors can hardly make their way in with their offerings. I see Tom carry in a blanket of unusual weave which Maria Antonia has had about for over a year. Finally the gifts fly out from the top of the shade. This time they are thrown hit or miss. Everybody gets some little thing, nobody seems to have a large accumulation. Tom tells me he gave the blanket with a number of other things to the man who gave him the steer.

As soon as the last gumdrop has had a welcome the highly populated flat quiets down. Many go to the trading-post half a mile away to trade or to watch others trade. Women settle with their babies in the shadow of their wagons, at home here as anywhere. If there is shade, so much the better, if not, they throw towels over their heads or draw up their blankets. The sun is hot, and a fierce wind is blowing; blankets form a bulwark against drifting sand.

It seems now that nothing is going on. I know, however, from previous experience that this morning a rite of great importance to the patients, and as far as they are individually concerned, their last one, is to be performed. I ask Tom to tell me when the "blackening" is to be done. He soon warns me, and I repair to the small open shade outside the ceremonial shelter. I expect to find Maria Antonia here attended by women, but she is not in sight. Nine sit formally in a semicircle, in the center of which is the little girl holding the trophy. I motion for permission to sit down at the corner of the shade, for there is silence when I arrive. The women begin to talk quietly. Since they are from Sunrise only one knows about me, none is acquainted with me. This one explains my presence, "She is Red-Point's granddaughter. She is just like a Navajo." Whereupon all smile benignly upon me.

Once in a while a man brings out some grease which the trophy-bearer rubs over a particular part of her face or anatomy, or some herb medicine which she must chew or drink. Her mother instructs her how to use each and is intolerant of slowness or of carelessness in holding the trophy stick. In about an hour warning comes from the shade, and the women all pull their blankets over their eyes. An old man nearly blind emerges and limps falteringly to the east so far that I can see only that he moves in a fumbling way, not what he is doing. Then the patients come out, one, two, three, four, blackened out of all semblance to themselves, blackened thus to keep the ghosts from recognizing them. This medicine is dangerous indeed, and an attendant bids me bend my curious head, cover my shifting eyes. The patients go to the east and return. They dress, and the rite is ended. They will keep the charcoal on for two days before they may wash.

Later I ask Marie why her mother was blackened in the ceremonial shade with the men. "Always when I saw this before, the men were inside and women blackened the women under a blanket in the outside shade."

"That is because one of the men was married," she replies. "This man is not married, so it is all right for all to be blackened inside together. His first wife died, and he does not live with his second any more."

I note also that this sing omitted the "naming." If people want to have sacred names which they have given to their children bestowed thus publicly, the old man may shout them as he points to the east and they are an additional aid in driving out the alien ghost.

XXXI

MARIE'S LITTLE LAMB

ORDINARILY the afternoon of the third day is given over to entertainment of some kind. It may be curative clowning, as when the Black Ears act foolish and toss into the air such patients as come for aid. They perform rarely, but Marie told me they would dance their Mud Dance today. Horse races and other field sports are the most common diversions, although there may even be a Girls' Dance. The guests appear with their accustomed regularity at the cooking shade about twelve o'clock. With their usual precision they eat too, heartily, but somewhat more hastily than usual. The young huskies omit their second table, and before long the place looks comparatively deserted. I announce that I am going to Ganado, and White-Haired-Woman persuades me to take her and a bunch of her friends to the celebration at Water-in-the-Ground opposite the trading-post. There is to be a dedication of a new day school and a community assembly hall. It is hardly out of my way and I consent, but I am only loading up when Marie, looking hurt, mentions imploringly that they wanted to go, too.

"I did not know it," I apologize, "and I have already promised these women. I will run them over. You get your crowd together, and I'll come back for you."

I do so, and we land at the community house with all the

women and children Jonathan can hold to find Maria Antonia and the fourteen-year-old boy there, too. Someone brought them in a wagon. There is a huge temporary dining-shade, for no celebration would be understood by the Navajo if food were absent. The reason the young blades bolted our food is that they do not want to insult their hosts by neglecting this feast in any way. Since it is run by the Government, there is a census of men, women, and children fed, and it reads 2,500. As we wait for the mess-shade to disgorge its visitors, many doubly replete, Marie whispers to me confidentially in a voice of deep indignation, "I found my pet lamb over here."

Surprised but amused, I ask, "But how did it get here?"

"That old woman brought it with her. She just took it from our shade. If we hadn't come here I would never have got it back."

"It *is* lucky we did, isn't it?" I reply rhetorically, as I dismiss the incident in my interest in the rug exhibit.

I see an old friend of mine who used to be my interpreter. He is busy organizing a dance he intends to put on after the speeches. As he opens a door of the community house, I notice his troupe is wearing shirts which are imitations of the buckskin shirts of the Plains Indians. Their heads are gay and heavy with feather bonnets. Thinking, "Et tu, Brute!" I turn to Marie. "I am going to Ganado. I know what this entertainment will be like, and tonight there will be only the Girls' Dance. I will be back early Monday to take my grandmother home," I promise, confirming a previous somewhat noncommittal agreement.

"All right," she smiles, and I am off.

Less than a mile from Water-in-the-Ground I leave behind the hot sand blown on to sticky sweating skin, the thick aimless crowds and the monotony of three days of ceremony. Traffic is heavy today on our road and I meet six cars and trucks altogether, all bound for the celebration. This number in fifteen miles does not make me feel at all cramped, and I drive on thinking thoughts to the rhythm of the motor. I have covered about six miles, and I have noticed no living thing in sight since I loose-herded our sheep, which were crossing the road several miles back. I hear, as if directly under my wheels, an insistent, plaintive, slightly aggrieved "Wä hä hä!" Penetrating it is, startling, even ghostlike. I have been buzzing along thoughtless of my driving; I had supposed I was automatic about it years ere this. "Could I have heedlessly run over a lamb?" I think as I jam on the brakes and come to a dead stop some feet from where I heard the cry.

I look back, see nothing dead, dying, or rolling in the road. I even get out to inspect more thoroughly. There is nothing. At the moment I try to convince myself there cannot possibly be ghosts, I think of Marie's rescue of her lamb and turn to the rear seat. As I lift up a tarpaulin which has taken an elevated position I exclaim, "Oh! Are *you* here?" and Marie's lamb answers piercingly, "Wä hä hä!"

All alone as I am, I burst into a series of hearty chuckles which follow one another in ever more rapid and deepening succession. What to do with a lamb? By this time my mind has passed the mouse-trap stage. My next thought is, "What would Marie do?" Simple enough—she'd take it along. So will I. The ranch I am visiting for the week-end is full of live things—what is one more? A bit of alfalfa and a pan of water in a vacant turkey-pen—what more does a lamb need?

XXXII

TRAGEDY

ON SUNDAY Old-Mexican's-Son is home with his brother, Big-Mexican. They had come by way of Water-in-the-Ground about midnight, and like all good Navajo they had stopped at the sing. Instead of monotonous dancing and a large jesting audience they had found a serious council of many men. Talk back and forth, forth and back, always controlled but in an atmosphere charged with deep emotion. After the celebration of the white people the crowds had increased; besides wagons and horsemen there were many automobiles. About nine o'clock a large one had turned around in a well worn auto track and had unknowingly run over a Navajo, Little-Singer, who had chosen that particular spot in which to lie down and go to sleep. Probably he had not chosen it. He was just there when he wanted to sleep, and so he lay down.

He was not killed. Hushed excitement attended the calling of the ambulance and the transporting of the injured man fifteen miles to the hospital. Several hours after, the guests convened to "talk it over." An injury or a death is bad enough at any time or under any circumstance, but for such a thing to happen at a sing held so that "all might be restored" —this is incredible, a bad omen, the bitterest blow fate can deal.

The orthodox accused the young sophisticates of causing it because they danced those steps in the summer. "They should only be danced in the winter, and that is the cause of this misfortune. Anyway we have too many white innovations. Automobiles are bad, but we are getting too many of them. They are bound to bring disaster."

The young educated men defended themselves reasonably: "You dance the dances of the Night Chant yourselves at the Ceremonial, and the snakes are not frozen up then, for it is only August. And if you are going to do away with everything you get from the white man you will have to give up all your silver, your sheep, and even your horses. We got all of them from the whites. Besides it isn't as if someone said, 'Don't do it.' Nobody said anything."

"And so the argument went on," report my friends. "You know those fellows can certainly bring out their points well."

"They surely do," I answer. "But what conclusion did they come to?"

"How could they come to any? The old men still believe the breakdown of custom is the cause of all disaster; the young ones do not believe it. It's the old story."

On Monday morning I go to Water-in-the-Ground, making a slight detour to deposit the lamb in Red-Point's shade. I find Marie's wagon at the trading-post. She tells me her mother is ill back there on the other wagon. This is not just "not feeling good." There is tension in the very air. Marie says Angela is with her, and if I will take her mother home she can rest better. I find Maria Antonia reclining against a pile of sheepskins and quilts in Atlnaba's wagon, feeling too wretched for even the faintest smile. She has a bad headache;

TWO OF MY SISTERS AND MY GIRL CHILDREN

A VERY LITTLE GIRL ON A VERY LARGE PLAY-
GROUND

THE FIFTEEN-FOOT LOOM

HASTIN-GANI'S-WIFE ATTACHES THE WARP CURLS

her cough is alarming; a knife stabs at her left side, sometimes even turns over slightly.

Angela helps her into the front seat of the car, and we
bundle her up in quilts. How many times in the last few days
I have bowled along this road considering it fairly smooth,
excellent indeed as roads go out here! Now as I drive as carefully as I can it seems to me each tiny stone is a boulder,
each groove a jolting rut. I realize the torture Maria Antonia
is going through, and I can do nothing to prevent it. In an
interminable half-hour we are back at the shade. Tenderly
Angela helps her grandmother and makes her as comfortable
as possible on her sheepskin bed. Djiba, as frisky as ever, wonders at her grandmother's lack of response to her many diversions but does not cease, in fact increases, her efforts to attract
attention.

I retire to my own bower, worried but helpless. Angela
struggles to make dinner out of nothing. Soon Djiba walks as
briskly and purposefully as Atlnaba to my abode. She clutches
in her tiny hand a note: "Will you please give us a match?
Angela." I wrap a few in the note, give her an orange, and
off she goes, her little full skirt swishing to the rhythm of her
diminutive bare feet, her bright face set in the direction of
her important errand.

On Tuesday I go to the shade to see how my grandmother
is. She is worse. "Has she been sick at her stomach since she
got home?"

"No," answers Marie, "it was just from the jolting of the
car, I guess."

Red-Point is glad I came. They are talking over a plan.

"You see we can't possibly take her to the hospital. Little-Singer died there yesterday afternoon."

I am shocked. I understand perfectly why my grandmother cannot go there. A place where one dies is contaminated, and if anyone goes there, he puts himself in the way of the worst. I know, too, as do they all, although they do not say it, that Little-Singer is the fourth person to die at the hospital within a week. After considering the implications I suggest, "But could the doctor come here to see her?"

"Yes, my father says that would be all right."

"Does he want to go down and get him? If so, I'll take him," I offer.

"He wants to go over toward Cornfields to get a man to sing. He sings the Knife Chant and he cured my mother twice before when she was like this."

Secretly I demur, as I suggest that we stop to get the doctor on the way. Red-Point agrees, but somewhat hesitatingly. I take him first to Old-Mexican's-Son, who persuades him, after a little talk, to get the doctor. As we drive nearer the hospital, Red-Point, this staunch independent veteran of life's wars, sinks in his seat. As I stop before the door, he is fairly cringing. Horses, warriors, shots he is brave enough to face, but this thing, Death! His only technique for it is avoidance. I do not even go in but call out my question. The doctor is not there. Perhaps he is at his house, and I hastily drive my grandfather away from this house that strikes him with terror. We do not go far, not even off the Mission campus, before he regains his composure.

Now, after using all our powers of persuasion trying to force our medicine upon him contrary to his confirmed belief, I spend forty-five minutes searching within a space of two acres for that doctor. There is a girl in charge here, she does not know where he is. Another is in charge of the office, phones, and does not know. No one even knows who might know. It would make a great difference in my decision if I knew whether he would be back in ten minutes, forty-five, or not until dark. As I fail in each inquiry to get any satisfaction whatsoever, Red-Point becomes visibly more cheerful.

Finally I give up as someone mentions that today is the Fourth of July. Perhaps the doctor is away for the day since it is a holiday. Grimly I reflect on the circumstance that here, as in the city I come from, one must get sick between ten and five of a Monday, Tuesday, Wednesday, Thursday, or Friday. Let him who gets his lungs pierced in the night or on a Saturday, Sunday, or holiday look to his own fate. By the time I have given up, Red-Point has himself and the situation in hand once more. I surrender to him. I drive him to the home of his Knife Chanter.

He is not home either, but his wife knows where he is, just about to ride out of sight under yonder cliff. Red-Point whoops and motions. In a twinkling he has turned his horse, and in no time he is back. Red-Point explains his errand, slips some money into his hand. He dismounts, darts into his hogan for his bundle which his wife has already reached down from its nail, and in less than ten minutes we are on our way back to Red-Point's.

At three o'clock the Knife Chanter begins to sing. Maria Antonia has high fever, and she can hardly breathe because of the pain in her side. There is no sun today; the sky is dark, and a strong wind is blowing. The ceremonial acts are neither new nor elaborate. There are no sand-paintings. But before anything else is done, Maria Antonia must bathe and shampoo her hair in the yucca suds. The basket is prepared with its attractive foam, its five pollen crosses and circle of yellow. There is quite a large expanse of clean sand behind it, and on it the Chanter has described four little crosses of yellow pollen.

He bids her walk around the basket on its sand foundation from east to south to west to north, placing each foot in a designated spot. She is so weak she staggers and cannot step carefully. I almost cry out as she goes on, no one helping her, and finally falls to her knees on the sand. She goes through with the shampoo, unties her own hair string, as the Chanter and Marie help her. Her hair is wet as the cold wind, touched with a few drops of rain, blows through the shade.

No one could be gentler or more tender than Marie as she finally helps her mother to her bed and wraps her up when the bathing is over, and the Chanter continues his steady singing to the accompaniment of his deerhoof rattle. Angela warms a piece of outing flannel at the fire and wraps it around her grandmother's feet. They are not cruel; their pity is as poignant as mine. The sing must be done properly, if at all; the details of it are no more cruel than the surgeon's scalpel. No one would rush in and grab it from him; it is just as unthinkable for the profane to step into the corner of the hut where only patient and Chanter should be.

This sing, even more than the others, furnishes opportunity as well as food for sober meditation. Here is no feast with merriment and sociability. This is a matter to be compared with the doctor's sitting, watch in hand, as he counts the beats of a vacillating pulse. My sympathy has run the gamut from the weakest sort of pity to bitterness at not finding the doctor, from grim fatalism at being compelled to fetch the Chanter to the most abject futility at watching Maria Antonia shampooing her hair in that wind. It now flares into feverish anger which dies down in despair as I see her rest once more disturbed, when she is forced by the tenets of the cure to sit up while the Chanter blows medicine—pine leaves floating on water—on her side where the pain torments her.

"After all," I ask myself, "is this more futile than the administration of oxygen or the shot of adrenalin, each of which is a hope against hope?"

But this is only rationalizing, for after all we do have a chance to cure pneumonia, and I am sure that is what my grandmother has.

The afternoon singing with very little business lasts a little over two hours. In the evening it begins about eight. One must not go to sleep in a place with a sick person; the children are carefully excluded. One may not come in while the singing is in progress, but one may go out when a particular song is finished and ere another has begun. I go out during a long intermission. From my bed I hear the burden and the rattle until after midnight.

Next morning Marie says her mother is a little better. My bitterness mellows to fatalistic tolerance as I hope Maria Antonia may recover. "Twice at least before she has survived not only the disease but the treatment. She is unbelievably wiry; perhaps she will again. Even if the doctor *had* come, what good could he have done? He would have ordered complete rest. They would have the sing anyway, and what hope could he have of success for his treatment? If she does not get over this, at least he will not be blamed. They are following their own creed. Whichever way the balance swings, they will be better satisfied so."

Red-Point has promised to sing for a man at Black Mountain. He has complete confidence in his friend, Knife Chanter, who will sing for four nights. He goes off to attend to his own duties.

XXXIII

DEATH

THE War Dance has kept me longer than I had planned to stay. On Thursday I leave Maria Antonia with grave misgivings. I am gone something over three weeks, during which she is continually on my mind. I meet someone from Ganado at Gallup, but he does not know how she is, was too busy to ask, never thought of it. At length toward the end of my absence I receive relief to my anxiety from my friend Little-Woman. "Marie says Maria Antonia is better." Consoled I say to myself, "She is a tough one all right."

In a few days I return to Ganado, and Little-Woman tells me, "Maria Antonia died at the hospital last night."

"I do not know what to do. Do you?" I ask my white friend, Big-Woman. "Do you know what Navajo do at a death? The only thing I can think of is to go up and see them."

"Yes, they will want to see you," she answers. "I will go with you. We shall have to cry with them."

Before dark we go. We meet Curley's-Son on his horse. Solemnly he shakes hands with both of us. We do not say much, but we can see his sorrow; and it is evident that he understands ours. We find all but Tom in Red-Point's shade, just sitting in a grief-stricken assemblage. The old woman who was a patient with Maria Antonia at the War Dance is here, and I wonder if there is a ceremonial reason. I go to the back of the fire where Red-Point is sitting, thrust out my hand to grasp his. He gently pulls me down, so I am kneeling, lays his head on my shoulder, and breaks into sobs. All I can say in those long minutes, is, "My grandfather, my grandfather!"

They are all crying quietly by this time, and at last I move over to Marie as my friend weeps with Red-Point. Putting her head on my breast, Marie sobs: "Oh, my sister, I am *so* glad to see you! Where have you been?"

"I'm back now," I assure her as she continues to weep bitterly for perhaps five minutes.

In turn I "cry with" Atlnaba and Ninaba, less long with Ben Wilson's wife, whom I do not know so well, and I finally take a place right next to my grandfather. Tom now comes in, quietly shakes hands with us, and we all sit silent. I have cigarettes, but I hesitate to break into the quiet. For twenty—perhaps it is only ten—minutes we sit there, the tears gradually lessening, sniffles eventually subsiding. It is Djiba who breaks the charged silence. In her serious businesslike manner which has more than once reminded me of her grandmother, she gets up, bustles to the woodpile, and places a huge piece of wood on the coals.

Red-Point breaks into a laugh, and we all smile at one another. He gets out his smokes, I have mine ready. "It is very hard for us," he begins in the exact vein I have heard from white people. "We did everything we could, but nothing seemed to help."

My friend and I agree that he did everything he possibly could. He goes on. "We want you to tell the white people that we are thankful for everything they did for us. Old-Mexican's-Son and the people at the hospital, they did all they could, and we appreciate it. The people at the hospital buried her for us. And they did it quick too, and we are glad for that. Be sure and tell them how thankful we feel for all they did."

Marie explains: "We were down at the hospital with my mother up to the time she died. She died just before midnight. You know after a death nobody in the family eats until after the body is buried."

"What time was she buried?" I ask.

"We could eat at eight," says Marie with the same satisfaction a white might take in a carload of flowers or a silver casket. They have friends; their friends have done for them the service they most dread, and they have done it speedily. The Navajo, if he can manage it in any way, leaves the last rites to someone else, anyone who will perform them.

"I was terribly shocked when I got here. Just a few days ago Little-Woman had written me that she was better. And I was so glad to hear. Ever since I left I was worried. Nobody I asked in Gallup knew. I didn't see Old-Mexican's-Son. Then I was much relieved at the good news."

"She was well, you know," Marie continues. "She was so she could walk around. That Knife Chanter sang for four days and nights, and he cured her. Then they had that Male Shooting Chant over at Sage-Woman's, and my father thought it would be good if they sang over my mother, too. And she was all right. But then she came home, and it rained; and she got wet. Then she got sick again the same way. My father wanted to have another sing, but she said, 'No!' After that she was hopeless, she didn't think she'd get well any more."

"Was she willing to go to the hospital?"

"Yes, but she did not believe they could help her."

"What did the doctor say she had?"

"Pneumonia."

"I thought so."

"But," expostulates Marie, "she got over that sickness she had when you were here. I think she would have been all right, if she hadn't got wet that time after the sing."

Red-Point takes the floor again. "I was waiting around the store this morning. Everybody who came in, Indians and whites alike, told me what a good woman she was, quiet, industrious, had good sense."

"She certainly was," chime Big-Woman and I in chorus. "Everybody had great respect for her."

"I don't know what those children are going to do," he speculates. "You know she was raising the three, Ninaba, Dan, and Djiba." This in the presence of their parents! "They miss her an awful lot. But we all do."

"We are so glad you came," says Marie. "We didn't know where you were. My mother was conscious up to the last. She would open her eyes and know us. The morning before she died she asked for you. Have you seen Angela? Does she know? She asked for her, too."

"No, I just heard it myself when I got here after four o'clock."

We leave finally, I promising to move back in a few days. As we drive back I grumble to my friend: "I was sure she had pneumonia. It seems she has had it before. I thought she was very ill, but I remembered how hardy she was and hoped she could get over this. There's a limit to what anyone can stand. Even if the doctor had been home on the Fourth of July he couldn't have kept them from having these sings."

"And getting wet in that rain! There they are without a house," she adds.

"Yes, and they have four perfectly good hogans over at White-Sands, yet they live in these shades, with no real protection. I don't understand it. I always used to think the Navajo left a place of death because they were afraid of it; but that cannot be the case. They go back nearly every day to get something; sometimes they stay a long time. There are four chickens there, and they feed them regularly. Tom said they were going to move the hogans over here, but they haven't even started yet."

"Of course, they have been much upset all summer, first by the little girl's death and now by Maria Antonia's illness. It is a lot of trouble for one family. It seems often to happen like that," concludes this sympathetic lady, whose own family has suffered blow after blow of the same kind.

I continue with my intolerance of death. "Another thing is, they never think of such a thing as rest or convalescence. They think if a person can walk around, she's well. The same way they never see that somebody's sick, until she's dead. I suppose as soon as Maria Antonia wanted to walk around and cook, they let her. I wouldn't even be surprised if she gathered wood. Not that she'd have to, but you know how she was."

XXXIV

COLLECTING PLANTS

THE trouble in Red-Point's family, the continual need for him to sing for others has made me despair of his advice in collecting the plants necessary for the vegetal dyes. Atlnaba and Marie know how they are made and what is used only in the most general way. Much travel will be necessary to secure the needed supplies. The reason blankets dyed with natural dyes are so few is that the materials are scarce and difficult to obtain. Now, too, the United States Government has begun to "lift the depression." The way it plans to do so for the Navajo is to have them work at making dams and on other water-conserving projects. There are too many hand laborers in proportion to wagons and teams. Consequently Tom, Curley's-Son, and Ben Wilson decide to take their teams and get work for themselves. This means that they are away from home from Monday morning to Friday night. It means that the usual efficiency of the household is cut down and the women have to do all the work—their own and that usually done by the men and horses. My sisters must therefore stay at home whereas formerly they were reasonably free to go away if they wished.

I secure as an interpreter a girl who has two-months-old twins. She wants to go with me; she knows some of the dyes; her mother will take care of the babies. We start on the colors made from plants which grow near her house. We spend a morning collecting leaves, stems, and flowers. We pound them on a smooth wooden stump and brew them over the fire. At the end of the day we have four shades, two of yellow made from different plants, two of pinkish brown, all satisfactory.

We are filled with ambition at our success and plan the next day to go farther afield for a rarer plant which makes the soft pink tan, my favorite color. The stepfather of the Twins'-Mother has told us where the mountain mahogany grows, and we will go for it. But today a sudden heavy rain has almost ruined our dyes, boiling over the outdoor fire. By dint of coaxing we have saved them, but the world has become muddy. We start out next day in the direction our mentor gave us, planning to stop at Hastin-Gani's hogan for more detailed information. This point is about eight miles from the house of the Twins'-Mother. We ride eagerly along in the crystal air cleared by the shower of the previous day and suddenly come to a harmless-looking mud puddle in the road. Jonathan has gone through worse before; he goes into this and stays.

The Twins'-Mother and I work for about two hours when a girl comes from a near-by hogan. She speaks perfect English and gives advice about backing, going forward, using sagebrush, and the poles we have found. She finally asks where we are going. "To Hastin-Gani's." "This isn't the road to Hastin-Gani's," she tells us. "You should have taken that one." And she points to a dry pleasant road a few yards to our left.

Three hours of my language, the patience of the Twins'-Mother, the advice of the strange girl, and the hard work of us all see us out of the mudhole and on our way to Hastin-Gani's, which is only a quarter of a mile away. We get a hearty laugh as we enter the house, for we are covered with red mud from head to foot and there is no portion of Jonathan unblemished. As we eat our lunch, the Twins'-Mother says she is not sure where the mountain mahogany is; she does not know exactly what it looks like; we should have to climb a long way on foot to get to it according to Hastin-Gani's-Wife's instructions. It is past two by this time and clouds are threatening in the direction where the mountain mahogany purports to be. We are both exhausted. I surmise this fact is the real reason for her excuses. So we decide to turn back.

Unavoidable interruptions due to the Conservation work, the weather, and the marital difficulties of the Twins'-Mother prevent us for a week from another attempt at the mountain mahogany. But her excuses the first day were real, and she has now secured help which will make us certain of getting our roots. She makes an agreement with her stepfather to meet us on a given day at a designated place on the road we must travel. He herds sheep there and will leave his horse, accompany us, dig the roots, and drop off the car again on the way back. On that day we start out anew. We have with us a pick and a pickax as well as a supply of coffee, sugar, and roasted prairie dog, supplies for the father, not to speak of lunch for us all.

The cheerful Navajo meets us according to his promise. We travel twenty miles over a road much roughened by rain and never repaired, until we come to the edge of Nazlini Cañon, where we stop and survey the world. Our guide points out places in the far and nearer distance and tells us some of their history. At our feet are cañon-desert plants and shrubs, and he tells us about these. There is a bush that looks much like the mountain mahogany but is not. This is very plentiful.

And here is the soft-gray-leaved, yellow-flowered plant the Navajo call "cactus-cleaner." It grows near the prickly pear, and in contrast with it is soft as a kitten's fur. He shows us how the Navajo pluck a few sprays of this plant, brush the tips lightly over the cactus fruit and are then able to pluck it with no fear of getting thorns in the fingers.

There is the aromatic sumac, used with another plant to make black dye and somewhat rare. This we gather, for we do not know when we shall come upon it again. I take samples of the other plants too, one a tiny yellow-flowered "medicine" with a pleasant fragrance called "breeze-through-rock." The Navajo say that if this is held at the side of a twenty- or thirty-foot sandstone boulder, the odor will penetrate to the opposite side of it at once and in twenty or thirty minutes the whole rock will be redolent. "Interesting," say I to myself, "but who except a Navajo would make that sort of observation?"

There is just one clump of mountain mahogany here, so we go back to a place where it grows thick on each side of a small gulch. The "real" and the "false" grow so close together that it takes the Twins'-Mother and me a little time to differentiate them with our unpractised eyes. Her father, however, shoulders the pickax and gets to work. He vigorously digs the roots for nearly an hour, when he returns with a sackful. They vary from hair thickness to about three or four inches in diameter and appear as dull brown with spots of bright rose. They resemble manzanita bark more than anything I have ever seen.

I preserve the specimens we have collected in my plant press as we wait. When our booty is secure, the laborers rest over lunch and cigarettes. This day has been successful.

[263]

I have decided to collect all our materials, and after they are assembled to spend the necessary time making the dyes. We shall need a great deal of water and wood, and it will be more efficient to make several kinds of dyes at once. We have located some of the plants we need not far from White-Sands; these we can gather whenever we wish.

One day White-Haired-White-Woman comes to the trading-post. She has been interested in the dyes for a long time and tells me to come to where she stays at Black Mountain, where her interpreter will instruct us. Like Short-Pants and Little-Man-with-the-Spectacles she furnishes me a short cut to information. So far we have never been away from home overnight. Although the twins' grandmother will care for them, I do not know how their mother will feel about leaving them. I broach the subject, and she says quietly, "Perhaps we can take one along." After all we live as the Navajo do. The baby secures its nourishment partly from its mother, partly from canned milk which is just the same at Black Mountain as here. We will try it.

This is the beginning of our travels with the baby. The only extra baggage it requires is a small corrugated cardboard box for its "clothes," and a small lard kettle in which its mother carries the few things necessary to feed it. The baby himself is tied to his cradleboard, which his mother holds on her lap. As the day passes and we jostle and jerk over sharp-cut washes and through—luckily—the muddy ones, he sleeps. We feed him at lunch time and he sleeps again. There is a period of five hours during which he never whimpers, puts in all his energy in sleeping and growing.

At Black Mountain we learn from the husband of a famous dyer the materials she uses and the way they are combined. All of the plants and mordants in season are easier to get at White-Sands than here. We can go nearer the source of supply with the car. Some plants can be used only in the spring, those we cannot get anyway. So with our formulæ carefully cherished we return home.

Hastin-Gani's-Wife has told us that her daughter makes the "vegetable dye" blankets and that most of the necessary materials are found near her house at the Haystacks. We set out on a day's excursion, for this is near the "highway" that runs to Gallup. We go first to Hastin-Gani's house to see if any of his family want to go with us. They *all* want to go. But his wife cannot because she is racing with time at her weaving. We take him and a daughter and a son. We come to his daughter's house but draw up on the opposite side of a deep wide wash, for the bridge has been washed out.

Hastin-Gani crosses the wash and investigates, finds no one at home. He suggests they may be in the field about a mile back. We go back to the temporary crossing, and as we return on the opposite side my passengers see a woman and a boy walking about half a mile away. We hail them and they turn out to be the woman we are looking for and her son. They were on their way to a baseball game. They are overjoyed to see their family; we add them to our capacity load and return to the daughter's house. It is on the side of a broad ravine shaded by unusually large piñons and junipers. The house is as attractive inside as out, clean and neat as a pin. The daughter sets immediately about making a fire and paring potatoes. We have brought our lunch, and she graciously accepts it to add to what she is serving. As the potatoes sizzle in the Dutch oven and the coffee comes to a boil, she shows us her supplies of roots and mordants and explains how they are used and where she finds them. The plants do not grow in many places. The deposits of the mordant, which is a mineral added to make the dye fast, are few, but where they do occur it is plentiful.

Because the mordant is found far down the cañon, but more particularly because the woman's husband considers the deposit as a kind of secret and individual possession, as he alone of the family knows where it is, I ask her to send me a supply of each thing we need. She agrees to do so but gives us a large sack of dock root, the most desirable of the plants for making yellow. She wants to go with us as far as St. Michael's to the ball game, about two miles. We take her only to find that the game is being played at Fort Defiance. All right! She will return with us to her mother's and help her with her weaving!

I shall not be satisfied until I know how the Hopi make their dyes. Big-Mexican has repeatedly invited me to come to Oraibi to look into this matter. The Twins'-Mother wants to go; the one twin has proved he will behave on a trip; but my own family also wants to go. We are to go just at the time of the Snake Dance, so there is an additional attraction. I am the only one who has seen it. We shall be gone three or four days, so we must have bedding and food. Jonathan this time has his maximum load, not in weight perhaps but in odds and ends. We outdo even the return trip from Sunrise, but we have no pop bottles. Blanket rolls on fenders and mudguards, sacks of corn and boiled mutton. Red-Point, Tom, Marie, Ben, and Dan in the back seat with the supplies, the Twins'-Mother with the babyboard and myself in front. The baby's luggage goes between his mother's feet.

We get to Oraibi, see our Hopi. We find that the Hopi use the same plants as the Navajo with few exceptions, but their process is different. It is applied to dyeing reeds rather than to wool, for the wool they use is Germantown already dyed or of the simplest colors. We attend the Snake Dance and return after three days without a single mishap, not even a flat tire. The Twins'-Mother finds the larger twin happy, and his grandmother reports that he has not cried at all, except when he was hungry.

The Twins'-Mother now spends some days at White-Sands with me, concocting dyes. We have the dried dock root given us by Hastin-Gani's daughter, and the large supply of mountain mahogany. These of all the plants we use require the greatest labor. The dock root must be ground; the bark must be pounded from the mountain mahogany. As I pound, the Twins'-Mother grinds; as she pounds, I grind. We take turns at renewing the fire and testing the wool immersed in the other dyes.

We have disappointments and surprises. The rose-sand dye made from our pet mountain mahogany is as we expected. We try a concoction of "owl's foot," a noxious weed. We use a large quantity of the stems and leaves, discarding the yellow flowers; we boil it all day in hope of getting green. We secure a beautiful yellow, the softest and loveliest we have made, but after all it is yellow. I surmise that a yellowish green might be secured if the plant were taken earlier in the year before the stems become hard and fibrous.

Purple dye is made with the petals of the four-o'clock. The Twins'-Mother gathered as many of these as she could find, but they were few indeed. We would try to dye a very small amount of wool with them. Our adviser had told us to boil them "just about fifteen minutes." Since we have such a small quantity we conclude that we will boil it longer to make it stronger. At first the dye water is light red; but as it boils longer it loses this shade and takes on a muddy yellowish color. The wool we dye with this becomes a desirable but peculiar shade of light brown. The general rule is that color will become darker the larger the amount of plant substance and the longer it is boiled. For our purple the first part of the rule holds but not the second.

Dye made from the dock root ranges anywhere from lemon-yellow, if a small amount is used with not too much boiling, to a deep orange if the amount is large and it is boiled an hour or longer. We were warned always to use an enamel vessel for dyeing. We have three of these but need another. The first dye we tried was that of the cliff rose. We cooked a portion of it in an enamel bucket and a part in an aluminum pail of mine. The dye made in the enamel kettle was a yellowish brown, that in the aluminum, a pinkish brown. On the basis of this experiment we decide to try the aluminum for the dock root. We put it into the boiling water, quite a large quantity. It looks more brown than yellow. We think the concentration will be strong. Old-fashioned and orthodox Navajo dyers use "rock-salt" for their mordant. Now the Navajo are taught by whites to use salt and soda for the same purpose. We used "rock-salt" given me by Hastin-Gani's daughter for the dye in the enamel kettle. Into the aluminum one we plunge the salt and soda (although many Navajo use no mordant with this plant), and what is our surprise to behold a dull mahogany color! If I had tried for months to achieve a shade like this, I should have considered it superb.

And here it is! We expect yellow—almost everything we get is nearer yellow than any other color—and this is what we get. This surprise cancels our disappointment over the purple.

I tell the Twins'-Mother this is the dominating color in the blanket an expert weaver has been exhibiting at various places this summer. She told me she achieved hers with mountain mahogany. In order to get the dark rich shade we have here she must have used a highly concentrated solution. We know how hard it is to find, the amount of labor it takes to dig it, pound the bark off the roots, and prepare it. After all of this very little remains for dye. The dock, once found, is easy to prepare, and a little goes a great way. So we seem to have hit upon something. I will not allow myself to believe it until we have immersed the wool and the dyeing is complete.

The Twins'-Mother can hardly wait until the dye is sufficiently boiled. She puts in an end of wool, squeezes it and finds a pale mahogany. After the skeins—we happen to have quite a lot of this good color—have been steeping for some time she squeezes an end on the batten she uses for a stirring stick. It is still the beautiful mahogany. Even though we allow for the fact that washing, rinsing, and drying will make it much lighter, we are finally satisfied that it has been boiled long enough. Subsequent washing with soapweed, and drying, prove us to be right, and the color resulting from this treatment satisfies me completely.

We have learned many things. We tell each other, "You never know what you are going to get." I put it differently to myself: "It is impossible to control conditions. When the supply of materials is as uncertain and as scattered as this, when the method of concoction so crude, one can never be sure of exactly duplicating the circumstances." I always knew that was the reason for the irregularity and variety of the colors in the blankets, but until now I had not comprehended the fact. Atlnaba and I, as well as the Twins'-Mother are fired with the ambition to try out all of the weeds that grow around our place.

I can readily understand how the natives happened upon the knowledge of the various mixtures they use. The dock root contains a large quantity of tannic acid and therefore needs no mordant, or fixer. I can imagine that some woman tried the dye without the mineral which makes it fast, perhaps because she had none. She discovered that the dye was as good as when she added it. Other women add it because it is necessary with the other dyes.

The age of experiment is not by any means gone. Every now and again a blanket in which a new color is used comes to the trading-post. One now in my possession contains a red indistinguishable from the Diamond dye red. The woman who made it secured it by mixing different plants; the formula she is keeping to herself.

Another woman at Black Mountain secures a gray-green in which there is very little yellow. Wild horses cannot drag the secret from her bosom. The reason I should like to pry it out is that all real greens I have seen or heard described depend upon indigo for their blue. Often those called "green" by the Navajo are nearer yellow although they may take on a greenish tinge. They consider the use of indigo legitimate in vegetal dye blankets for good reasons: it is really a vegetal dye, and it is old. But it is not native and for this reason I am only casually interested in it.

Woman-of-Red-Streak-Clan visits us. I am shocked at her appearance. The first year I was at Ganado, eight years ago,

I had seen her as the woman who had charge of "the blackening" of the patient's wife at a War Dance. She was noble in bearing, slim but well-proportioned, energetic. Her hair even then was white, her face had an expression of calm determination and complete capability. A white man had said to me with no trace of banter, "That woman could be the dean of a college." I had seen her often since at the trading-post or on horseback. Always she had the appearance of perfect dignity and self-assurance. This afternoon, when she comes with Marie to see our yarns, I can hardly believe it is the same woman. She is thin and old, not wrinkled in a timeless inevitable way like Red-Point, who has been that way for years, not graciously old with mellowness, but aged in a year with worry and inability to bow to the inexorability of fate.

All her life she has been accustomed to dominating her family and even her community. Everyone regards her with respect, says she is fair-minded and direct, but at the same time all are a little afraid of her. About a year ago death claimed her only daughter, who was twenty-one years old. "She just can't get over it," explains Marie. "She cries all the time. She never weaves any more, she can't stay at anything. She just cries."

Her response to our inquiry as to how to make blue is consistent with all the others. She will not tell us, but if we give her the wool she will dye it for us. When I say, "You use urine to make it fast, do you not?" she answers, "Yes." The word is more than she can utter to a white person. In the old days blue was dyed by placing indigo in a urine bath. Only the urine of small children would do. If that from a person no longer virgin were used, the wool would become streaked. Children were trained to urinate in special pots kept in the houses for this purpose. The wool was immersed in the mixture of indigo and urine and allowed to stand for days. About two weeks were required for navy. When the desired shade was secured the wool was washed "fifteen times." I have never seen it done, but I am sure I could use the present tense of the verbs in every case where I have used the past.

To secure green my informants steep the yarn in indigo until a light shade of blue is secured; then they give it a regular bath in the dock-root dye.

At first it seems strange that we secure much of our information about dyes from men. They are interested in all activities, no matter by whom they are carried out. They set up the loomframes when they are at home. They help the women set up the big looms; they make the implements; they furnish the drawings for the sand-painting tapestries. They are the ones who go farthest afield for weeds to be used as medicine; some of the mordants are minerals, as are the colors for the sand-paintings.

The relationship between the materials that men use for their religious activities and those that women use for weaving is close. Both kinds may be gathered at the same place. Not only are the native products similar; processes are sometimes identical. Medicine-men concoct and brew, furthermore they burn plants and minerals for ceremonial purposes, as did Red-Point for his daughter's prayer. So it happens that Red-Point promises to show us how to burn the plants, the gum, and the "rock-salt" to make black, the most complicated of all the dyes.

Many of our visitors are old women. There is nothing like a start to keep the ball of information rolling. Marie and I secure many checks on these, our experiments, after the

Twins'-Mother leaves us. Most women have refinements of their own as well as their secrets, but the essentials are the same. Most weeds yield yellow, and weavers use the kinds nearest home.

One old woman, asking if we have yet made black, tells us that we must be sure that none of us having to do with it is menstruating. If anyone is, "the yarn will not get black." I have no doubt that bits of folklore like this will crop up, no matter how long I continue weaving.

XXXV

FATHER'S SISTER

DURING the intervals between my trips with the Twins'-Mother, Marie visits me frequently. She seems to want someone to whom she can talk about her mother. Atlnaba, who looks thin, drawn, and old, often joins us. Marie goes over all the circumstances of the illness to reason out the ultimate cause of the fatality. "The doctor said my mother had tuberculosis, but she didn't die of that. She wouldn't have died if she hadn't got pneumonia. About two years ago when she was lifting a heavy load of wood, she broke a rib. It punched into her like a knife, and she was sick after that. But that Knife Chanter cured her. I don't think, though, that her rib ever healed right, because she often complained of pain in that side. Then she broke it again before you came. It got better, but she said when the singer pressed her at that War Dance, that is when she felt it punch her lung again."

"That is probably what caused it," I agree.

"But then she was well again after that man sang. She could walk around, and it didn't hurt her. Then she had that sing. I think she would still be living if she hadn't got wet. Then she gave up too; she had no more hope."

"She always worked too hard. You know she always wanted to do more than she should or could do. Atlnaba is like that, and so is your father—most worth-while people are. Then

[274]

they overdo, and they die young. But I am sure your mother was happier doing what she wanted to do."

"That old woman who is here, she was just coming to see my mother at the hospital. She did not get there in time, so she has been staying with us since then. Everybody came to see my mother. The night before she died, Tom, his brother, and Ben Wilson all dressed up in their best clothes and went in to see her," she states with the greatest pride, as though greater honor was never accorded any woman.

"Did she like that?" I ask.

"Oh, yes! When she opened her eyes and saw them she smiled. She couldn't talk much, but she said, 'My sons.'"

"What did she call them usually?"

"She always said 'my son,' and they said 'my mother.' Of course she should have said 'my son-in-law,' and they, 'the one whom I do not see'; but she thought too much of them for that."

Tom comes up. It is Friday night and he is tired from a week's work. As he smokes, I get out my photos. One of Yikadezba is especially good, and I think of suppressing it. But they see it and scrutinize it eagerly. Finally Tom says: "It just seems to me she is still running around and I might see her any time. I can't believe she is gone."

I return about six-thirty one evening, tired, hot, hungry. I can hardly tell whether it is hunger or fatigue which makes me so exhausted. A fierce, hot, sandy wind has been blowing all day. I go to Red-Point's shade to take a letter to Marie, and she asks with her customary persuasiveness: "This old woman wants to go home tonight. Won't you take her?"

It has become almost as difficult for me as for a Navajo to

say "No." This time, however, I do not yield. "Oh, Marie! I am just dead. Tell her I'll take her tomorrow morning."

I have recovered after "a little coffee"; my ailment *was* hunger. As I lie on my stomach on my nice woolly sheepskin I hear footsteps and the soft murmur of voices. It is too dark for my reading. Marie and the old woman sit near me as the darkness falls. It is too warm for a fire. The wind has quieted after a day's fury. The stars are far away. We know one another's whereabouts only by sounds and the flash of a cigarette.

The old woman took a fancy to me at the War Dance, and I thought she was sweet. But she does not know me, or why I am here. "She says she thinks it is nice you are here and one of our family. She is glad you learned to weave, but she can't understand why you thought of coming here to live."

I explain that white people have notions about Indians derived from seeing them at trading-posts or in the towns, that their notions are not particularly flattering. I was interested in learning all about their clans, their kinship, and many other things. But I wanted most to see what they were like at home. People say they are lazy. I did not think that was true, because if they were they could not get so much done. They say also that Indians are unfriendly. Well, I knew that was not true, but I wanted to see. And besides I wanted to weave.

"You have relatives," she says. "Grandfather, sisters, and children. But you have no father. It is good to have a father, you know." She refers not to the fact of illegitimacy—that does not matter so much—but rather to the Navajo custom whereby a father's clanfolk owe a particular debt of hospitality and good will to "son's children."

"I know. I have often thought of it and thought I ought

to have one. But how can I do that? Have you any suggestion?"

Quick as a flash she answers: "Take your grandfather's clan for your father's. His clan is Place-of-Walking-About, my clan is Place-of-Walking-About; he is my brother, therefore you are my brother's child. You call me father's-sister, I call you the same and you call my children 'cousin.'"

So saying, she rises and shakes hands with me, thus formally making me a relative of hers and her children. I rise and gladly accept the neat, spontaneous recommendation. The darkness covers my surprise.

One Friday about two weeks after Maria Antonia's death Tom announces: "We are going to move Sunday while we have the wagons. We will start early, and you can come later when we are settled. I have chosen a place for you."

"Where are you moving to?" I ask.

"Not far, just down near the garden."

Now I know it is not the fear of death which makes them move. If it were, they would not have stayed a minute, nor would they come back. They have shown that inconveniences are nothing in the conflict with custom and belief. If Maria Antonia's spirit were haunting this place, it would not begin now; it would have been here for the last two weeks. It is simply that "it seems as if she were walking around." Out of hopeful and loving expectation comes ghastly silence; instead of natural bustling activity there is only baffling stillness. They do not, like us, try to "stick it"; they simply move away, leaving the disconcerting hush to consort with the abominable quiet.

XXXVI

DEGREE IN WEAVING

IN THE time I have spent with the Navajo I have seen numerous large rugs either finished or in the process of being woven, but I have never seen one being strung up. One day Old-Mexican's-Son tells me that Hastin-Gani's-Wife wants long poles so she can start a large sand-painting tapestry. Before he gets them she finds some herself, and on the day scheduled we make our way to her place.

There is no difference in the manner of stringing the rug, which is fourteen feet square. There is merely added difficulty of manipulation. All four poles are fifteen or sixteen feet long. The weaver uses the same ones for the temporary frame and for the permanent bars. It is not to be expected that she can run the warp ball over the end bars of the temporary loom alone. She sits at one end and throws the ball to her daughter at the other, who in turn adjusts the warp properly and throws the ball back.

Perhaps the most difficult part is to keep the large mass of warp from tangling from the time it is taken from the temporary frame until it is fastened to the permanent one. All of this Hastin-Gani's-Wife achieves with perfect skill, and with what seems to be ease. The whole effect of her behavior is that of complete control. She does not hurry, but her work proceeds unbelievably fast.

She has decided to have the entire length of her warp stretched instead of rolling it around the warp beam at the top as many women do. Her loomframe therefore juts far above the shade where she plans to work. Her son helps her to adjust the loom to the loomframe, and he, like his mother, works with exact knowledge of what he is to do and how. A small ladder leans against the outside of the shade, and by means of it he reaches the top beam of the loomframe. As he stands on top of the structure his mother throws the rope which regulates the tension up to him from inside. He runs it over the stringer so that it remains an even distance from the last coil and throws it back to her. They proceed thus until the warp stands high and loosely stretched in place.

Hastin-Gani's-Wife now pauses to make some two-ply cord. I have never seen this done either, but luckily Marie has shown me how to make three-ply just the day before, and the twisting is the same. In the midst of it Hastin-Gani's-Wife is called out. She hands the spindle to me in the most matter-of-fact manner. I am flattered at her belief in my ability and fearful lest I fail her. But she stays quite a while, and by the time she gets back I have the knack of this spinning on the thigh. It involves only twisting, has nothing to do with splicing.

I help her a little about fastening the edge cords which we have just spun. She sits before the loom to make the heald loops. As I watch her I pick up a spindle on which someone is spinning warp. I have never spun warp, but the first thick rove is so evenly made that I am surprised to find myself doing very well. This Sunday, during which everything has gone so pleasantly and quietly, seems to be the day for my comprehensive examination in rug-making.

As she passes her loops over her rods Hastin-Gani's-Wife remarks: "You can make the diamond saddle blanket. Will you show me how to do it?" She does not know that this innocent remark is more precious to me than my degree from college. She, acknowledged among the best weavers of the tribe because of her skill and dexterity, asking *me* to show *her* how to make a saddle blanket!

The Twins'-Mother and I have dyed only a sample of each color we tried. By the time we cease our experiments I have many small skeins, no one of them of much use but altogether a goodly amount of yarn. I decide to weave them into a kind of Joseph's coat cushion top. All summer Marie and Atlnaba have been threatening to put up a loom. Before their mother's death there was no time; since, they have wanted to do so but somehow lacked the will to get at it. Marie mentions again her desire to learn the saddle-blanket weaves. One day when I am ready, I announce: "This would be a good place for a loom, don't you think, between these two trees? I want to make a cushion top and put all these colors in it. But first I am going to make you a sample of each of the fancy weaves. We will put them on the sticks and then leave them unfinished so you can always count them when you need them. This will be your notebook."

We get the poles from White-Sands. Curley's-Son is working only two miles away this week, so he comes home every night. He makes the lower beam of the loomframe rigid and fastens the topmost one firmly to the two trees. We can manage the rest.

I start with "braided," the simplest of the diagonal weaves. I count off the warps for the first heald and find them wrong.

I start all over and again make a mistake. I finally think I have the counts for one heald right and count off those for another. Mistake follows mistake until I am impatient and cross. I continue, however, and finally have the counts for the four healds correct. I weave a few rows to show Marie, and then she tries. After she has woven a little it is time for dinner, and we both take a rest. When we try it again in the afternoon we both find it wearing and difficult. The sun has moved over the piñon and is shining through our warps.

I hang a plain dark blanket behind the loom, and our troubles are over. They were due to the light. I now feel more tolerant and understanding of Mrs. Kinni's-Son. Perhaps this is the reason she had such a bad time counting the warps when she was showing me. We keep the blanket behind our loom, and when I count out the diamond I experience no unpleasantness or delay.

When we take out the heald loops of one harness to prepare for another we substitute a string for the healds and push it up to the top of the loom. This will remain the permanent count for Marie to refer to. As I count the warp for the diamond I explain to her the general principles I have worked out. She grasps them and uses them at once although she cannot formulate them. I sit beside her and spin. She thinks it is hard to keep track of the healds and the weft reeds and to get them in exactly the right order. I do not wish to bother her and speak only when she asks, "Which one is next?" She weaves about four inches of "diamond" on top of about the same portion of "braided." I look at it, and to my great satisfaction it is drawing in. This part of the weaving must be at least an inch narrower than it was when we began.

Gloatingly I say, "Look at your edge, Marie!"

She jerks her hand, still holding the comb, over her mouth as she gives vent to a hearty chuckle. "I was so interested in getting the weaving right, I forgot all about the edge." This would have been balm to the troubled soul of my first summer but even now does not pass me by unappreciated.

This is an appropriate time for Marie to learn because there are constant interruptions which make it impossible to accomplish much. It is the corn season; there is an excellent crop, and Atlnaba spends long days making a corn confection whose name I cannot translate. I call it "green-corn macaroon." Marie helps her as does Ninaba when she is not out with the sheep.

When the women husk the corn, they lay aside the tender light green inner leaves, placing them carefully so they do not accumulate sand, ashes, or other dirt. Someone cuts off huge dishpanfuls of the milky kernels. Another of the group grinds them on the metate, which has been set on a clean sheepskin, smooth side up. After a large mass of the thin batter is ready, all set about preparing it for the baking. The worker transfers a handful to a clean curved cornhusk. She gets it all in the husk—there is none dripping around the edges. She folds it over, places another husk on top, folds *it* back, then secures the whole by lapping back the pointed tips. She lays the "macaroon" on a board which is fast becoming heaped with the fresh neat luxuries.

Meanwhile Atlnaba has had a hot fire burning over a space with a large circumference. When the confections are ready she shovels away the unburnt wood and the coals and digs out a shallow place for an oven. Everyone now takes up a position near this and lays the filled husks in accurate rows until the space is filled. Atlnaba shovels the sand over them again, distributes the coals evenly over it, and keeps wood burning at the side so she will have fresh coals when these burn out.

The sand oven is left with but occasional attention to the fire for about three hours. Then the stuffed husks come out, golden brown in color, solid where they were soft before. Whenever we are in doubt during the corn season we eat one of these confections. They have much the consistency of a macaroon, they are slightly sweet; the flavor is between that of baked and parched corn. After eating one I feel as if I should not need food again for a whole day at least; it is completely satisfying.

Everybody eats as many of these as she wishes. These bakings are, however, primarily to preserve corn for the winter. The bulk of them, therefore, is placed to dry where the goats cannot reach, then stored away against the winter, when they will be cracked up and boiled for a staple dish.

Atlnaba superintends also the preparation of great quantities of corn baked in the same way but in a deep pit. The labor connected with this is in creating a fire hot enough to penetrate three feet or so in depth and, after the corn has baked for perhaps a day or longer, in husking the savory ears. The children are almost always chewing on an ear of corn. If Djiba gets tired of hers before she has eaten it all she lays it aside until she wants it again. If, by that time, it has disappeared—perhaps Dan or Ben finished it!—she stands and screams vociferously.

Marie comes to my home and I expect her to weave as usual. Instead she says: "My father is singing the Bead Chant over there where we went the first year you were here. They are having the sand-painting today." And she adds wistfully, "I have never seen it."

"Do you want to go?"

"Yes."

"When should we start?"

"Soon now."

I remember this is the place where several girls live of whom Marie is very fond. When we arrive Marie falls onto the bosom of her favorite, and for twenty minutes at least they cry together. Another one cries with Atlnaba. This is the first time they have seen one another since the death of Maria Antonia. Our own callers have shown me that after a death, women greet relatives, and even friends, with tears. The tears are shed with each in proportion to the closeness of the friendship.

Red-Point concentrates on the songs for this painting very carefully. He keeps his eyes closed most of the time. Although he does not hesitate, neither does he joke or banter, and it seems as if he pulls the ritual from the remotest cubicles of his memory. The confidence and assurance of the Shooting Chant are noticeably absent. The songs are so different that even I notice them. Later, as we eat in the adjoining shade, he complains: "It is very difficult for me to sing this. I don't sing it very often, and I don't even know it all. I have to think hard about it all."

On our way home, Marie elucidates further: "Poor Leo! He is sick again. They are just trying this for two days to see if it does any good. In a few weeks he will have the War Dance. Then if he gets better, they will have the whole nine days of the Bead Chant next winter. They can't have it in the summer."

Interruptions are not confined to the daytime. I lie sound asleep about eleven-thirty one night when I am gently awakened by Marie. She scares me nearly to death by this visit at what to me is the middle of the night. I can see there is a woman with her. As I come to a sense of realization, Marie explains: "This is one of our relatives from over near where Tom's brother is working. Her daughter is awful sick. She rode over here to get help. She wants you to take her to Ganado to get her husband, Black-Moustache, to go for a singer who lives up on the mountain."

I can think of nothing I should less rather do. I argue for a time, then, knowing that the moment is impossible for civilized medical treatment, agree to go. I do not know how ill her daughter is, but if she is riding like this at night, she must be greatly alarmed. Even if it does no good, she will feel she did all she could.

We drive to Ganado, Black-Moustache's-Wife sitting erect and tense in the back seat, Marie in front to direct me. No one is home at the first hogan we try; at the second we get the report that Black-Moustache has gone up to the mountain for the medicine-man. We return home and to bed. The woman rides alone into the night.

The next morning Marie comes with the announcement, "Black-Moustache's daughter died before her mother got home, at midnight."

Spinning is as suitable as weaving miscellaneous patterns for these days filled with harvest activities and emergencies. I spin more than usual this summer, and I find my yarn becoming constantly more satisfactory. Marie remarks this and points with pride to what I have done, calling it to Atlnaba's attention. She adds, "I couldn't spin real nice until I was nineteen."

Whereupon I naturally ask, "How old were you when you began?"

"Ten."

I reflect that she has spun continuously, that the hours I have put in on it are actually very few, in the wintertime none at all; and I see no reason to be discouraged.

When Marie thoroughly understands the "diamonds," we substitute strings for healds, and I count off the warps for the "double-faced." Between times Marie says repeatedly: "I am so glad to know how to make these weaves. My mother knew how, and I have always intended to learn but somehow we never got at it."

I am weaving at the "double-faced" when Djiba's-Mother comes to see us. She remarks to Marie, "She is beating us."

"No," I reply, "if you were weaving the same thing yours would be more even, and your edge would be better. I just know the way to do it, you know how to make a good blanket."

To Marie I add, "That is always the way with a good teacher; she learns from her pupils."

Marie then confessed with a kind of wistful satisfaction, showing this was *her* examination as well as mine: "You remember that day when Old-Mexican's-Son brought you up here and said we must teach you to weave. I didn't sleep very well that night, and I worried: 'What if we shouldn't be able to teach her? Maybe we can't.'"

Marie and her sister will doubtless never realize how I bless them for the conscientiousness with which they accepted the responsibility thrust upon them: if I had failed, they would have acknowledged the failure as theirs.

One day I tell Marie how enthusiastic some of my white friends are about weaving. I add, "But they will never really learn to weave because they don't stay with it. It is like anything else: you can't learn it without practise, and you must be willing to give it time."

"I know," says Marie. "Mrs. C., for whom I worked in Los Angeles, said she wanted to learn. She tried it once and then said she couldn't. That is what we all thought you might do."

I then tell her the story of Mrs. Kinni's-Son and her fear of white women as competitors. At this Marie only laughs and says her own experience trying to teach white women re-assures her on that score. Even though I have learned she is sure I will not become a rival because it takes me too long to spin and weave. I could not earn my living at it.

Index: